HINDUISM

HINDUISM

The Eternal Tradition
(*Sanatana Dharma*)

David Frawley
(Vamadeva Shastri)

VOICE OF INDIA
New Delhi

First Published: 1995
First Reprint: 1997
Second Reprint: 2000

ISBN 81-85990-29-8

Published by Voice of India, 2/18, Ansari Road, New Delhi – 110 002
and printed at Rajkamal Electric Press, Delhi – 110 033

Contents

Part III. Appendices

Preface

Today there is a new worldwide seeking for a universal form of spirituality above and beyond the limitations of organized religion. To meet the challenge of the global culture dawning today we must create a universal spiritual tradition that can encompass all the diversity of human culture both religious and secular. Yet the idea of a universal tradition is not new. It is the very foundation of one of the world's great religions, the most diverse and oldest, the religion known as Hinduism, whose original name is Sanatana Dharma or "the eternal tradition of Truth."

To renew such a universal tradition it is important that we look to its already existent formulations which, though distorted by time, still contain a solid foundation and enduring structure on which to build. It is not surprising therefore that the idea of the unity of all Truth has most been promoted in modern times primarily by Hindus like Ramakrishna, Vivekananda, and Gandhi, as this view is part of the Hindu heritage.

Having personally experienced the universal basis of Hinduism and having tried to present various facets of it in books on various aspects of Vedic knowledge, I felt it necessary to write a book expressing this discovery. My search for a universal tradition and comprehensive spiritual science led me to various Hindu-based teachings, which culminated in an encounter with the universal view, Sanatana Dharma, behind these teachings. As few people today, including the great majority of Hindus, understand the background of this complex religion and culture, I have tried to present the universal view behind it, that others might share in my discovery.

I am not writing about Hinduism from an academic perspective which, however interesting, is a second hand view. The academic view is not the view of the artist but the art critic. It is not the view of the practitioner at work in the field but the scholar peering in the distance. Hinduism affords endless ground for academic investigation, which has its own value, but such an approach will not provide a first hand understanding of the teaching. It is at best introductory or peripheral for those who want to get to the core of the teaching and its living relevance.

I am writing about Hinduism as an individual born in the West who has not only immersed himself in the Hindu tradition, but has discovered that tradition within himself, not as a novel identity but as part of a discovery of the true Self that transcends birth and death. I am not writing about Hinduism merely as a particular religion but about the universal culture behind it which is relevant to everyone. I am not writing about something that concerns only people of a specific faith only but about the spiritual issues we all must come to examine if we want to know the Truth.

Many Hindus, both in the United States and in India, have requested for me to write such a book expressing their tradition to the modern mind. They have told me that the inner truth of Hinduism spoken by a Westerner is much more likely to be believed in, even by Hindus, than the same truth expressed by a Hindu. If a Hindu gives value to his or her own tradition, it is regarded as mere traditionalism. But if a Westerner expresses its importance, it is taken seriously. This is rather sad but it does appear to be a fact in the modern age where everything Western is looked upon as better, even things like spirituality that the Western world has not given much importance to. Hindu friends in India requested such a book for the sake of Western educated Hindus for whom it is fashionable to denigrate their own tradition, without having really examined it. Hindu friends in the United States requested it for their children, particularly those in college, to help them preserve their spiritual heritage in a materialistic world.

Fortunately I have been able to visit with people in India from all backgrounds, including swamis, yogis, traditional Brahmin priests, Hindu social activists and political leaders,

Ayurvedic doctors, Vedic astrologers, Hindu musicians, and modern Westernized Hindus of all types, including writers and journalists. I have also made it a point to study the Hindu tradition from its Vedic and Puranic roots including Vedanta, Sankhya, Yoga, Buddhism, and Tantra, examining the original Sanskrit texts when I have been able. In this process I discovered that a tremendous gap exists between what the Hindu tradition is and how it is understood in the modern world. Hopefully the work I have done in explaining the tradition in a more appropriate light can be useful for others. I hope that it will encourage similar studies.

Naturally much of this great tradition cannot be dealt with in a single book. This book does not attempt to discuss the main teachings of Hinduism, its teachers, scriptures and so on. This has been examined in my book *From the River of Heaven: Hindu and Vedic Knowldge for the Modern Age.* I have also dealt with the historical issues of Hindus in *Gods, Sages and Kings: Vedic Secrets of Ancient Civilization.* Another book, published in India only, *Arise Arjuna: Hinduism and the Modern World* provides a Hindu perspective on different religions and the current social issues facing Hinduism in this materialistic age.

The present volume is a series of reflections, as well as questions and answers, on Sanatana Dharma, the universal tradition behind Hinduism and the yogic spirituality that derives from it. It is not about Hinduism as a religious belief as opposed to others (which exists more in the minds of non-Hindus than in the minds of those we would consider themselves to be Hindus). Yet it does recognize the value and importance of the Hindu tradition and its special corpus of knowledge. It is meant to present Hinduism in its true light, which is a spiritual art and science designed to connect us to our original nature as Pure Consciousness.

I am writing this book as one who is Hindu in religion, though not by birth. I am not afraid of identifying myself with this tradition. I understand Hinduism as a universal approach, but I also understand the structure of Hinduism with its complete spiritual science and culture. I view Hinduism as a integral formulation of the universal tradition developed through thousands of years of experience by various yogis and sages, not merely just an idea or speculation about it.

This universalism of Hinduism is not a universalism of merely accepting all things as they appear but one that has given the appropriate place for each aspect of life and every type of spiritual practice. In this regard I see Hinduism as the religion of both the past and the future, as it shows the appropriate place for every spiritual practice within the greater science of Self-realization. I also see that the encounter of the West with Hinduism will eventually transform Western religious and spiritual systems into a form of Sanatana Dharma, or the universal view of Hinduism, that will become the world religion of the future, not by converting people but by incorporating all religion, arts and sciences into a higher view.

For this book I would like to thank Dr.B.L.Vashta who first encouraged me in this direction and Avadhuta Shastri who brought me into his family and gave me his family name. Ram Swarup's studies of Hinduism have helped deepen my thought and he also kindly allowed me to use his Great Refuge from his unpublished *Anusmiriti and Anudhyayana* in the appendix of the book. Swami Radhananda was helpful for his encouragement after going over the manuscript, and Swami Satyananda of the Ramanashram provided additional crucial encouragement on tackling these difficult issues. Many others helped in various ways, particularly my Hindu friends all over the world. Above all, I must acknowledge the great teachers of India from the ancient Vedic rishis to the great modern gurus and the great Deities who have worked through them.

Let us reexamine humanity's oldest and most enduring spiritual tradition, which of the religions of the world can perhaps most rightfully can call itself "the Eternal Tradition," in order to help understand our own deeper and greater spiritual potential. This eternal teaching begins and ends with the Self, the revelation of our True Being, which is pure consciousness, freedom, bliss and immortality.

May all beings come to recognize That Self!
May all cultures come to build their societies upon It!

Namaskaram!

Santa Fe, New Mexico,
U.S.A.,
November, 1994

David Frawley
(Vamadeva Shastri)

Part I

The Universal Dharma

Truth alone wins, not untruth. By Truth is established the path that leads to the Divine, by which the seers, who have fulfilled their desires, reach to the Supreme abode of Truth.
Mundaka Upanishad III.1.6

Self-knowledge is the basis of all knowledge.
Upanishads

There is no attainment higher than Self-knowledge.
Shankaracharya, Upadesha Sahasri II.17.4

1.1 Perennial Wisdom

Throughout history wise and discriminating people of all lands have sought a Truth which is Universal and Eternal. Yet this has been the main quest not only of philosophers and mystics but of all of us in life's more profound moments. Deep inside ourselves we all long for an Absolute Truth through which we can transcend suffering and death and gain bliss and immortality. Many great thinkers, looking beyond the names and forms of the various religions and philosophies which have existed through history, have looked for a tradition of knowledge which reflects the Universal Truth and allows people of every generation to connect with It.

Truth, after all, is that which is eternal and unchanging. It remains the same for all times and all people. Truth is not a fad or opinion of the moment, but the very law and ground of existence. Truth is not something that exists at one place only but can be found everywhere, if one knows how to look. Truth is the universal presence in which all creation exists. Such an Eternal Truth must maintain an ongoing presence in society for civilization to have any real meaning.

The quest for Universal Truth, and a tradition to sustain it, is not merely a spiritual quest, it is the essence of all human culture. In any field of knowledge we are seeking universal truth —an unfoldment of universal laws, which like gravity, are common to all human beings regardless of their background. Science formulates itself as an understanding of universal physical laws. Art portrays the creative forces of the universe.

All religions base themselves upon something universal. After all, religion addresses God or the Spiritual Reality behind the workings of the universe, which is not limited by time or space. The attempt to connect human beings with the Eternal is the very essence of true religion. Yet religions as they have been institutionalized generally remain bound to a particular savior, holy book, or church, which removes them from universality into partiality. They have functioned in the world not so much to create universality but to breed division, the conflict between the believers and the non-believers.

Religion has generally turned into dogma, authority, or vested interest in which discovery of Truth has been set aside for mere belief as a representative of Truth. Such a materialization of the spiritual into particular time-space coordinates is the very denial of its transcendent reality. But such a limited view of truth is easier for the human mind to appreciate, dominated as it is by ego or self-sense which is extremely hard to overcome. For this reason individuals seeking the higher Truth have always looked beyond organized religion to various mystical and spiritual paths, which formulate themselves with a greater universal sense than institutionalized creeds.

Formulations of an eternal tradition or perennial wisdom most commonly come from two areas. The first is the perennial philosophy of various philosophers. The second is an eternal, often secret, wisdom tradition of humanity.

A perennial philosophy has been looked to as the core of truth behind the thoughts of all great thinkers, who obviously share much in common in their understanding of life. Yet however profound and noble such a philosophical endeavor may be, the Universal Truth is not mere philosophy. It is not a special broad mindedness to be found among various intellectuals. It is not a matter of mere ideas but encompasses the whole of life and consciousness. It is more a matter of feeling or intuition than discursive thought. It requires spiritual practice and realization, not merely a good education or an open mind. Without actually experiencing the Universal Truth we cannot truly talk about it. This requires purification of body and mind, while mere philosophizing, trapped as it is in the realm of ideas, can be an obstacle to it.

As thought is conditioned by time, space, causation and language, all formulations of mind must remain partial. No philosophy can or should be acceptable to everyone, any more than we must all like the same food. While a philosophy of the Eternal should be developed, it must remain adaptable. It can only be preliminary, a helpful preparation of the mind. More important is an inner purification, which alone leads to real meditation, and this requires that the mind be humbled before the Infinite it can never grasp.

The idea of a tradition of universal spiritual wisdom is closer to a real eternal teaching. This idea of a universal can be found in mystical groups throughout the world which base themselves upon the pursuit of higher consciousness. Unfortunately, such wisdom tends to be defined on an occult level through psychic powers, magic, miracles and other subtle phenomena rather than through a deep knowledge of consciousness which is its real basis. There is a tendency to identify it with an invisible hierarchy of various ascended masters, which different groups remake in their own image. Such masters may exist — not in the form they are portrayed in the popular imagination as supermen, but as beings who have transcended the ego — but a universal tradition would not rest upon them. A universal tradition must rest on Universal Truth and its immutable laws, not on a particular set of leaders, who could never be the same for all people.

Perhaps the most clearly developed traditions of spiritual knowledge are the yogic systems. In these we find a deeper presentation of an eternal wisdom tradition, a science of cosmic and Self-knowledge. If we don't first know ourselves and the workings of our own minds we cannot know anything else. Such Self-knowledge is the knowledge of our eternal being, not merely knowledge of our outer personality which is constantly changing. Our true Self transcends the fluctuating and conditioned body-mind complex. The mind-body complex, being a product of circumstances, can never be universal or eternal. Only consciousness, being formless, is beyond such time-space limitations.

In this regard we must discriminate a tradition of occult knowledge from one of Self-knowledge. The former deals with knowledge of the subtle worlds and hidden powers of nature. The latter alone deals with the highest Truth of consciousness. The two traditions can be integrated and each has its place, but the highest knowledge belongs only to the tradition of Self-knowledge which goes to the heart of who we really are.

Such a universal tradition cannot be created. If we look deeply we see that it must always exist, just as the universe always exists. A universal teaching need not be invented, nor can it ever be the product of human thought, which is inherently limited. We must attune ourselves with the self-existent reality of the Universal Truth. Should we try to make it up we will remain caught in the preconceived pattern of our own minds.

How then do we discover this wisdom tradition? It is not merely a human phenomenon but is inherent in the cosmic mind. It is the basis of all creation and the very intelligence behind the workings of nature. Only through diving deep into the cosmic mind through profound meditation can we approach this universal knowledge. It requires divesting ourselves of all beliefs and preconceptions and coming into contact with the ground of Being itself. Then such Truth can come through us apart from the limitations of our human mind and personality.

The conscious seeking of universal spiritual Truth, however, has not always been the isolated phenomenon that it has been in the Western world, which has been dominated either by belief-oriented religion or materialistic science. There is one religion which has always formulated itself as a universal tradition. This is the religion we know as Hinduism, whose correct name is Sanatana Dharma, literally "the universal or eternal tradition." Hinduism does not rest upon any singular formation or belief system but has remained open to all approaches to Truth, through a great variety of spiritual teachers and practices apart from any organized dogma.

On an inner level, Hinduism defines itself through Self-knowledge, which is the basis of the system of Vedanta, the summit (*anta*) of spiritual knowledge or wisdom (*veda*). As the higher and inward aspect of the Vedic teaching, Vedanta remains relevant to everyone, including those who find the outer forms of Hinduism difficult to understand.

The Hindu tradition, being a conscious formulation of a universal tradition of Self-knowledge, carried on by many yogis and sages of all temperaments since the dawn of history, provides a good foundation on which to renew a global formulation of the tradition of perennial wisdom. This is not to say that Hinduism is the sole representative of the universal tradition. Obviously a universal tradition cannot be owned by anyone, or reduced to any region of the globe. Yet the beauty of Hinduism is that it is a religion which is open to the universal and not closed in an exclusive belief system. Hinduism is not centered on any single figure like Christ, Mohammed or Buddha. It has no standard creed or practice. It is an open tradition of spiritual search that accepts all true human aspiration regardless of its name and form.

Nor is all that we know of as Hinduism such a formulation

of Universal Truth. The formulation of a universal tradition, being bound by time, must contain elements which are not universal. It must have teachings relative to particular people, places and cultures. Yet its foundation should be universal and that foundation in Hinduism is still intact and, in fact, in resurgence, in the process of reclaiming its greater universality as the many modern Yoga teachers from India indicate.

There are those today who want to create a new universal tradition by combining together all the religions of the world. This is a valuable endeavor, but we must recognize that what has been formulated in a fragmentary way cannot lead to wholeness. We cannot create the universal through putting together the particulars. We cannot create the unity of a tree through gathering together the leaves which have fallen from it. It would be like trying to create a universal government by giving a place to all the existent governments of the world and their vested interests, including those which are inefficient, or corrupt.

Such an approach may in fact be self-defeating. By validating various particular or limited approaches, we may emphasize their differences in which there can never be unity. Similarly, we may never be able to arrive at a common humanity by trying to accommodate or give equal importance to every different human group in terms of race, language, religion, culture or life-style. This can only occur when we set aside our differences and recognize the essence of consciousness which is our true nature, in which all outward differences lose their significance.

More importantly we should recognize what is universal in the different teachings of the world — which is to discard that which is not universal. The real unity is self-existent at the core of who we are. It cannot be fabricated by validating the differences that exist at the surface. The unity of the ocean exists at its depth, not at the level of the waves, which must ever remain turbulent.

There are others who want to create a universal tradition

anew by discarding the religions of the world, recognizing that all the religions we possess have become limiting identities. Yet this would be like trying to create a new science by discarding all that science has previously discovered. We must take what is universal in the teachings of the world, neither validating them at the level of their surface differences, nor discarding all that they have to offer.

As such a tradition always exists in the cosmic mind we only need to restore its outer functioning. To do this we must recognize the tradition which has existed and the forms it has created. For this a reencounter with Sanatana Dharma — the perennial wisdom tradition of the great sages of India — is helpful, if not essential, however we choose to try to reestablish such a tradition. On this foundation, let us examine more deeply the whole issue of religion and spirituality, through the foundation of India's eternal tradition and its global relevance.

The Conscious Being alone is all this, what has been and what will be.

Rig Veda X.90.2

All this universe is God. The Self of all beings is God.

Mandukya Upanishad I.2

He who sees the Self in all beings and all beings in the Self, henceforth has no more remorse.

Isha Upanishad

Hatred never ends by hatred but only by love, that is the eternal law (Sanatana Dharma).

Buddha, Dhammapada I.5

1.2
Sanatana Dharma: Hinduism in a Universal Light

The Himalayas are the world's greatest mountains, extending over fifteen hundred miles on the north of the subcontinent of India, with hundreds of massive snow peaks jutting above over twenty thousand feet. These great mountains are the source of the most extensive river systems in the world, the great rivers like the Ganges, Brahmaputra, Indus, Amu Darya, Yangtze and Mekong, which feed Asia, the world's largest continent. Looking at the Himalayas from the standpoint of sacred geography — which conceives the entire planet as a single being — we could say that these mountains at the roof of the world represent the crown chakra or head center of the planet. We would, therefore, expect powerful spiritual energies to consistently emanate from them.

Not surprisingly, from these massive snowy peaks has come perhaps the greatest spiritual tradition in the world, as well as what is probably the oldest — the teachings of the great yogis, rishis and bodhisattvas who have lived in this region since time immemorial. From the Himalayas this teaching has spread out to many lands and many centers throughout the world, particularly through India, which lodged beneath the Himalayas to the tropical south receives the greatest portion of its waters.

This Himalayan tradition, perhaps because of its very depth, richness and diversity, has seldom been understood as a whole. The largest part of the tradition — what has been called Hinduism by the proximity of the Himalayas to India — remains the most enigmatic and misunderstood of all religions, largely because it is not a religion in the Western sense of the term but a spiritual path wedded to the whole of life and nature.

Because of the misconceptions associated with the term Hindu — which many people, owing to its misleading name, regard as an ethnic religion, rather than the universal teaching that it really is — this spiritual tradition has been propagated in the modern world mainly under the name of Yoga. Yoga is the main practice of the Himalayan tradition, which aims at guiding us to our own spiritual realization.

Vedanta is another term for the Himalayan tradition as Vedanta represents its highest knowledge, its peak experience, the unity of the individual self with the Universal Being. Vedanta shows us the path of Self-knowledge that leads us to our true nature which transcends time, space and limited embodiment and, beyond even the cosmic Creator, unites us with the Absolute.

The term "Vedic knowledge" is also used for the tradition, as Veda, spiritual knowledge, indicates the full range of spiritual and occult sciences at its foundation. The Vedas are also particular texts, the oldest teaching to come from the Himalayas and from India. Dating back over six thousand years the Vedas are the oldest books in the world, the most ancient spiritual legacy of humanity.

Such spiritual terms — like Yoga, Veda and Vedanta —

better communicate the essence of this nameless tradition than the limited designation Hindu. When the first teachers of the tradition, like Swami Vivekananda, came to the West in the late nineteenth century, they began emphasizing these terms, though they often used the term Hinduism with an equivalent meaning, particularly in India.

The real name for the Himalayan based tradition is Sanatana Dharma, which literally means the "eternal or universal truth," sometimes translated as the "perennial wisdom." Sanatana Dharma is a tradition conceived as inherent in the cosmic mind, arising with creation itself. Sanatana Dharma is a set of teachings which comprehend Universal Life and Consciousness, including religion, yoga and mysticism, philosophy, science, art and culture as part of a single reality. Yet as the term Sanatana Dharma is unfamiliar and rather complex it has seldom been emphasized in teachings given in the West.

The term dharma itself has been gradually introduced, not only relative to Hindu teachings but in regard to Buddhism, whose original name is Buddha Dharma, literally the "truth of enlightenment," but which has often been shortened to the Dharma. An understanding of dharma, which more specifically means "natural law," is crucial to this greater Himalayan tradition. Hinduism has also been called "Hindu Dharma." Some Hindus object to the name Hinduism because Hindu Dharma is not an ism or ideology but a way of life.

The term Yoga, the science of union with the Divine, was found to have a special appeal to the Western mind because Yoga as the practical side of Sanatana Dharma contains an aspect of physical culture, the science of asanas or yogic postures in Hatha Yoga, which is attractive to and has become emphasized by the physically minded Western world. Yet while the use of the term Yoga has been helpful in communicating aspects of Sanatana Dharma without confusing it with a religion in the sense of a belief system, it has its limitations. Yoga, which properly refers to the practice of Sanatana Dharma or the universal tradition, which is primarily meditation, has largely been identified with yogic postures and is now looked upon as a kind of physical culture. Hatha Yoga, the Yoga of physical culture and personal effort, was originally used to orient us physically toward the pursuit of higher states of consciousness. It was not used as an end in itself, nor did it stand apart from the science of meditation or other aspects of the spiritual tradition from which it arose. Its goal is Self-realization, not merely health or flexibility.

After having been exposed to various Yoga teachings for over a century now in the West, it is important that Westerners come to recognize the greater background of Yoga and the full tradition from which it comes, including related arts and science like Ayurveda (Vedic medicine), Sanskrit, Vedic astrology, Indian music and dance, the greater system of Vedic knowledge, Vedantic philosophy and, above all, the full breadth of the yogic paths of knowledge (*jñana*), devotion (*bhakti*), service (*karma*) and psycho-physical technique (*rājayoga*). It is equally important that Hindus in India see behind the forms and rituals of their religion these great yogic and Vedantic truths, and not simply judge their tradition by its outward dimension.

We could call the greater tradition of Sanatana Dharma "Yogic culture" or "Yogic science," which embraces the whole of life. For example, the same approach that appears in yogic postures occurs in Indian dance. The same philosophy that occurs in Yoga serves as the background for Ayurvedic medicine. The study of the Sanskrit language, which mirrors cosmic sound, is itself a path of Yoga. Meditation is a way of bringing peace and equipoise to the mind, just as yogic postures serve to do so to the physical body.

Hinduism reflects this universal yogic tradition. Even what appear to be extraneous cultural aspects of it — like the depictions of deities or rules of diet — reflect an understanding of the real nature (*dharma*) of things, and are not arbitrary rules and customs. Those who want to understand the greater yogic teaching need to reexamine what is called Hinduism, not as an organized belief system with a dogma and hierarchy (which is the pattern of Western religions), but as a complete spiritual culture that can be adapted by people in all circumstances. This requires not merely doing yogic postures or meditation but establishing a spiritual culture and life-style, which gives meaning to all that we do individually and collectively.

Many Westerners have adapted aspects of Hindu teachings like the practice of Yoga, the philosophy of Vedanta, or Ayurvedic medicine. They may follow guru-lines originating from India, if not teachers who were born there. A number of Westerners have taken Sanskrit names. Yet very few would call themselves Hindus. Some would be opposed to the appellation, which they would identify with assuming a foreign or restrictive religious identity. Yet if one explains the concept of Sanatana Dharma to such people, most would regard themselves as followers of this universal tradition.

Hindu as a particular ethnic type born in India, believing in caste and untouchability, economically, socially and intellectually backward — which is how this religion has been generally presented to the modern mind — is indeed a narrow and unappealing concept for anyone. Sanatana Dharma — the idea of an eternal or universal tradition of Self-realization — on the other hand, represents the deepest aspirations and perceptions of the human heart, which all sincerely aspiring people must recognize.

The broad and open collection of spiritual teachings which occurs in the greater Hindu tradition appears as the planetary incarnation of Sanatana Dharma or the Eternal Truth. It is not limited to any messiah, prophet, scripture, or church, not restricted to any particularly community or looking toward any particular historical end. It contains numerous teachings and revelations, and is ever being reformulated in light of the experience of living Self-realized teachers. It embraces all aspiration toward the Divine or supreme Being by all creatures, not only human beings but plants and animals and the creatures, godly or ungodly, of subtle worlds beyond our physical senses. It maintains our connection with the universal tradition through all worlds and all time, to the ancient past and the distant future in the vision of a timeless self-renewing reality (Brahman).

Hinduism is like a great Mother and the other religions are like her children. Like a mother she does not criticize her children but tries to nourish and support them, though occasionally she must discipline them. Through her we can understand the ground from which all religions spring and which is their real goal.

Truth is the Sanatana Dharma or eternal tradition. It is not limited to any religion or spiritual path, nor to any name, form, person or group, nor is all that might be called Hinduism true. Yet the idea of Universal Truth is inherent in the very concept of Hinduism as Sanatana Dharma. Sanatana Dharma tells us that dharma or Truth is eternal and universal (*Sanātana*) the very perennial essence at work in all beings. It tells us that Truth is beyond limitation, cannot be possessed by anyone, and is ultimately a matter of direct experience for each individual, which must be unique.

Sanatana Dharma is a way of knowledge without limits, yet it does possess unchanging principles. It recognizes the great laws of Nature and Consciousness, like the law of karma — the idea that as we sow so shall we reap, not only in the present but in future lives. It respects the cosmic intelligence working through Nature and seeks to harmonize human life with the universal energy. For this it encourages us to honor and worship the Divine principles (Gods or Devatas) working through the forces of Nature, including respecting our Mother Earth, which includes making regular offerings and prayers to these deities.

Sanatana Dharma, moreover, is a practical way of knowledge,

not a theoretical system or ideology that can be embraced merely on a conceptual or emotional level. It aims at providing us with practices that enable us to discover Truth for ourselves, rather than merely telling us what Truth is supposed to be. Such practices are quite diverse and cannot be limited to any set formulation or standardized approach. They include yogic postures, breathing exercises, ritual, mantra and meditation, which allow the individual to directly perceive the Universal Truth. Sanatana Dharma also shows us the ethical disciplines necessary to use these tools correctly, like the practices of non-violence (*ahiṁsā*) and truthfulness, or the following of a vegetarian diet. It directs us toward our own spiritual practice and realization as the true goal of our lives and does not leave us with a mere belief to save us.

What we know of as Hinduism contains a model for Sanatana Dharma, which however tarnished by time, remains the best working model that exists today. Hinduism contains the greatest diversity and freedom in the spiritual life that can be found in any of the religions on the planet. It allows the Divine to be worshipped in any name or form, or beyond form. It allows us to see God as father, mother, brother, sister, friend or master, and ultimately requires that we see God as everything, above all as our very own Self. It says that whatever leads us to our deeper Self, which is the true Divinity, is good, regardless of the form that it takes, which is a matter of no real significance by itself.

If we look at the religions of the ancient world — before the advent of credal, dogmatic and convert seeking cults — we find that they resemble Hinduism. The religion of the ancient Greeks and Romans had similar temples and image worship as that found in Hinduism today. So did the ancient Egyptians and Babylonians, and the Taoists of China, as well as Native Americans like the Mayas and Incas. The indigenous religions of Africa and of the Pacific Islands are of a similar nature. Even Judaism has much in common with the Hindu view — religion as culture or a way of life, rather than an artificial belief system.

If we examine native and tribal beliefs of all continents with their connection to the Earth and their occult and shamanic knowledge, we find much that resembles Hinduism. Hinduism thus contains much of the greater and deeper roots of human spirituality before and beyond limiting dogmas. As globally we move out of domination by religious dogma, the spiritual roots of all civilizations in Sanatana Dharma must once more emerge.

For this reason a redefinition and new understanding of Hinduism is perhaps the most important matter in religious thought. Hinduism alone of the world's predominant religions has yet to really define itself. It has not yet articulated itself clearly to the modern mind. Even Hindus with a modern Western education usually do not understand their own tradition. Its teachings have been set forth, often quite clearly, by the many great teachers since Vivekananda, but there has been such a vastness and diversity of teachings, aiming more at spiritual practice, that the underlying tradition has become obscured by the very luxuriance of its growths.

Most of us, at least with a little reading, are able to define what Christianity, Islam, Judaism or even Buddhism are. We can study the life of Christ, Mohammed, Moses or Buddha as the model for the entire religion. But how many of us, even those of us who may have studied teachings which derive from the Hindu tradition, like Yoga or Vedanta, can define what Hinduism is? How many of us are aware of its true name as Sanatana Dharma or the Universal Dharma? How many of those born as Hindus know this? The very beauty of Hinduism is that it cannot be defined in any simplistic manner. It contains all the mystery and complexity of life itself. Yet without understanding it we cannot claim to know what religion really is.

However, to understand Hinduism we must understand its recent history. India was not only under British colonial rule for two hundred years, but under Islamic rule for over five hundred years before that. During this period Hinduism was actively suppressed.

Hindus were often prevented, or at least discouraged, from practicing their religion in public and forceful attempts were made to convert them which, under Islamic rulers, resulted in one of the worst genocides in the history of the human race. Economic pressure was applied to them by an Islamic religious tax imposed upon non-Muslims in India, and by the British in their commercial exploitation of the land. Even today billions of dollars are being spent yearly by Christian and Islamic missionaries to try to convert Hindus.

The result has been that Hinduism went underground and became contracted in itself. Not only were the governments and the courts of India dominated by foreign rulers and their hostile religions, even the academic establishments came under the control of forces which discouraged Hindus from articulating their religion, while encouraging negative stereotypes of it. This British system of education, or the Catholic school system, still dominate India today.

Not surprisingly, much of our view of Hinduism has come from missionaries and colonialists who were trying to convert or rule India, and were certainly not qualified to present its ancient spiritual culture. The idea of Hindus as primitive, polytheists, idolaters, devil worshippers, and so on are missionary stereotypes whose motivation is not to understand this profound religion but to discredit it in order to gain converts. Such people did not study the great sages of India, or seek to learn Yoga and meditation under them, but cast Hinduism in the same negative light as they did the religions of the Native Americans, the Chinese and other non-white peoples. How many of us would go to Christian missionaries to find out what Islam or Buddhism are? Yet many of the people we look to for a definition of Hinduism, like Griffith, Monier-Williams, Max Muller and most of the Western Vedic scholars, have neither been Hindus, nor even wanted that religion to continue but were consciously plotting its destruction.

Modern India has had a strong leftist and communist element, particularly in the universities, which with its atheistic bent could not be appreciative of Hinduism either. The result is that the view of Hinduism taught in India today is more leftist than Hindu, and often about as sensitive towards Hinduism, as the Marxist interpretation of the Bible is toward Christianity. This necessitates a reexamination of Hinduism by those who have studied it according to the present academic world and its limited views.

Hinduism today is no longer limited to the region of India. There are Hindu minorities in all continents, and Hindu-based spiritual teachings have been adapted by people of all lands. In fact, of the religions that exist in the world today Hinduism is perhaps the most likely to become the religion of the future. The reason for this is not that Hindus have the most money or the most missionaries, or are the most strongly motivated to take over the world. The reason is that Hinduism, as a conscious formulation of the universal tradition, has the breadth to encompass, integrate and transcend all existent religions. It has a wideness of cosmic vision which can not only embrace but extend the field of modern science into spiritual domains.

Therefore it is important that we go beyond the usual idea of religion and come to recognize once more the need for Sanatana Dharma. This will enable us to integrate all useful teachings, whether of the East or the West, the past or the present, into a valid system of spiritual culture and universal knowledge, based upon the foundation provided for us by the Himalayan sages.

Let us therefore enter into an examination — a meditative inquiry if you will — into what a universal tradition should be, into how Sanatana Dharma through Hinduism has attempted to create it and what elements of it remain. To do this we must look to the main issues of spirituality and religion both individually and collectively. Through this examination we can perhaps gain the foundation to restore a universal tradition.

Come together, speak together, together let your minds arrive at a common understanding, just as the ancient Divinities in a common knowing honor the same Good.

Rig Veda X.191.2

He who does not know the Imperishable Word of the chant that dwells in the supreme ether, in which all the Divinities reside, what can he do with the Vedas? Those who know That, let them gather together here.

Rig Veda I.164.39

1.3 Religion and Spirituality: The Search for Universality

Religion is the most profound and uplifting aspect of human life, as well as the most ambiguous and contradictory. Religions have, more than any other domain of human culture, served to instil ethical values and raise human beings to higher levels of consciousness. We see this in the mystics, saints, sages, seers and yogis who have existed to some degree throughout the various religious traditions of the world. On the other hand, religions have been the main cause of misunderstanding, mistrust and hatred between human beings, and have been responsible for the greatest violence and inhumanity, which persists to the present day. We see this in the propaganda, forceful conversions, inquisitions, crusades, holy wars, and terrorism perpetrated in the name of religion which often has no respect for life.

Religion means "to unite," referring to the unification of the soul, the essence of our being, with God, the Supreme Universal Principle. This definition of religion is the same as that of Yoga, which refers to uniting the individual with the Supreme Reality. Religion — properly understood as a means of union with our fellow human beings and with the underlying Divinity — has brought many people to the awareness of the Divine as their true nature. Religion — improperly understood as an exclusive belief system which places us against those who think differently — has become the basis for murder, pillage, genocide, wrecking entire cultures, and condemning to hell our fellow human beings, our own brothers and sisters.

Perhaps nothing more so than religion stimulates the passions of humanity toward either higher or lower actions. This is because religion introduces absolutes into human life. Religion sets up a standard of judgement that goes beyond life and death and all the limited values of our transient existence. Such a standard can deepen our sensitivity or can breed fanaticism and bigotry, depending upon whether we use these absolutes to provide a higher standard for our own behavior or to become harsher in our criticism of those who think differently than we do. True religion directs us to the Absolute, which requires that we cleanse our minds of our limited opinions and judgements. False or imperfect religion tries to make absolute these very prejudices, opinions and limitations.

To understand religion, we must look at religion as a whole, not as a belief system but as a way of life, a system of ethical, mental and spiritual culture — what is called in the Eastern world, dharma or the guiding law of our being. Otherwise we will be unable to extract the essence of religion from its mass of conflicting beliefs. This requires that we look at our own lives as a whole, and that we examine religion as a living phenomenon, as part of our greater human potential, our inner dharma, from whatever different land or culture it may arise. We must learn to look at religion as a way of connecting with Reality through our own consciousness, which is the view of the science of Yoga. This is the view of religion that India has given us, the land wherein human beings have spent the most time in pursuit of the sacred, not to convert others, but to realize the Truth.

We may think that it is best not to examine religion, which

is after all a matter of faith. Let each person follow whatever faith he or she prefers, we may think. However in the modern world we must strive to understand all people and all cultures. To compartmentalize religion into various faiths, each of which leaves the others alone, would be like saying let each country speak its own language, and we will speak our own, but let us not try to learn the language of others or strive to develop any global language. It is like accepting the boundaries that exist between nations as real boundaries and staying within our own particular frontiers. This superficial sense of tolerance is a contraction of fear and insecurity. As human beings all religions and all cultures belong to each one of us and we should be free to examine each for whatever value it may have, just as all of science should be there for us to examine without any boundaries.

Religion, properly speaking, concerns the ultimate questions of life and death. To approach it we must question deeply, including questioning religion and, above all, questioning ourselves. We must ask: What it is that we are really seeking through religion? Are we really seeking the Truth or to know God? Or is religion merely something to believe in and then stop searching?

Is religion something to belong to, a new identity, to be part of a group of people who like us and make us feel good about ourselves? Is religion a social movement to take over the world and convert it to a belief that is meant to arouse our missionary zeal? Is religion the certainty that we will have ultimate salvation or happiness, and that those we don't like will be punished by God? These are emotional and vital urges which, however comforting, have little to do with the search for Truth, which being universal cannot cater to human partialities. Such urges cause us to distort Reality according to our personal and collective desires. They are not part of a genuine seeking of Truth or God, but a further development of our egoistic urges, which have no real place in the spiritual realm. Religion should be the human search, within our own being, for the Truth of this wonderful universe in which we live, its indwelling Spirit. Otherwise we should probably call it something else.

And what is religion meant to provide us? Is it merely a safe haven, a supportive community, or secure ideology? Is it a book that makes it so we don't have to think for ourselves any more? Is it a hero figure who substitutes for our own inner growth and self-responsibility, who saves us by merely believing in him? Is what we are looking through religion merely human or is it a transcendence of all social conditioning, including culturally conditioned ideas of God? Can our religions as we have formulated them lead us beyond death, hatred and suffering? Can they bring the peace and love that we all long for? Are they based upon a respect for all beings and an openness to Truth from wherever it may come? If not, is it not truly religious to look beyond our given religions?

What kinds of ideas and practices should we call religion? Is it merely acting good, or thinking good thoughts, but remaining in the limited field of the mind and ego? Is it converting others to our idea of the good, making others think, act and perceive the world in the same pattern that we do, which may destroy other cultures and ways of thought different than our own? Is religion an external action like going to a church or temple. Is it a change of our beliefs, or a total revolution in consciousness? Is promoting a belief or performing some form of worship enough or does religion require spiritual practices like Yoga and meditation?

What is the universal element in religion, which like the universal element in art can reveal its essence? Can the essence of religion be found in the churches, holy books, or the priests? Does it lie in religious controversies, conflicts and holy wars? Or does it reside in the intimate yearning of our deepest heart which no single group can own or dispense? Is the Truth of religion unique to one religion or is it present to some extent in all religions?

Or does it perhaps exist beyond all of them? Has our religious urge existed because of or in spite of what society has institutionalized and enforced as religion? Is religion as we commonly think of it a formulation of spiritual aspiration, or a deformation and perversion of it? What is the basis for a real spirituality and can it be found within the confines of organized religion? Is spirituality nurtured or suppressed by the religions we have in the world today?

If we look deeply into ourselves we will observe that we are not really interested in religion, and perhaps wisely so. Business, sports, entertainment, politics and other outward aspects of life are the focus of our attention in the modern world, and these are less controversial and divisive than religion, which appears to be a hold over from the dark and troubled Middle Ages. Given the nature of what we call religion with its sin, guilt, fear, and even vengeance, there appears to be little reason why we should take much interest in it. It appears as an emotional negativity devoid of common courtesy, not to speak of love, compassion and humanity. Not surprisingly, many people today have a greater sense of loyalty to their football team than to their church. Most people have a greater adulation for their favorite movie star than for their religious leader, should they have one.

And if we are interested in religion it is usually not the Universal Truth that concerns us. It is our particular church or hierarchy, the religion of our fathers, our nation or our people, promoting our belief, defending our religion politically, militarily, and so on. We do not spend our time in meditation or even in prayer (except to ask God to do what we want) but in criticizing what are, from the standpoint of our particular religious bias, irreligious people. These may be criminals, those of different life-styles, or simply the followers of different religions, which groups we may lump together as one homogenous mass of evil. Meanwhile we ourselves are narrow-minded, judgmental, lacking in any real love, peace or wisdom, and yet may regard that such attitudes are justified by God and his Word.

Fortunately, in the modern age we are passing out of the domination of institutionalized religions which have controlled the world over the last two thousand years. Religion as a belief system — the idea that one religion owns the Divine or Truth as if it were a kind of property — is a medieval phenomenon that is now out of date, the product of a dark age of lack of scientific knowledge and global communication. The division of religion appears on par with the division of nations, languages and currencies, which are bound to disappear in time.

Religion as it is generally known in the Western world, and its culture which now dominates the world, projects an exclusive truth for a particular leader, book, or group of people and the need to convert the world to it — which is contrary to the idea that there is a Universal Truth. It formulates truth as an external authority rather than an inner experience and thereby denies any real inward search for God. This exclusivist idea of religion may have one God but it has two humanities — the believers and the non-believers - and regards the non-believers as inferior or sinful — to be converted or conquered — which leads to every sort of misunderstanding and exploitation. Its concern is not union with God but elimination of the non-believers. It does not aim at making us better people but at changing those who do not outwardly conform to what we think is religious. As we are beginning to come together as a planet and recognizing our common humanity, such divisions can no longer be accepted. They no longer appear religious but inhumane.

In a number of Western countries today only a small portion of the population attends any church on a regular basis. Even if many people may still allow themselves to be called Christians, the designation is often nominal at best, and it is very difficult to find a person who could be called pious in the orthodox sense. In fact, for many people in the West religion is a regressive word and church is synonymous with boredom or oppression. We can no longer believe that only one religion is true. Some of us may doubt whether any religion is true.

Asia is following a similar movement. The younger generation is more interested in the pop culture imported from the West than in its own traditional religious or spiritual culture. The educated elite is proud of its modern, scientific, and humanitarian views which often criticize or denigrate their traditional religious backgrounds.

In this age of open communication and critical scrutiny we have become painfully aware of the limitations of organized religion and its herding of people into hostile camps. We have come to recognize that behind the rhetoric of God and religion is often political, economic or sexual exploitation — not an enlightened or humanitarian force, but one of darkness and oppression. Compared to such divisive creeds, science and humanitarianism, even of an atheistic bent, appears more compassionate and enlightened.

Yet though the bonds of organized religion are breaking down the long term human seeking for the Eternal and Infinite, which is the essence of human nature, continues to exist and appears to be growing. More and more people are seeking experiential forms of spirituality to satisfy this internal longing. It is not so much that religion has failed us or become out of date, but that religion as we know it is no longer relevant either to our outer or inner needs. Religion as belief is breaking down but religion as the seeking for direct knowledge of cosmic reality is undergoing a revival. There is a search for a new religion not as a new church, but as a universal spirituality beyond all organization. It is a return to Dharma, a rediscovery of the laws of life.

We can foresee the breakdown of the monolithic world religions which have dominated the world, along with their massive organizations, and their dogmatic hold on the minds of people. Their power is on the wane, particularly in the lands of their origin. The waves of missionary conversion, which have left the

Western world and moved to Asia and Africa — and are still very active trying to undermine the traditional cultures of these lands — will also soon have to come to a halt. We are beginning to become open to the spiritual ideas of other people instead of trying to impose our own beliefs upon them (which generally occurs without having even looked at what they already believe in).

It is true that there has been a recent upsurge in religious fundamentalism, particularly in Islamic and Christian countries. Such fundamentalism is far from any real spiritual regeneration. It is a reaction to the modern Western popular culture that is sweeping over the planet and threatening the existence of old cherished belief systems.

Christian fundamentalism in America itself is a pop religion of TV preachers accompanied by Country and Western singers, with instantaneous conversion at football stadiums or even in front of the television, with wild prophecies, and make believe miracles. Its preachers are often found to be involved in financial and sexual improprieties of various types. Such religion is hardly the piety of the Middle Ages and is accompanied by little soul searching, and no real spiritual practices, much less any asceticism. It appears as much as a modern distortion as any traditional religiosity. For most people it is a temporary or occassional fad, not anything really enduring or profound.

Islamic fundamentalism is more militant and traditional, and perhaps more dangerous as it does not hesitate to resort to violence, not only in Islamic countries but all over the world. Yet it also appears to be colored by the age of technology into as much a media show as a religious reaction. One wonders if the terrorists it has produced would be so active, if the mass media did not so well broadcast and thereby sustain their cause.

This fundamentalist reaction does have a justifiable cause. Western popular culture with its lack of spiritual values is limited and can lead to a spiritual and moral wasteland. The criticism of immorality against it leveled by the fundamentalists is, to a great extent, correct, even when their dogmatic and violent reactions are wrong. We do need to reconsider our relationship with the Divine, which we have sadly ignored. But the correct force to counter modern materialism is a new spirituality, not a retreat into old religious prejudices. Religious fundamentalism only succeeds in making people backward and isolated from the progressive movement of evolution and communication, which renders their cultures regressive and sterile. It only serves to make materialism look more humane by countering it with a force of superstition.

One can foresee the collapse of religious fundamentalism all over the world in the coming decades, perhaps sooner than we think, just as communism has quickly and unexpectedly recently collapsed. It will not be long before fundamentalist regimes will fall either internally owing to the oppression they bring on their own people, or externally for the warlike actions they bring on the world as a whole.

We must soon pass out of this duality of dogmatic religion (which itself is a form of materialism or belief in institutions) or scientific materialism (which is invested with a religious aura of truth and universality). One can foresee a future age of world peace and harmony wherein what is valuable in each religion is honored, and serious individuals will seek Self-realization through meditational paths beyond the bounds of organized beliefs. We can no longer look upon the time of some ancient prophet and his small following as the golden age for humanity. We have been too exposed to the rest of the world through the mass media to pretend in a medieval way that our particular community is the only valid one. We can paint our enemy as the devil but no one is going to believe it anymore. That we are all human beings with the same basic drives and potential is evident to all open minds. The ugly head of religious fundamentalism has a fair amount of bigotry and a number of terrorist tactics left but this is only a sign that it is being rejected.

We now live in a global age wherein we must come together as a planet. For this new era we need a universal spiritual tradition that recognizes the sacred nature of all human beings regardless of their beliefs, and which is founded on immutable cosmic laws. Different cultures have developed different spiritual approaches which we must come to understand and respect. This is the same as different cultures have developed different types of art, music, literature, or philosophy. We can no longer say that only European art is good and that Chinese or Indian art is barbaric, for example, though even in the last century many educated Europeans had such beliefs. We now recognize that as human beings we share a common planet and that there is much delight in sharing foreign cultures. We should have at least the same openness in the spiritual realm. Unfortunately the spiritual realm is where we have the most intolerance though, as the domain of life that deals with the infinite, it is a place where intolerance has no real place.

In the seeking for a new spirituality we must remember that there are spiritual traditions that have survived to the present day, which though tainted or regressive in outer aspects, can provide the foundation for a new spirituality. The spiritual traditions of East Asia, particularly of India and Tibet, show the way to a global spirituality. They have never formulated themselves as exclusive belief systems, but have remained open as universal meditation paths. They have preserved living traditions of spiritual realization, the millennial heritage of humanity, with great living spiritual masters. Such teachers are necessary for all of us to learn from to develop an authentic experiential spirituality, rather than just some speculative or imaginary creation of our own thoughts and opinions. As Western science moves to the East, Eastern spirituality and its science of Yoga is coming to the West. This can serve to link up the two sides of human knowledge for the coming age.

The Western world has prided itself in modernity and rationality. After all it invented these things. Yet if we look at Western culture it is obvious that it has been guilty of various forms of prejudice and narrow mindedness, a Eurocentricism in religion, art and culture. We have been forced to recognize the inhumanity committed in the colonial era, which led to slavery and genocide, and still is producing economic exploitation. We must come to recognize the cultural imperialism which has gone along with it that has portrayed non-European cultures in a negative light, particularly their spiritual traditions, and has reduced their histories to mere footnotes to events in Europe. The judgement of Eastern religions as pagan, polytheist, idolatrous, and primitive, now appears on par with the judgement of Asian and African peoples as racially inferior — not an enlightened judgement but an embarrassing prejudice. The attempt to discredit venerable and profound oriental cultures as inferior, which is still going on by missionary movements today, has been never motivated by the seeking of any real understanding but by political, economic and religious ambitions toward domination. The negative judgement of these cultures is not the product of an enlightened rationality but of a cultural prejudice and limited religious belief systems that does not want to recognize the validity of other points of view.

The West can no longer look down upon Asian culture. The Japanese have shown how well the Asians can compete with us on all levels of modern culture. The Chinese and the Indians may not be far behind. We have come to recognize the value of Asian systems of Yoga, meditation, natural healing, martial arts, music and painting, and so on. We have also seen the skill of Easterners as scientists, artists, doctors, and businessmen. We have seen that Asians, like the Japanese, can be competitive in the modern world without giving up their traditional cultures or customs.

In this regard we must reexamine the Eastern idea of religion — which is not religion as commonly known in the West — but a way of truth and natural law, dharma. Dharma is religion or the pursuit of enlightenment by how we live, not merely by what we may say or believe. It is religion as a striving to attune ourselves with cosmic law, not the imposition of a belief or ideology made up by human beings or by the God we have created in our image. The time of belief-oriented religions is coming to an end but the age of dharma is beginning.

Religion in the coming age will be very different than what it is today. The predominant world religions will break down into smaller groups wherein a particular religious identity is no longer important or will even be regarded as regressive. People all over the world will begin to experiment with different religions just as we now do with different forms of art or science.

Asia, Africa and South America will experience a revival in the coming century applying modern technology but along with their own cultural, religious and spiritual bases. This may present the Western world with a scientifically and economically more advanced third world following older non-Western spiritual traditions. This will be accompanied by a greater adaptation of Asian meditational traditions in the Western world. Then the whole barrier of East and West will disappear.

Older indigenous religions as a whole will experience a revival. Europe will once more reencounter and reintegrate its pre-Christian past. The spiritual depth of ancient myths and rituals will become obvious to a deeper psychological vision. The Middle East and North Africa will have to deal with their pre-Islamic past, particularly the Egyptian and Babylonian traditions that modern archeology has once more uncovered, and come to recognize the value of their older images and icons. The mystical side of all religions will become prominent and the ritualistic and ideological side will recede. Spiritual, yogic and occult movements of all kinds will gain much interest all over the world. Syncretic religious movements combining various teachings will continue. Futuristic religious ideas will become evident with a seeking to contact the greater reality of the mysterious universe in which we live.

There are many signs of such a new awakening. The already existing interest in Eastern (dharmic) religions of Hinduism, Buddhism and Taoism indicates this trend. The upsurge of interest in Native American traditions, Western occultism, Pagan practices, and Shamanism is another indication. A renewed interest in the mystical side of predominant Western religions is another. Another is a seeking of spirituality through modern psychology or modern science.

There will be much in this movement that will be superficial, wrongly formulated or misleading and that will have to be rejected in the long run. Religions may be combined superficially, the occult may be explored from a naive or egoistic standpoint that leads to confusion or exploitation. Experiential spirituality may be confused with the adaptation of new ideas or the taking on of new identities. Spirituality may be donned as another external appearance, and there will be those of strong egoistic natures who will use this new spirituality to take advantage of others and promote themselves. These trends are already evident, so much so that there may be those who may wish to reject the new spirituality altogether.

However, these limitations are part of a slow awakening to true spirituality from a non-spiritual basis that must first misinterpret or misuse spirituality before really coming to understand it. The influence of mass media-oriented commerciality, the dominant force of the age, will naturally taint this renascent spirituality, yet the long term trend will bring greater light, depth, clarity and understanding through all such initial difficulties and pain of new birth. Though as a planet we may still be decades, if not centuries, from a truly spiritual culture, that is the eventual goal of all our individual and collective striving which at least the more aware among us must recognize, wherever in the world we may live.

One of the religions which will greatly benefit from the new spirituality is Hinduism, whose universality is inherent in its original formulation as Sanatana Dharma, the eternal tradition of Truth and natural law. Modern spiritual teachers from the Hindu tradition — like Ramakrishna, Vivekananda, Aurobindo, Yogananda, Shivananda and Gandhi, to mention a few — have been at the forefront of the new universality in religion and experiential forms of spirituality. Sanskrit terms like yoga, karma, gurus, mantras, Kundalini and chakras have entered into common parlance and become the basis for many new insights.

Hinduism — which has appeared as a contracted religion, in retreat, and perhaps on the verge of self-destruction for the last few centuries — is experiencing a new revival and expanding its influence all over the world. Its related teachings under different garbs — like Vedanta, Yoga, Tantra, and Ayurveda — are one of the main thrusts of the new spirituality. In its modern renaissance Hinduism has not ceased to be a belief-oriented religion, it never was one. As Sanatana Dharma or the universal tradition, it has always been an open tradition, accepting the best in science and religion, and allowing great freedom in its approach to the spiritual life.

A Hindu spirit, a sense of universality, tolerance and non-exclusivism is arising in the minds of people throughout the world. Therefore it is important that we reexamine this spiritual tradition. Sanatana Dharma, the oldest of the world's religions and perhaps the most dynamic, helps us in this process of universalization because it is a religion that has emphasized spiritual aspiration over the clinging to particular forms. So let us dive deeper into this great legacy in order to discover our greater potential, which is not merely human but Divine.

Where all books of knowledge become one, that is the conscious Self of all beings.

Taittiriya Aranyaka III.11.20

Yoga is the calming of the disturbances of the heart.

Patanjali, Yoga Sutras I.2

The teacher guides the student in the meaning of the Vedas: speak the Truth, practice the Dharma, do not be heedless in your self-study.

Taittiriya Upanishad I.19

Neither agency, nor action does the Lord create for the world, nor the experience of the fruits of action. All this occurs according to the nature of things.
The Lord does not recognize the good or evil done by anyone. Knowledge is covered by ignorance, by which creatures become deluded.
But those whose ignorance is destroyed by knowledge of the Self, for them like the Sun, that knowledge reveals the Supreme.

Bhagavad Gita V.14-16

1.4
Religion or Dharma: Belief or the Nature of Truth

In the Western world religion is associated with a belief in something unseen, miraculous, or perhaps even irrational. For the Western mind religion is something removed from ordinary existence, and apart from the world of Nature, something supernatural, like the miracle of Christ of turning water into wine. The fruits of our religious practice are gained after death, in heaven, and seem little related to the events of this life. Such religion is different than religion in the Eastern or Hindu sense, and appears artificial and imaginary, rather than the product of any profound meditation.

There is no such term as religion in this sense in the teachings of India. The term for a spiritual teaching is Dharma, the natural law of Truth and its universal and eternal principles. The so-called religions of India — like Hinduism and Buddhism — are not religious belief systems but ways of cultivating dharma, ways of developing higher awareness. To follow the Dharma requires living in harmony with the universe attuned to the consciousness of the Universal Being. Discovery of the Dharma is possible only through direct perception, which requires freeing the mind from its conditioned responses. It does not rest upon belief or speculation. The cultivation of Dharma, which is religion in the sense of the Himalayan sages, means developing an awareness which is clear enough to perceive things as they are. If we emphasize Dharma rather than religion there will be no more religious conflicts in the world. In fact, religion as we have known it will disappear into a real search for Truth through Yoga and meditation.

True religion is to recognize the Dharma, the underlying Universal Truth, and to build our life and culture around it. Just as the same physical laws, like gravity, are in operation for all human beings regardless of race, nationality or religion, so the same spiritual laws, like the law of karma, are in effect for everyone. These are the dharmas that we must discover through inquiry into the nature of Reality. For this we must approach the universe with an open mind and heart, not seeking to impose any belief or theory upon life but allowing the being of life to reveal itself to us in silent receptivity.

Dharma as the nature of things is the eternal constant, the Self-existent Reality. No one doubts that fire burns, its very existence proclaims it. Each thing similarly proclaims its dharma or place in the universal order through the qualities which compose it. Each person has his or her own dharma, a unique place and function in the cosmic rhythm. To know the Dharma is to discover not only the unity of Truth but all of its variations upon this overflowing oneness of Self-existence.

Yet while we can perceive the nature of physical objects fairly easily it is difficult to perceive our mental states and their consequences. We do not perceive the results of our actions, like the effects on ourselves of the violence we perpetrate against others, because these effects manifest only through time (and sometimes not until future lives). To see the real consequences of what we are doing, we must purify our minds and hearts by both right living and meditation. Just as a person who puts his hand in a fire must suffer (though there is no intent on the part of fire to hurt anyone), so when we violate natural law we must suffer. Greed, anger, and hatred are negative forces that harm us as well as those we injure.

We have only one basic choice in life. We can choose to be dharmic, which is to follow the laws of the universe, or we can choose to be adharmic, which is to try to impose our personal desires on life and thereby separate ourselves from the great stream of creation. To be religious in the true sense is to be dharmic, which is to recognize the sacred nature of all beings and embrace all that is. Unfortunately, to be irreligious has been portrayed by organized religion as the rejection of some arbitrary dogma (like the divinity of one particular human being), rather than living out of harmony with the universe (like being violent or greedy). This view must be changed if we are to discover what is really true. Religion must base itself upon the pillar of natural law and immutable truth, not on human opinion and transient convention. Otherwise it is not wholesome and real but artificial and arbitrary and must lead us down the road of decay and destruction.

The Dharma of the Human Being

As human beings we are in doubt as to our true nature. This is a simple fact that each one of us can observe. We do not know who we really are or our real purpose in life. We do not know what happened to us before we were born or what will happen to us after we die. Individually, we think that it is our purpose in life to achieve various outer goals like pleasure, wealth, fame, or power. Yet none of these achievements brings lasting happiness as we can easily see by examining the lives of the people who have achieved them. Collectively, we also seek to gain power, territory, or mastery of the external world, which similarly does not lead to any real peace or happiness, or to a harmonious society, as the crime and wars in the world reveals. Unlike the rest of nature, we human beings appear not to know our place in the universe or how we can find happiness, and we are perpetually seeking something we do not have.

There is a reason for this uncertainty about ourselves. The dharma of the human being is to discover the Universal Truth. We have no outer dharma, no instinctual programming like animals which we cannot deviate from, but only an inner dharma, an openness of nature which gives the capacity to evolve a higher consciousness — or if we fail to recognize it, which allows us to follow our lower tendencies that debase us. For human beings our dharma is to bring consciousness into the world, which means to bring an awareness of the inner Self into all our activities. While the nature of other creatures is evident, our human dharma must be created, must be won, and requires a labor to bring forth. This is the work of spiritual practice or sadhana.

The spiritual life exists beyond the names and forms of objective and material existence and their limitations. Dharma is not a mere name but the indicator of this Eternal Truth behind the name and form. In Sanatana Dharma or the Universal Truth it is not name and form, which being limited cannot be universal, that is emphasized, but the underlying reality which transcends all appearances. The name or form of one's spiritual practice is not what matters, but our real character, who we really are, and what we are actually doing in life, our daily activity. It doesn't matter if we are called pious according to one religious authority or excommunicated by another. The real issue is whether we are introducing a greater consciousness into the world through how we live.

Whatever name or form one may look up to in religion is not of ultimate significance but how the name and form is used to approach the Inner Reality. If concentrating on God in the form of a monkey aids in preparing the mind for meditation, such a monkey is a great dharma, a great truth. On the other hand, if the idea of God encourages only dogmatism and sectarianism, such a God is an obstacle to our spiritual life that must be cast aside.

In this regard it is more important to recognize God in the world, in Nature, in human beings, and in oneself, than to worship God beyond the world, apart from other people, apart from Nature and ourselves. If we can't recognize the immanent Divine, the Divine within us and within the world, we are not even entitled to talk about the Transcendent. If we can't perceive the Dharma we cannot find That which is beyond all laws and limitations.

Dharma and the Religions of the World

The different religions of the world, to the extent that they represent a higher path, represent different dharmas or approaches to Ultimate Truth. The different religions can be viewed as aspects of Sanatana Dharma or the Universal Truth. The great sages of all lands have been aware of a universal tradition of Truth, beyond name and form. Without such an awareness no real wisdom, which requires going beyond personal or social limitations, would be possible.

The religions that have their origins in India have always emphasized Dharma. Buddhism is called Buddha Dharma, the law or truth taught by the Buddha or the enlightened one, the Dharma of Enlightenment. Jainism is called the Jain Dharma, the truth or teaching of the Jina or the one who has conquered his own nature. Sanatana Dharma, or the Universal Dharma, is the basis of Hinduism and explains why it is the most comprehensive syncretic of all religious traditions. The great sages of India have never regarded themselves as limited to a belief that we would call Hindu, people following a particular ethnic religion limited to the Indian subcontinent. They have looked upon themselves as followers of Sanatana Dharma, the universal tradition of Truth. The term Sanatana Dharma can be found in Buddhist and Jain teachings as well, as the movement toward universality is part of the spirituality of India and the Himalayan region as a whole.

We could say, therefore, that there are two basic types of religious teachings in the world. The first are the belief-oriented systems that predominate in organized Western religions, which emphasize sin and salvation leading to either hell or heaven. Their idea of cosmic law is something imposed from above by the will of God, which may appear to be arbitrary or even vengeful. The world of Nature is looked upon not as part of our own being but as a hostile reality to be controlled or conquered, or as a realm of temptation.

Second are the dharmic traditions of the Eastern world which emphasize natural law, meditation and Yoga leading to Self-realization. Dharmic traditions seek to know the truth of things and do not set any dogma over our own inquiry. Most indigenous and tribal religions, with their connection to natural law, could be considered as dharmic type of teachings, though they are not always articulated to the same degree as the systems of India.

Yet among the mystics of Western religious traditions we find a respect for life and a practice of meditation similar to the dharmic traditions of the East. Among these have been various Jewish and Christian mystics, Sufis, and numerous mystical groups outside of organized religions, like the Rosicrucians and Theosophists, many of which recognize karma and rebirth that characterizes dharmic traditions. One could argue that Dharma is the real impetus behind Western religions as well but that it was distorted by various vested interests into dogma and authority.

While other religions are specific formulations relating to a particular founder, Hinduism as Sanatana Dharma remains generic. It is not a particular dharma but the Dharma as such, which is its concern. For this reason, Hinduism is not a particular religion but encompasses all that could be called religion. Sanatana Dharma is an attempt to be open to and embrace all dharmas, not to set up one against another. So too, our concern in religious study should be with religion as whole, not with one religion or another. We should ask not what is the truth of this or that religion but what is the truth of religion? Then alone can we find the Universal Truth.

Religion and Belief

Religion as generally known in the Western world is defined rather neatly, but perhaps simplistically, by belief-oriented religions — particularly Christianity and Islam — as Judaism is more a culture than a belief. Such religions identify religion with belief in One God, one primary representative of him, and one book of revelation from him. The right belief is said to bring about salvation. The wrong belief is thought to be the worst of all sins and bring about damnation. Such religions are trying to convert the entire world to their belief, which conversion they view as salvation for humanity.

While such monolithic belief systems can state their beliefs in clear and uncomplicated terms, they often sound more like slogans or stereotypes — absolute statements that appeal to an emotional need for certainty and security but fail to deal with the complexity of life itself. Is Truth really that simplistic or have we narrowed it down according to our own bias which, however well intentioned, falls short of what life in its abundance really is?

Why should God have only one Son when all things come

from Him? Why should there be a final prophet when there were previous prophets, and while the capacity of spiritual knowledge can be found in all people? Why should God only be addressed in the masculine tense when the infinite must be beyond sexual characteristics and possesses as many feminine as masculine qualities? Why should there be only one bible or religious book when any number of books on other subjects are possible? Is the Word of God so simple that it can be put into one book. Can it be reduced to human language at all? And is it salvation that we need or self-understanding? Does mere belief change us or is a more intimate contact with the truth of our being through meditation necessary?

A statement of exclusive absolutes about religion is not possible for dharmic traditions like Hinduism, nor would Hindus find it desirable. Coming from a universal background such restrictions appear arbitrary. They appear not as a deep understanding of the Infinite but as the attempt to arrive at a mental or emotional formulation that satisfies not the soul's longing to merge into the Divine, but the ego's need for certainty, security and control.

Only that which is absolute can be absolute. The Eternal can be absolute, but to assert finality for a particular person or event in the historical realm, is to try to make absolute that which is relative. This is not spirituality, but spiritual materialism, confusing the absolute which is formless with a particular form.

And why should a belief be asserted? Rather the Dharma should be recognized. Why should any Truth have to be asserted at all? Does not the truth of things speak for itself if we are open to it? We don't have to proclaim that fire burns. We don't have to shout to the world that the sun shines. It is an experiential fact. So too, spiritual realities should be approached as experiential facts. The insistence on belief indicates lack of experience, and leads to ignoring what experience teaches us.

Belief is not knowledge. A belief is an assumption, which if treated as a working proposition can at times help us find the truth. But if we take it as true in its own right it becomes a preconception that clouds our vision. For example, in order to climb a mountain I must first believe I am capable of it or I will not be able to put forth the effort to attempt it. But if I regard that believing I can climb the mountain is the same as actually climbing the mountain, then my belief is a delusion which breeds not only incapacity but unreality. While belief may have some preliminary value it must be discarded as we move along the path.

Belief in God is not knowing God, though it may assert what God is supposed to have said. And how can we know what someone has said if we don't know who they really are? Merely because it is written in a particular book? If we ourselves do not know God, how can we fulfill his will? And if we don't know God within ourselves, how can we know his reality outside ourselves? Such belief does not take us to truth but presumes to tell us what it is as a mere verbal formation. Belief becomes a substitute for knowledge which prevents us from discovering truth.

To know a particular food, like grapes, we must actually get them and eat them. It is not merely enough to believe in grapes or believe in another person who once ate them. Belief is no substitute for knowledge and by itself it cannot destroy our ignorance. The process of belief building is the very essence of the ignorance of the mind which asserts its mental and emotional patterns as truth.

Any number of beliefs are possible because all beliefs are speculative, with no certainty for any of them. One religion has one set of beliefs, which are said to be the absolute truth. Another religion has a different set of beliefs claimed to be equally true. One proclaims that God is only this and another proclaims that God is only something else. One makes a particular representative of God final, the other does so with another figure who may have a different teaching. The process of belief building leads to division within humanity. As belief is not knowledge but emotional assertion, belief leads us to the battlefield to determine not which belief is true but which will dominate the world (which is the real goal of belief). It leads us away from spiritual experience which it opposes, because any real spiritual experience will cause us to question all beliefs.

Belief and Faith

However, we must discriminate between belief and faith, which are not the same thing. Belief is the identification of God or truth with a book, person, church or religion. Faith in the true sense is an openness of the heart to truth, which looks beyond belief to communion with That which transcends names and forms. True faith is the same in all beings, it is the aspiration to the Divine or Truth. Belief can be in any number of things and has no finality. To have true faith we must give up our beliefs. Faith is to accept the Divine nature of all beings and to be open to Divine grace in all places. It is to orient the mind not in its own conclusions and beliefs, but in a recognition that Truth transcends all human opinions.

Dharmic traditions recognize the importance of faith over belief. Whereas the articles of belief are particular, faith itself is universal. We should all have faith in the Divine or Truth and our ability to realize it, but when we believe in someone or something as the truth, rather than seeking ourselves to discover the truth, we are breeding illusion.

True faith is in the Dharma, in the nature of things, which is self-evident, and in the understanding that the nature of things is beneficent and sacred, blissful and liberating. True faith is not in an external formulation but in the perception of inner reality. It does not arise from wishful thinking but from an openness to the Self-existent Truth.

Theological Ethics and Dharma

Belief-oriented religions, when they formulate themselves in an exclusive manner, project their own particular theological ethics which may be apart from, or even contrary to any universal ethics. They hold that if a person does not believe in a particular formulation of God, in one specific representative of him, in one book which contains his word, or other such particular dogmas, that the person will suffer or go to hell, whatever else the individual may do — however good, kind, compassionate, generous, or selfless he or she may otherwise be. This is what could be called "theological ethics," the judgement of people not by their behavior but by their beliefs, which makes not having certain beliefs on par with doing harmful actions. Raised as an orthodox Catholic, for example, I was taught that to not to accept the unique divinity of Christ was a mortal sin, along with things like theft or murder. Theological ethics may be confused with universal ethics, as if not following the articles of belief of a particular religion was a universal failing or a moral depravity. Sanatana Dharma does not accept any particular theological morality. It says that we raise ourselves by good actions and lower ourselves by actions which are bad. It does not matter what we believe in but how we live. Hinduism says that a person who leads a good life, even if he or she has never come into contact with any scripture and has no religious beliefs at all, will come to a good end. On the other hand, a person who leads a bad or harmful life will come to a bad end, even if he believes in what he thinks is the true religion.

It is not irreligious activity that we need to be afraid of — the breaking the codes of belief, ritual or prayer of a particular church — but adharmic (non-dharmic) activity, which is living out of harmony with the Universal Truth and contrary to the nature of things. In this regard confining ourselves to one belief as opposed to others is contrary to Dharma, is out of harmony with the universe, which includes all beings, and like the sun shines on all alike.

Theological ethics divides humanity into the believers and

the non-believers, which may be Christians and heathens, Muslims and Kafirs, or simply the people of God and those of the devil, or whatever the religion decides, including condemning different sects within one's own religion as heretical. This division is equated with a real division in behavior between good and evil, holy and unholy, as if only the members of a particular religion can be truly good and those of other beliefs must be evil, however good they may appear.

Dharmic traditions, on the other hand, differentiate human behavior into dharmic and adharmic actions, actions which further the Truth and those which promote ignorance and illusion. There is no division of humanity into dharmic and adharmic souls because the soul, our inner nature is inherently dharmic. The soul is our dharma. The only division is between people who know their true nature and those who do not. Knowledge or ignorance is a capacity of all human beings, and we must all move from the ignorance to the knowledge, if not in this lifetime than in a future one. Hence Dharma can never divide people into warring beliefs.

If there is only One God or Truth then there cannot be two humanities, the believers and the non-believers. If reality is one then humanity must also be one. To connect to the oneness of reality, we must first recognize the unity of human beings. If we cannot see the unity of human beings — including our unity with those of different religious persuasions — then we cannot talk of the unity of God. This requires recognizing the common dharma of human nature, which is to seek the eternal, not to place people under restrictive religious identities.

The Culture of the Dharma

Culture appears to be a purely outward thing, the various changing codes and customs of different peoples, times and countries. If we look at the different peoples of the world, we see every sort of cultural variation in terms of language, clothes, diet, art, religion and so on. The spiritual path as something timeless and universal should be beyond culture and to begin only when we set cultural prejudices aside.

Yet culture has another meaning. The spiritual life is a form of cultivation. To flower in truth we must cultivate our nature, we must create a field for the soul to grow that pervades our whole life, both individual and collective. Dharma as a way of life is a culture as well. Culture thus ultimately refers to how we live. Our culture is the field that we create by the circumstances and modalities of our lives. Naturally this should have a certain harmony to it, not a rigid order but an organic development like a plant.

Many modern spiritual teachers, particularly coming from India, have tried to purify their teachings of extraneous cultural factors. They have provided teachings and practices that can be applied irrespective of cultural context. This allows people to apply various meditation approaches without having to consider the more transient and outward side of the teachings, like rituals. They can adapt meditation practices without having to change jobs, residence or relationship. They don't have to become Hindus but can adapt Hindu insights in a way that enhances their lives as they are already developing from their own background. Even in India the spiritual teachings have become more distant from their cultural matrix.

While this non-cultural approach has its value, it does have its limitation. Many people today, particularly in the West, have rejected the cultural side of spiritual teachings, not to transcend culture but to remain immersed in materialistic or intellectual cultural patterns which are contrary to the spiritual path. They have not taken up a spiritual culture, like the study of yogic teachings, chanting, ritual, spiritual art, but instead have continued with the popular culture of entertainment or an intellectual culture of art and science. Some people in India are following this trend as well.

It is important that we recognize the nature of the culture we surround ourselves with and are clear as to its values and how they affect us. While we can apply spiritual teachings outside of any particular cultural context this does require that we ignore the culture we follow. We cannot graft spiritual teachings onto a non-spiritual culture and life-style and expect them to work. Nor do we need to reject the cultural side of spiritual teachings when it may be useful in enriching our lives.

We are all surrounded by culture, the collective culture we live in and the personal culture created by our daily activities. Culture is our environment and life-style which determines our nature and consciousness on a subtle level. We are all creators of culture both for ourselves and for the world. The culture we create is the forms and actions we follow and thereby allow to spread. Our culture is the food we eat, how we exercise, the entertainment we seek, the programs we watch, the books we read, our meditations, and all else that we do. It is important therefore that we are conscious creators of culture and not just mechanically or passively follow the cultural influences around us, which in the modern world are generally negative to deeper spiritual values.

Different spiritual traditions have created different cultures. Yet of the world's cultures, the richest and most spiritual is probably that of India, which has placed the greatest emphasis on spiritual realization. This is the culture of Yoga, the culture of the Dharma. The culture of the Dharma is the richest of all cultures because it is a universal culture. It is the civilization of the cosmic mind which transcends all the limitations of mere human social structures. It includes systems of physical, mental, and spiritual culture. It contains art, music, poetry, philosophy, medicine, and astrology. It provides a rich field in which all parts of our being can grow toward the light. While this spiritual culture has entered into the general culture of India, it has a purity and elevation that remains above any mass culture, which tends to limit, stereotype or distort it.

Many of us today practice certain spiritual teachings but remain otherwise immersed in a materialistic cultural matrix. This is true not only of Westerners but of Hindus, particularly those who reside in the West. The general cultural field in which most people live, modern technological and pop culture, consists of mass media influences and various scientific developments. There is the general intellectual climate, the books or trends which are popular, and the major political and social movements of the day. Many of us are identified with these and follow their activities. In this process we may be coming under the influence of their values, which may be contrary to any spiritual practices.

Therefore we should examine our time and see how much of it we spend in areas of culture which are unspiritual and do not promote Self-knowledge. If we don't nourish a dharmic culture in our lives, then we will not be able to lead a dharmic life or create a dharmic society.

If we are going to immerse ourselves in a culture, let it be the culture of the Dharma. This may require doing daily yogic practices, mantra, meditation, chanting, devotional singing, pujas, rituals, satsangs, and pilgrimages. It may include studying or practicing the dharmic systems of music, dance and poetry. It may mean following an Ayurvedic life style or healing practices.

Unless we develop the culture of the Dharma we cannot expect our culture to change nor can we expect spiritual teachings to really enter our life and society. The Dharma has a rich culture and many sides. Dharma itself is our support, but we must support the Dharma for it to uphold us. For India this means an interrelated spiritual and cultural renaissance is required. Those who see the necessity for this must take action to bring it about.

As rivers flowing to the sea discard their names and forms, so the person of spiritual knowledge, liberated from name and form enters into that celestial Being who transcends all.

Mundaka Upanishad III.2.8

That which they call Indra, Mitra, Varuna, and Agni, as also the celestial beautiful feathered eagle — That which is the One Being, the sages declare in manifold ways.

Rig Veda I.164.46

He whom the Shaivites worship as Shiva, whom the Vedantins call Brahman, whom the Buddhists call Buddha, whom the Naiyayikas call the creator, whom the Jains call the Arhat, whom the Mimamsakas call karma, may that Vishnu, the Lord of the three worlds, grant you the object of your desire.

Stotra to Vishnu

1.5
The Eternal Tradition of Hinduism

Hinduism is the oldest, most complex and enigmatic of the world's major religions and the most atypical compared to predominant Western belief systems. Hinduism represents the other side of religion — the ancient, imagistic, occult, mystical and yogic side that Western monotheistic religions have tried to supplant, if not exterminate. Pagan religions, of which Hinduism is the main representative in the world today, are not simply primitive, immoral or oppressive as they have been portrayed by their detractors. As the unknown, the other and as the religions they sought to replace, monotheistic beliefs projected their own fears and suspicions upon Pagan religions and their different approaches to reality. Predominant Western religions have seen Hinduism according to the limited perception caused by their monolithic beliefs which, like a particular language, condition us to see the world according to a particular point of view.

Dharmic traditions are experiential rather than belief-oriented — as we see among the Hindus, Buddhists and Taoists. They are open, creative and meditative in their approach, an attitude often shared by Western pagan religions and philosophies as well. Such experiential traditions have a great appeal to the inquiring spirit, with their knowledge of deeper levels of consciousness and extrasensory powers. They have a greater history of tolerance and respect for other beliefs, a necessary attitude in the multi-cultural world order in which we live today. Hinduism as Sanatana Dharma has always been able to accommodate many different religious and spiritual approaches. From its standpoint religious beliefs are not absolutes but merely theories, working models, guides to practice, which must eventually be left behind.

Hinduism abounds with every possible name and form for Truth or the Divine. This is because Hinduism requires that we see the same reality in all the diversity of creation — that we see the same Self in all beings. It is not because Hinduism is trapped in the diversity of name and form but because its sense of unity is inclusive, not exclusive. As a formulation of Sanatana Dharma, Hinduism is not attached even to its own names and forms, however diverse. It can accommodate the names and forms of all religions into its comprehensive view. This universal view permeates the form of the teachings of Hinduism, which consists of many different approaches to the same One Reality. It allows the teaching of Hinduism to encompass all time and all religion, and affords it a characteristic tolerance and syncretic view of life.

However the Western mind — caught in an historically based religion or tied to modern scientific materialism, which both view time and humanity in a linear way — has tried to reduce religion to a particular name and form. It has tried to compartmentalize Hinduism as a religion the way Christianity and Islam appear to be, seeking to find in all religions a particularized belief system. Looking for a code of beliefs such people have regarded the diversity and freedom of Hinduism as confusion, contradiction, or lack of consistency — as a sign that there is really no tradition of Hinduism as such but just a collection of cults. Yet this seeming chaos is the field of a universal tradition that cannot allow itself to be reduced to any stereotypal pattern.

Sanatana Dharma as an open tradition does not exclude any useful way of approaching the truth of the vast universe in which we live. It does not define itself against something else but includes all that is useful to the spiritual life. Yet this does not mean that a universal tradition accepts other religions as they see themselves. This is not possible, as exclusive views which insist that their point of view alone is correct are mutually contradictory. In accepting the value of all sincere approaches to the Divine, Sanatana Dharma cannot sanction the exclusivism of any particular group. That Sanatana Dharma accepts Christ as a great saint, for example, does not mean that it accepts the Christian claim that Christ is the only Son of God.

Sanatana Dharma accepts faith and devotion but not the limited form with which it is identified. Sanatana Dharma accepts all sincere efforts to find truth or to help other human beings. In this regard Hinduism can honor atheists, if they are doing good or searching for the truth. Hinduism values doing good more than the mere belief in God, which can be used as a mask for doing harm. It holds that a person who does good, be he an atheist or agnostic, is better than a person who does harm, be he a firm believer in God. Yet beyond valuing what is good, Hinduism values spiritual knowledge. It says that a single person of real spiritual perception is more significant than any number of mere believers or good people. All the good and bad actions of people are ultimately illusory as the Divine is the only true reality. One who knows that is the real teacher.

The Name Hinduism

It is strange to note that Hinduism — the main religion in the world which has defined itself as a universal tradition — has come to be viewed as a narrow ethnic belief system. There are several reasons for this, not the least of which is an inability to recognize an open spiritual tradition by those who have been dominated by exclusive belief systems. Perhaps the main factor that causes us to misunderstand the connection between the eternal tradition and Hinduism is that Hinduism is a religion without a name, a religion in fact beyond names.

The name Hinduism suggests a belief limited to a certain geographical region, ethnic group or nation — the religion of the people who inhabit the Indian subcontinent, who are sometimes regarded as a certain primitive dark-skinned racial type. This is a misconception that reflects little knowledge of Hinduism or India and its inhabitants. It would be like calling Islam "the religion of the Arabs," or Christianity "the Greek religion," which terms were historically used for these religions when they were more circumscribed in the regions which followed them.

India is not a small and homogeneous country like France, Germany or Great Britain but a subcontinent like Europe. In fact India contains more different ethnic groups and languages than that of Europe as a whole. Modern India has fourteen official state languages which have a variety of scripts. The Punjabis of North India and the Tamils of the South are more distinct peoples than the Swedes of Northern Europe from the Greeks of Southern Europe.

Hindus come from a number of different races and ethnic groups even within India. The people of Nepal, though a Mongolian race like the Tibetan and Chinese, are predominately Hindus in religion. The tribal groups of India, many of which are not Caucasian or Mongolian but of the Austric race, are predominately Hindus. Hinduism remains in Bali in Indonesia, which region it once predominated, and has left an important imprint upon the entire culture of the area. Hinduism once dominated Indochina wherein the Ankor Wat temple complex abounds with Hindu temples. Vietnam was a Hindu country up into the seventeenth century. Afghanistan was dominated by Hinduism into the tenth century. Hindu influence existed in Persia, Central Asia and the Middle East, not only by Hindu traders but with Hindu converts. Even a number of ancient Greeks became Hindus.

The name Hinduism is a misnomer and a foreign invention. It goes back to the ancient Persians who called the land of India, the land of the Hindus as they contacted India through the Indus river, the western most large river of India. The Sanskrit name of the Indus, Sindhu, gave rise to both Indus (and India) and Hindu (the Persians pronounced Sindhu as Hindu). Hinduism is thus a geographical term. It does not define the Hindu religion but simply identifies the region from which Western cultures have contacted it.

The term Hindu cannot be found in any of the classical texts of Hinduism. It is nowhere in the Vedas, Upanishads, Bhagavad Gita, or the classical books on Yoga. Hindu texts do not contain the idea of different religious identities but only of a common human religious aspiration. As Sanatana Dharma or the universal tradition, Hinduism does not need to represent itself as one religious identity as opposed to others. If we live in the ocean, for example, do we have to give water a name? It is only those who live on different rivers that must give their water a special name. Hinduism has never separated itself off from the universal truth and formulated itself as one point of view regarded as exclusively true.

Sanatana Dharma and Time

From the standpoint of Sanatana Dharma and its eternal vision, history is not a linear or progressive development but a cyclic return, symbolized by the lotus which is the most enduring symbol of Hinduism. We are ever moving around the great center of Truth which lies within us. While we may try to divide people up into different identities, religious or otherwise, we are thereby only fragmenting our own deeper universal nature. While we may place human beings on a time line leading to heaven or utopia, we are only removing ourselves from Eternity, in which alone is liberation.

The timeless view of Sanatana Dharma affords two aspects to its teachings. First the same basic or eternal teaching endures throughout all the diverse layers of the Dharma, like a single thread on which many gems are woven. Second, and complementary to this, the teaching is reformulated anew with every generation, in fact with every practitioner. Each practitioner must gain his or her own realization and cannot merely be saved through belief or by the action of another, however great. The teaching of Sanatana Dharma is thereby both eternal and ever-new. This is its twofold beauty. It abides in the timeless present.

In this regard the Hindu tradition is not only the oldest of the world's religions, it is also the newest. On one hand, having no founder it goes back to beginningless time. On the other hand, being recast by living sages in every generation it reflects the present moment. The Hindu religion provides not only the oldest teachings in the world but living exponents of them in every age, great gurus who have realized the Divine Self. In fact Sanatana Dharma teaches that we are all that Divine Being and that we must realize That in our own lives. It is a religion that is coterminous with Life itself and with our own individual life.

Seeing no final goal within the realm of time, Hinduism is thought by some to be outside of the progressive movement of history. However, being oriented in the Eternal, Hinduism sees the final goal existent each instant of time. It is not bound to a history that makes us look to the future rather than to the present, but teaches that the Eternal itself pervades all the waves of time.

A New Look at Hinduism

There is, unfortunately, little good literature available in

English on Hinduism and little understanding of its meaning as Sanatana Dharma. There has been an attempt to fit Hinduism into the mold of Western religions, which it does not resemble. Those who attempt this generally criticize Hinduism for not living up to a standard it never had, expecting it to have a clearly defined dogma of One God, One representative of him, and One Book. While there is a significant literature on the different branches of Hinduism like Yoga and Vedanta, there is little that explains their position within the greater Hindu tradition.

Hindus themselves, with an open and inclusive tradition have seldom found it necessary to define what a Hindu actually is. To many Hindus, Hinduism as a universal tradition includes everyone except those who willfully exclude themselves from it, and Hindus may not regard such exclusion as real. Some Hindus do not even like to be called Hindus because they think the name detracts from the universality of their teaching.

Academic views of Hinduism focus on various aspects of this broad tradition and seldom address it as a whole. They rarely discuss the idea of Sanatana Dharma. Few books have attempted to define what all Hindus have in common. Hinduism, like its Motherland India itself, is like a tropical jungle, extending up to the highest mountains in the world, which no simplistic views can adequately characterize.

Most of the prevalent views and studies of Hinduism available in the West remain limited and unreliable. They fail to see the unity of the tradition and merely examine formal differences within various teachings, and may even regard the different teachings of Sanatana Dharma as in conflict with one another. Instead of looking for the common thread they try to divide off Veda and Tantra, or Vedanta and Yoga, often on merely semantic grounds. These are just exercises in the discriminating intellect of academicians which miss the real truth of the teaching. Another vision is required, not merely for better understanding Hinduism but for better understanding our own reality, which is what Sanatana Dharma is really all about.

Hinduism and Organized Religion

Hinduism is not an organized religion such as we ordinarily consider one to be. There is no Hindu church, no Hindu Pope, no Hindu Rome, Jerusalem or Mecca that all Hindus should go to, no Hindu messiah or prophet all Hindus must revere, no one Hindu Bible all Hindus must read. Hinduism has no prescribed day of the week for worship, no one prescribed mass, ritual or call to prayer that everyone must do. The different sects within Hinduism have their different ashrams, temples, leaders, holy places, holy days and holy books, but there is no one set of these for all Hindus.

We could say therefore that Hinduism is the greatest disorganized religion in the world. It has never organized itself along monolithic lines, with a set dogma and specific canon of beliefs. It has remained decentralized and localized, which is perhaps why of all the ancient imagistic and mystical religions, it alone has survived through the millennia. Therefore, Hinduism as an open tradition appeals to all those who are looking for a religious tradition with a great diversity of teachings that does not require any exclusive loyalty. Hinduism is the religion of the individual and allows each person to choose his or her own approach to Divinity based upon various teachings that encompass all human capacities.

However, Hinduism is organized in the sense that it contains systematic teachings for all manner of temperaments and all stages of life. As Sanatana Dharma it has teachings that encompass all of human life and culture from medicine and science, art and music, occultism, spirituality and Yoga. In this regard Hinduism has probably the best organized and most complete teachings of all religions and has addressed in detail all aspects of our existence, including those considered to be outside the domain of religion in other cultures. The literature of Hinduism in these different fields is both much older and much larger than that of any other religion. Hinduism is not organized as a belief or social institution but as a vast set of teachings that we are free to approach from our own angle.

Some people have wondered if Hinduism is a religion at all. They state that its very absence of organization and its non-seeking of converts disqualifies it from being a religion in the common sense of the word, and that it thereby fails to have a world view. They would see it just a collection of local cults from the Indian subcontinent, with every sort of primitive ritual and superstition that has long been discarded in the Western world.

On the other hand, Hinduism contains some of the world's most profound spiritual philosophies, like Vedanta, which have inspired many great Western thinkers including Thoreau, Emerson, Goethe, Schopenhauer, and a number of modern physicists. Hindu sages themselves have looked upon the West itself as spiritually primitive and lacking in any real experience of the Divine or higher states of consciousness, for which even terms are lacking in European languages.

Hinduism as a religion sees the validity of all aspects of human spiritual aspiration, from the use of simple images to the most exalted formless meditational approaches. Those who judge it by one side only reveal their own lack of comprehension. Hinduism is a multidimensional tradition that no form of linear thinking, whether scientific or theological can grasp.

Certainly Hinduism stretches the limit of the idea of religion. Yet the very things that make Hinduism different from organized creeds provides it with a greater claim to be a religion in the true sense of the word, which is a teaching that helps us to unite with Truth or God. Though Hinduism is not a religion as a convenient and exclusive set of dogmas, it is a religion in that it addresses all the prime issues of life and death, God and immortality. Hinduism contains a consistent set of insights, principles and practices that reveal the highest truths of Self and cosmic knowledge. It provides various methodologies or paths of Yoga to enable us to perceive this truth in our own consciousness.

Hinduism has its particular spirit, its universality, spirituality and yogic view. This goes back to the most ancient Vedic texts and their ability to identify any name or form of the Divine with all others, as when the Vedas proclaim the Sacred Fire, Agni, includes within itself all the Gods or Divine powers. Hinduism is a vibrant ocean of spiritual, religious and occult insights and practices, woven into a vast culture. It has the complexity of life itself, which cannot be reduced to a formula, understood in a single book, or controlled by any church or organization. Have you ever looked at the complexity of a tree, with its roots, bark, branches, leaves, flowers and fruit? Then look at the complexity of other trees and plants in the forest. The universe contains great diversity and uniqueness everywhere but with an underlying unity. The Divine similarly has various layers and dimensions as part of an Eternal and Infinite Being and Consciousness which defies all definitions, however clever, rational or appealing.

The Religions of Hinduism

There is perhaps a greater diversity of religions inside of Hinduism than outside of it. The different religions of the world — Judaism, Christianity, Islam, Buddhism and Taoism — do not have any greater variety of forms and practices than do the different sects of Hinduism — the Vaishnava, Shaivite, Shakta, Ganapata, Brahmanical, and so on.

Hinduism has been regarded as a collection of sects, not as a singularly formulated religion. More properly speaking, as Sanatana Dharma or a universal approach, Hinduism is a collection of religions rather than a single religion as commonly understood. Yet it is more than a collection of religions. These different religions of Hinduism are integrated into a greater and more universal Truth, and not merely haphazardly thrown together.

Each of the main sects of Hinduism can be seen as a religion in its own right. Several sects of Hinduism, like the Shaivite and Vaishnava, have a longer tradition and a more extensive literature than the predominant Western religions.

Almost whatever is found in any religion by way of forms of worship or view of the Reality worshipped — including rituals, prayers, yogic practices and meditations of all kinds, monotheism, pantheism, polytheism, agnosticism, atheism, and monism — can be found in Hinduism. Each is respected according to its place in human development and none is allowed to be the last word for all people. This is not to say that all views and practices are regarded as equal or the same — generally meditation is the highest practice and Self-realization the highest goal — but each practice is given its appropriate place.

One Christian fundamentalist group has said that there are only two religions in the world, Hinduism which absorbs everything and Christianity which excludes everything. One can be a Hindu and practice whatever religious teachings one finds beneficial, whether they arise from the Hindu tradition or outside of it. Hinduism defines itself as a pursuit of Truth, not the insistence upon a particular belief. Another of its names is the religion of Truth, Satya Dharma. It says that Truth alone wins, not untruth. One does not cease to be a Hindu by pursuing truth in different forms but only by ceasing to pursue Truth and instead promoting dogma.

India, the Land of Religion and Spirituality

The universal spirit of Hinduism is manifest in India, which contains more religions than all the rest of the world put together. All the religions of the world are present in India but in no other country. Besides the many branches of Hinduism, India contains the Sikhs, Jains and Buddhists, which originated from the country. India has become the land of refuge for many religious groups. It contains the last remaining Parsees, representatives of the ancient Zoroastrian religion of Persia, which itself is very similar in language and deities to the ancient Vedic religion of India. There is an ancient Jewish tradition in India going back to pre-Christian eras and a Syrian Christian tradition going back to the fourth century. Surprisingly, there is a greater diversity of Islamic groups in India than in any Islamic country in the world, which includes Sunnis, Shias, Ahmadiyas, Ismaelis, Bohras, and Sufis, a number of which, as unorthodox Muslims, are banned in orthodox Islamic countries like Saudi Arabia and Pakistan. The largest Bahai temple in the world is in Delhi and the Theosophists have perhaps their largest following in India. The acceptance of such diversity is explicable only through the open tradition of Hinduism, as non-Hindu countries do not have such diversity of religious practices or groups.

The World View of Hinduism

The Hindu world view rests upon an ultimate and impersonal Reality or Brahman, and sees the world as transient, as possessing no independent reality of its own. It says that God is the only Truth. For this view, Hinduism is accused of rejecting the world, denying life, and not giving proper importance to the individual, while religions that fail to recognize such a Transcendent Reality may be considered progressive, compassionate and concerned about the welfare of the individual because they rest upon a personal and historical concept of the Divine.

Such thinking remains superficial because Hinduism does not reject the world but only the idea that it exists apart from the Divine. Hinduism abounds with reverence for the Divine in all the forms of life and all aspects of nature — including animals, plants, rivers and mountains. It honors all aspects of the personal worship of the Divine with forms of the Divine Father, Mother, Lover, Friend, and Lord. Moreover it says that the individual is God (*aham Brahmo'smi, ayam Ātmā Brahma*). It values the individual over the entire universe. It emphasizes the full realization of the Divine in the Universal Being that is our true nature as an individual.

These two most salient features of Sanatana Dharma — its seeing of the Divine in innumerable forms and its recognition of the Divine reality that transcends all forms — are not contradictory but the two sides of the same vision which not only recognizes the Absolute Truth but finds it in all creation. Not surprisingly, Hinduism is not only criticized for its transcendent impersonality but for its many gods and worship of Nature — which is a criticism of an opposite nature. Those who see Hinduism as caught in the formless or as caught in the diversity of form only reveal their inability to understand its teaching. How can the same teaching be criticized in such opposite ways? It is like criticizing a person for being both too impersonal and too personal at the same time.

Owing to its otherworldly nature and rejection of mundane goals (including heaven, which as another world is also a mundane goal) as the highest reality, Hinduism is said to be pessimistic or anti-life. This appears in a stereotypical image of Hindu yogis mortifying themselves, closing their senses, fasting and weakening the body. This is perhaps the most misinformed of the judgements against Hinduism. Hinduism teaches that we are all God, that we contain within ourselves all time and creation, that our nature is Infinite Bliss inherently transcending all sorrow and limitation.

To call a teaching which says that our nature is Infinite Bliss pessimistic, while religions that teach we are sinners or materialistic science that teaches we are only biochemical reactions, optimistic, is absurd. Hinduism says that all life arises from joy and that we will all eventually return to Eternal Joy, however great a sinner we may temporarily appear to be. Religions that teach an eternal hell for anyone are the real pessimists, and those that teach an eternal heaven that still depends upon a body (which can never be eternal) are also pessimistic. Those who limit our being to this transient life are the worst pessimists of all.

Universality in Religion and Conversion

Hinduism has been criticized as not being a universal religion because it does not seek converts or send out missionaries. Hinduism does not seek converts, but this is because of its universality, not owing to a lack of it. Its very universal view which sees the Divine in all prevents it from becoming a religion of conversion. From its point of view the seeking of converts is a sin against the Divine in others, a kind of salesmanship, which fails to recognize the Divine Presence which is already there. Hinduism shares its knowledge with those who are receptive but it does not believe in proselytizing or propaganda. It is more concerned with communicating the essence of Truth than getting people to change their religious labels. It regards Truth as something we should search out inside ourselves, not try to impose on others as if it were an external thing.

Conversion is actually the denial of universality and an assertion of partiality. If Truth is universal who are we going to convert and to what? Hinduism emphasizes recognizing the Truth. We cannot be converted to Truth but only to a belief, which is a form of falsehood. A truly universal religion does not need to seek converts because it recognizes that we are always part of Universal Reality. From the point of view of Universal Reality all people are always within it. No one can be excluded from it, though we may try to live apart from it.

From the Hindu standpoint most attempts at religious conversion are forms of violence, particularly on a psychological level but often outwardly as well. They are attempts to impose an external belief or code upon a person, not to help them understand their inherent Divinity. They do not serve to awaken the Divine Self in people but to subordinate them to some institution or dogma. This violates the principle of ahimsa, or non-violence, in Hindu thought, and reflects a lack of understanding of the deeper consciousness in all creatures.

Hinduism has not sought to convert the world by preachers or by armies (which usually go together). It grows organically among people as part of a spiritual culture and way of life that affirms the Inner Truth and does not require that people abandon their native beliefs. Wherever Hinduism has gone it has preserved the indigenous culture of the people. It has sought to promote Nature and the Self everywhere, to help all beings develop their inherent potential, rather than to impose a belief, ideology or discipline from the outside. Hinduism as a religion of life cannot simply be grafted on by changing one's beliefs. It must be integrated into our very daily activity, not only personally but with our entire culture, greater humanity, and all of Mother Nature. It is concerned with a genuine spiritual development, not merely a change of names or clothes.

Yet it is wrong to think that people cannot formally become Hindus, regardless of their land of birth. This requires preliminary preparation including study and meditation as well as following a particular life-style and ethical discipline. It is usually not given instantaneously or overnight. Once these preliminaries are fulfilled a simple ceremony called Shuddhi is performed which makes one into a Hindu. There are a number of groups in India and the West who do this, though they seldom advertise or wave a flag about it.

Shuddhi means purification, not conversion. According to Hinduism we cannot be converted to anything, just as we cannot change our nature. It is not a question of becoming converted from one identity to another but of discovering what our real identity has always been. To become a Hindu all that we need to do is purify our minds and hearts so that we can recognize our Eternal Being. This is not to assume a new identity but to discover the Divine within us. Such conversion does not require denying any truth. It only requires giving up exclusive beliefs that cloud our perception.

Today Hindu spiritual teachers travel all over the world to share their knowledge and have disciples of all backgrounds and religions. They have not insisted that people formally convert to Hinduism in order to benefit from their teachings or follow its practices. Many Westerners practice Yoga and meditation, chant Om and other Hindu mantras, and visit sacred sites in India but have not had to become Hindus to do this. This is because Hindu teachers see more value in sharing spiritual practices than in getting people to assume different identities.

Universality and Monotheism

Western religious thinkers generally identify universality in religion with monotheism — the idea that there is only One God and hold that all truly religious human beings should worship this same Supreme Being. Yet this insistence on monotheism is exclusive, not universal. It rejects polytheism, pantheism, monism (the idea that there is only One Reality), and other forms of spiritual experience. Such extreme monotheism reduces the Divine to a single formulation, insisting on one savior, one final prophet or one book for all people. Such a One God is not a truth of unity, which is universal, but the assertion of a single thing, which is opposed to all else. True unity is universality, it is not one thing as opposed to an other, but the One that is everything.

The partiality of exclusive monotheistic belief is revealed in how it fragments itself further into warring monotheistic creeds (which is why monotheists are always fighting with each other as to whose One God, or view of the One God, is correct). Such extreme monotheism is generally a religion of warlike people. It promotes conquests and aims at the building up of empires. The religion of One God is reflected in one state and one leader, and the denial of dissent. Not surprisingly, historically Western monotheism has appeared as the religious counterpart of political imperialism and empire-building, and its expansion to absorb all other countries and cultures. History has revealed how monotheism has been allied with invasions, colonialism and genocide, which may not be an accident but the very end result of a rigid, one-sided and therefore ultimately violent view of the Divine.

The One God becomes an abstraction to which actual people are sacrificed. He becomes jealous, wrathful and communal and promotes such action among his special followers. He is opposed to any creativity or spirituality and insists upon his law, ritual and theology as the unquestioned truth. While this may not have been the intention of the mystics who emphasized the One, it has often become the behavior of his literal-minded followers. Such monolithic views are out of harmony with the cultural diversity of the modern world, and represent a medieval and authoritarian standard that usually has a patriarchal bias.

Hinduism, on the other hand, contains the diversity needed for a global age. Hinduism as Sanatana Dharma cannot be limited to belief in One God, but it acknowledges monotheism as an important approach to the spiritual life. In this regard Hinduism is also a monotheistic religion but not exclusively so and has created a number of wonderful monotheistic approaches including that of the Divine Mother. While accepting monotheism as one major approach, Hindus do not always regard it as the highest. Many Hindu teachings regard monism, or the idea that there is only One Truth, as the highest truth and as transcending any monotheistic or personal God.

Hinduism does not project a monolithic standard which discredits other views of reality. It recognizes the Divine in many names and forms, as possessing both unity and multiplicity, and as both personal and impersonal. It is not troubled by any contradiction between the One and the Many. It regards the Many as various appearances or manifestations of the One, which is not one in the sense of one thing opposed to others but a unity that includes diversity without being limited by it.

Hindu forms of monotheism exist in abundance. Most followers of Shiva or Vishnu hold a theistic view of reality with the Divine called Shiva or Vishnu. But Hindu theism is very different from Western monotheism. It allows for the existence of a multiplicity of names and forms of the Deity and of secondary manifestations as various Gods and Goddesses under its power. Hindu theism is also a yogic path that emphasizes devotion to the deity and personal communion with it through meditation and samadhi. It is not a monolithic belief system but an experiential monotheism of the Divine Beloved.

Multiplicity in Unity

Multiplicity arises from unity. The one itself becomes the many just as a single seed becomes a tree in all of its luxuriant growth of roots, trunk, branches, leaves, flowers and fruit. The many are not opposed to the One. The many are the One. The key is to see the One in the many and the many in the One, not to try to reduce the many to the One. The former is universality. The latter is a dead uniformity.

Hinduism is noted for the complexity of its views of reality, which seem bewildering for a mind trained to think that there is only One God. Its many names and forms for the Divine, its numerous great teachers from the most ancient times to the present generation, and its many practices and paths of Yoga encompassing all human temperaments — is difficult even for a broad mind to comprehend. While other religions have a single strand, Hinduism appears like the tail of peacock.

Hinduism recognizes many great spiritual teachers and leaders, saints, sages, seers, prophets, incarnations, yogis and siddhas through the millennia. There are several figures — like Krishna and Rama, the avatars of Vishnu, or Shankaracharya, the great teacher of Advaita Vedanta — who are of particular importance in Hinduism but none that dominate it so exclusively as Christ, Mohammed or Buddha dominate their religions. Each region of India has its important saints and sages of the last few centuries like Tulsi Das and Kabir in the north, Narsi Mehta and Mira Bai in Gujarat, Nanak for Sind and Punjab, Jnaneshvara and Tukaram of Maharashtra.

Hinduism has many new sects, and does not limit itself merely to the teachers of the past. The Swami Narayan movement starting in Gujarat in the late eighteenth century, the Ramakrishna-Vivekananda movement starting from Bengal in the late nineteenth century, the Arya Samaj movement founded by Swami Dayananda Sarasvati in north India in the mid-nineteenth century, are only a few of such groups which now have wide followings of their own.

Many modern Hindu teachers have become known in the modern world like Ramakrishna, Vivekananda, Gandhi, Aurobindo, Ramana Maharshi, Shivananda and countless more. Yet they are not known as mere propagators of Hinduism but as world teachers, proponents of Yoga, meditation, and universal spiritual principles. Such spiritual teachers see themselves as part of a universal tradition, not the proponents of a particular religion against others. This is no mere accident. It is part of the universal formulation of Hinduism which is not closed along particular lines.

Freedom: the Goal of Religion

Sanatana Dharma holds that freedom or liberation is the true goal of life. True freedom is freedom from all external conditioning influences, whether of body or mind. This is the freedom of Self-realization, complete independence of time, space and causation. We are all seeking freedom. No one of us is happy with boundaries or limitations. No one wants to live in a small and cramped room, or have no space in which to grow or express themselves.

Unfortunately we are seeking freedom in the outer world, through more possessions, power or pleasure, which are all forms of bondage and limitation. Hinduism says we need to redirect this seeking of freedom within, where alone it can be truly realized. Freedom is not the ability to have more things or gain more experiences but the inner fullness which no longer requires such external supports for our happiness. A universal tradition emphasizes freedom, which includes freedom from religion as well as religion as a means of gaining freedom. If we remain tied to a church, book or savior our religion has failed us, or we have failed our religion.

Hindus have complete freedom in their spiritual life. They have any number of holy books to choose from and are not required to literally believe in any one of them. They have any number of avatars and gurus to choose from, and aren't required to follow any one of them exclusively. They have their sacred sites everywhere that they live. Their spiritual practices are done in their own homes on a daily basis and require no church.

In the modern world we pride ourselves in our freedom of choice. We can choose where to travel, where to work, what to read, and so on , but in religion we still have little choice. We may be able to choose what church to join, but how much freedom do we have to choose our relationship with God? If we want to worship the Divine as Mother, what choice do we have in Christianity or Islam, for example? We are given different ways of approaching Christ but how many of our churches offer other great teachers who we can connect? And how many of them teach us to contact the Divine within ourselves?

As part of Sanatana Dharma, Hindus are not restricted from studying other religions or respecting Truth wherever and in whomever they see it. Hinduism does not have any word like heretic, pagan, or kafir. Hindus have never invaded any country and tried to force people to adopt their religion. There is no excommunication in Hinduism, nor do Hindus ever condemn anyone to eternal hell. Hindu leaders do not issue proclamations restricting the forms of worship that can be practiced by Hindus. Hindus do not have blasphemy laws that prevent anyone from criticizing Hindu teachings.

Hinduism does not require that we all have the same view of Divinity but encourages unique and diverse views for the full unfoldment of creative intelligence. It says that there is something unique about each person, which is their special connection with the Divine, and that there should be no standardized religion for all people.

Hindus are not required to agree with one another on religious matters but are encouraged to develop their own insights. Hindus respect original and honest thinking, rather than merely parroting what someone else, however great, has said. If two Hindus do not follow the same guru, worship the Divine in the same form, or study the same scripture, it is not a problem. They will not fight with or try to convert the other person. They respect their diversity as part of the great abundance of life.

Hinduism as Sanatana Dharma has developed an unparalleled freedom in the religious and spiritual realm, as Western culture has done in the scientific and material realm. It would be of great benefit to humanity to combine them. To the Hindu the spiritual realm is an inner universe to be explored, not merely a dogma to believe in. Hinduism provides the tools of Yoga and meditation so that we can make this exploration for ourselves. As such Hinduism is a way of spiritual knowledge, a universal teaching and yogic technology that any individual can adopt. It is not another religion fighting for converts or seeking to impose its ideas on the minds of people. Hinduism has as its highest goal liberation, which includes going beyond all religious teachers, holy books and churches, to the Divine presence at the heart of each individual.

On the other shore of the waters, in the center of the Earth, on the ridge of Heaven, greater than the great, by luminous seed having entered into the lights of the senses, the Lord of Creation stirs within the child.

Mahanarayana Upanishad I.1

There is only One Divinity hidden in all beings, who pervades all, the Self of all beings. He is the overseer of all actions, who dwells in all beings, the witness, the sole consciousness beyond all attributes.

Svetasavatara Upanishad VI.11

The Self is the Divinity that exists in all directions, born in the beginning, he moves within the child. He alone has been born and he alone will be born. He faces all creatures whose face is to every side.

Svetasavatara Upanishad II.16

Who One only like a magician rules all the worlds with his ruling powers, who One only exists in the arising and birth of all beings: those who know Him become immortal.

Svetasavatara Upanishad III.1

1.6 Sanatana Dharma and the Religions of the World

Sanatana Dharma as a universal tradition has room for all faiths and all religious and spiritual practices regardless of the time or country of their origin. Yet it places religious and spiritual teachings in their appropriate place relative to the ultimate goal of Self-realization, to which secondary practices are subordinated. Sanatana Dharma also recognizes that the greater portion of human religious aspiration has always been unknown, undefined, and outside of any institutionalized belief. Sanatana Dharma thereby gives reverence to individual spiritual experience over any formal religious doctrine. Wherever the Universal

Truth is manifest, there is Sanatana Dharma — whether it is in a field of religion, art or science, or in the life of a person or community. Wherever the Universal Truth is not recognized, or is scaled down and limited to a particular group, book or person, even if done so in the name of God, there Sanatana Dharma ceases to function, whatever the activity is called.

The Religions of India: Hinduism and Sanatana Dharma

India has been a great land of spirituality and mysticism since time immemorial. It is not merely a country but a subcontinent held together not by a force of arms but by a common spiritual aspiration. The great beings of this land, men and women, have focused on the spiritual life, the development of higher consciousness as their primary pursuit, giving military expansion, economic development, intellectual pursuits and religious ritual — the prime goals of other cultures — a secondary role. Because of the emphasis on spiritual experience in all its forms, India has promoted the idea of a universal tradition and has given birth to a number of religions and to the greatest diversity of spiritual teachings and yogic practices in the world.

Hinduism itself is not merely a single religion, one among many, but a harmony of many different religious teachings that maintained a peaceful coexistence with each other as parts of a universal tradition. It has not forced or molded these different teachings into uniformity, in fact this diversity itself has manifested because of the universality of the Hindu view, which is that it is not the many who become One but the One that expresses itself as all. This recognition of the One in all and all in One is the basis of the creative and yet synthetic Hindu vision that can produce ever new teachings without losing track of the underlying eternality of Truth.

One could divide Hinduism into a Vedic (Brahmanical) religion, a Shaivite (Shiva) religion, a Vaishnava (Vishnu) religion, a Goddess (Shakta) religion, a Ganesh religion, a solar

(Saura) religion, and various local or regional systems, including new spiritual movements which may have no defined affiliation. These different teachings have neither merged into one common belief, nor separated off into conflicting creeds. They have come together while maintaining their particular approaches, in the recognition that true unity includes the fullness of diversity. They have realized that the truth of any religion need not exclude the truth of others because all religions are merely aids to the unfoldment of the universal, which is the real goal and origin of all.

This harmony between the different religions of Hinduism can be used as a model to integrate the different religions of the world. It would not require any religion giving up its distinctive spiritual flavor but only recognizing the validity of other approaches in the Universal Self which is the real aim of all spiritual practices.

Hinduism's Spread through History

Hinduism is often erroneously looked at as restricted to the subcontinent of India. However, historically Hinduism has been practiced throughout much of the world, and teachings of the same order as Hinduism have flourished everywhere. Hinduism has never formulated itself as restricted to a particular geographical region but as relevant to all beings. Nor has it frozen itself in time. It has continued to grow and absorb additional spiritual and cultural impulses into itself, developing in an organic way.

Hinduism has spread in three main waves through history. The first wave occurred during ancient history and prehistory. It is difficult to define but is clearly evidenced by the common language, culture and religion found from Bengal to Ireland among peoples speaking Indo-European languages. Regions of ancient Indo-European culture consist of Europe (including Greece, Rome, the ancient Germans, Celts and Slavs), Anatolia (Modern Turkey, until the Turkish invasions of the Middle

Ages), Syria (the Mittani Era, second millennium BC), Iraq (the Kassite Era of the second millennium BC), Armenia, Persia, Afghanistan, Central Asia, Western China (the Tarim Basin and further east), and North India (to the Krishna river).

In addition similar practices to the Hindu can be found in all ancient cultures, including the Egyptians, Babylonians, Sumerians, Chinese and Meso-americans with their common solar religions, fire offerings, and tripartite social system of priests, warriors and common people. This early phase of Hinduism, or Vedic culture, existed from perhaps as early as 7000 BC to as late as 500 BC. It was the ancient phase of Hinduism, evidenced by the Vedas, the oldest books in the world, particularly the oldest Rig Veda.

The second phase involved a diversification of Sanatana Dharma, with the development of many religions, philosophies, mythologies, monastic and spiritual movements through Hinduism, Buddhism and Jainism. Its main movement was to the East with Buddhism spreading to Tibet, China, Korea, and Japan, and both Hinduism and Buddhism spreading to Burma, Thailand, Indochina, Indonesia, and even into Polynesia. There was at this time a secondary spread of dharmic teachings to the West into Central Asia, which was predominately Buddhist but had Hindu elements as well. A yet lesser diffusion occurred to Persia and Europe, mainly through various mystical movements.

This was the classical age of Hindu-Buddhist culture which came to dominate Asia. It began around 500 BC, overlapping with the first wave. It began to decline with the Islamic invasions of India around 700 AD and came to an end around 1500 AD with the Islamic conquest of India and Indonesia, which involved massive destruction of temples, and genocide of people, and a policy of forced conversion to Islam that caused the Hindu religion to contract in order to preserve itself and which eliminated Buddhism from India as it did from Central Asia.

The third phase is occurring today as part of one of the most important spiritual movements of modern times, the expansion of Eastern meditational teachings throughout the world. It also shows a combination of Hinduism and Buddhism, as well as aspects of Taoism or all the main Himalayan spiritual traditions. This phase began with the dissemination of Hindu teachings to the West through the eighteenth and nineteenth centuries. Vedantic influences reached many Western thinkers including Goethe, Schopenhauer, Emerson, and Thoreau through various translations of the Upanishads and Bhagavad Gita. This phase started in earnest with Vivekananda's trip to the West in 1893. There are now various Yoga, Vedantic, Vedic, Tantric and Buddhist centers in most countries and most major cities of the world. Along with it has been a modern migration of Hindus to different countries with significant Hindu populations in Canada, USA, the Caribbean, South America, Africa, and Europe. This movement is likely to last for many centuries to come. It will help create a global spiritual tradition, though this may take decades or centuries to accomplish.

Yet Sanatana Dharma is more than what is commonly regarded as Hinduism. It reflects the spiritual approach of the sages of India and the Himalayan region whatever their outward religion. All the religious traditions of India have at least at times reflected the universality of Sanatana Dharma. The Christians and Muslims of India, particularly a number of Sufis, often reflect Sanatana Dharma in their mystical teachings more so than their own less experiential orthodox traditions. They demonstrate a greater openness to Truth and seeking for spiritual realization than is characteristic of their religions as a whole. They have their own meditation practices, which are often more typically Hindu in nature and almost unknown in other countries dominated by their religions. This is because Sanatana Dharma can link one to the essence of spirituality, whatever religion one comes from originally.

As a conscious formulation of Sanatana Dharma, Hinduism

remains close to its basic principles of universality and eternity. This universality even encompasses partiality. Hinduism holds that it is alright for any one of us to think that our particular religion is the best, or that our teacher is the highest, if such thoughts increase faith and concentration in our inner practices. But we should recognize the right of others to think the same of their teachings, and not try to impose our point of view upon them. Sanatana Dharma requires that we respect the sacred nature of each individual and his or her own private relationship with Divinity, which it is not for us to judge.

Hinduism and Particular Religions

BUDDHISM

Buddhism formulates itself as Buddha Dharma, "the way or Dharma of enlightenment." Starting as a monastic reform movement within the field of Hindu teachings, Buddhism gradually developed a separate existence of its own apart from the common stream of Sanatana Dharma, though it never entirely gave up its roots. Indian Buddhism and its direct offshoots, like Tibetan Buddhism, contain much of the greater Hindu tradition or Sanatana Dharma with the use of Sanskrit mantras, Yoga techniques, Vedic fire rituals, Ayurvedic medicine and Vedic astrology, and a common iconography and temple worship with the Hindus. Buddhist traditions of more distant lands, like China and Japan, maintain many of these same practices but adapted over time to their own cultures.

Buddhism and Hinduism have much in common and their differences are often merely semantic or variant lines of approach. In fact there are greater differences among teachings in each tradition than between the two, as both traditions contain considerable diversity. While Hindus and Buddhists may disagree as to the nature of enlightenment or liberation, not only with each other but among themselves, all their various branches accept spiritual realization through meditation as the goal of life.

The Buddha is not portrayed as the only Son of God, the last prophet, or the only Buddha. He is simply the main representative of enlightenment in this era, the ideal sage or yogi. He is often regarded more as an inner archetype than an historical person. There are said to be Buddhas teaching in all worlds, not just this Earth. Previous Buddhas are recognized and many of these, like the Buddha Kashyapa, which is the name of one of the seven seers of the Vedas, have the names of great Hindu sages. Hindus recognize Buddha as an avatar of Vishnu and Buddhists recognize the Hindu avatar Rama as a Bodhisattva or enlightened being. There are many sages and yogis honored in both traditions.

Sanatana Dharma or the eternal tradition can be called Buddha Dharma or the enlightenment tradition. There is no conflict between Sanatana and Buddha Dharma as both emphasize dharma. Only if there is an insistence that one tradition or the other has an exclusive hold on truth or enlightenment do they have any real conflict with one another.

JAINISM

Jainism is another great religion of India that did not entirely merge into the common fold of Sanatana Dharma until recent times. Mahatma Gandhi has been called the greatest modern Jain, for his championing of non-violence, though he was actually a Hindu. The Jains base their teachings on various Tirthankaras, who like Buddhas, are great enlightened teachers going back to ancient times. They have similar yogic values and practices as other Hindu and Buddhist teachings. In fact, much that is regarded as typically Buddhist, like the emphasis on non-violence, karma, and the rejection of a personal God, were originally Jain teachings, which predate the Buddhist by some centuries. Jainism can also be seen as an aspect of Sanatana Dharma, not a separate religion. The Jains have included some of the greatest minds of India, including poets, mathematicians, astronomers and philosophers.

THE SIKHS

The Sikhs were originally a sect of the Hindus. It was a custom to make the eldest son into a Sikh or a defender of the faith. This was to counter the Islamic invaders who tried to force conversion upon the people of India. The Sikhs arose as defenders of Hinduism or Sanatana Dharma against this Islamic invasion from Central Asia.

Some modern Sikhs consider that they have a separate religion outside of Hinduism. However, if we examine the sacred books of the Sikhs we find that they are filled with references to Hindu names for God, like Ram and Hari, and Hindu holy books, like the Vedas and Puranas, and are composed by various saints and sages, like Nanak, who are equally revered by the Hindus. The Sikh holy books are written in a language, Gurumukhi, that has much in common with Sanskrit. Many Sikhs still consider themselves to be a sect of the Hindus and hold to the idea of Sanatana Dharma.

Some people hold that the Sikhs combined Hinduism and Islam but the Sikh holy books have very few references to Islam, Allah or Mohammed. The Sikhs fought against the Muslims and were their main opponents in northwest India. But the Sikhs like the Hindus accepted Muslims into their culture if they were peaceful and respected the spiritual traditions of Islam, like Sufism.

TAOISM

Taoism arose in China not India, yet there were considerable contacts between Taoism and the Indic traditions, and both arose in the Himalayan region. Buddhism and Taoism in China influenced each other considerably and often merged into a single teaching. Hinduism had contact with Taoism from a pre-Buddhist era, which was maintained through the Buddhist era.

Taoism can also be considered to be a dharmic tradition. It has its yogic and meditation practices much like the Hindu and Buddhist, as well as its tradition of occult knowledge. Like the Vedic tradition it looks back to an earlier enlightened age of humanity before what we know of as civilization began. Like Hinduism Taoism is a religion of life and Nature that seeks to grow organically. It does not proselytize or seek converts. It has no dogma or ideology and promotes a universality of vision. Like Hinduism it has its folk religion of various Gods, Goddesses and nature spirits, with a similar form of temple worship being offered to them.

The Shinto religion of Japan, which has much in common with Taoism, and interacted with Buddhism, can similarly be regarded as part of the Eastern dharmic traditions.

ZOROASTRIANISM

The Zoroastrian or ancient Persian religion still survives in India as the Parsees, who took refuge in India in the eighth century after the Islamic conquest of Persia. Their religion is very similar to the Vedic in language and concepts, particularly in its emphasis on fire worship, and hence can perhaps be counted as another dharmic tradition. It also had a strong influence on the Greeks, Romans, Jews, Christians and Muslims and brought many Vedic/Hindu ideas to them. Its influence even spread to China. Western India was often under Persian rulership in ancient times and brought about yet a further exchange of ideas and practices.

PAGAN RELIGIONS

The pagan religions of Greece and Rome, and those of the ancient Celts, Germans, Slavs and Baltic peoples (Lithuanians and Latvians) have much in common with the Hindu, particularly through their similar Indo-European languages and cultures. The ancient Greek culture has many affinities with that of ancient India. Both had temple worship of Gods and Goddesses, many with common names or characteristics, had elaborate mythological systems, deep philosophical traditions and a love of astrology. Much of this older European religion can be better understood through looking at Hinduism. A study of Hinduism — wherein these traditions are still alive — can aid in the restoration of this older European tradition in which many of the keys of Western mysticism, Goddess worship, spiritual art, philosophy and science lay hidden and ready to return.

This same worship of Gods and Goddesses, temples, magic and mysticism can be found among the Egyptians and Babylonians. In this regard Hinduism as the most ancient of living religions can help us understand and perhaps even recreate other ancient traditions like those of Greece, Egypt and Babylonia.

While Christianity looks down upon pagan religions, we should note that Christian theology and philosophy relies heavily on Plato, Aristotle and Plotinus, who were pagan philosophers. The philosophy, medicine and science of both Christianity and Islam has a pagan Greek basis from which came modern science and most of modern European intellectual culture, art and poetry. Science and its empiricism developed from a pagan basis, reflecting the concern of indigenous traditions with understanding of the world of Nature. Hence it may not be surprising that the keys to a spiritual science can be found within these same pagan traditions. In this regard the resurrection of Greek and other pre-Christian religions of Europe is an important part of the spiritual awakening today.

Christian and Islamic mysticism has also maintained connections with the pagan mystical traditions of the Hindus, Egyptians, Greeks and Persians. Pagan cultures thus are not simply primitive but capable of great spiritual, philosophical, and scientific sophistication. On the other hand, the non-pagan beliefs have been noted, particularly in the Middle Ages, for oppression of art, science, and mysticism, destruction of libraries and colleges and an anti-learning attitude which has not aided in the unfoldment of true knowledge for humanity.

JUDAISM

Judaism as an ancient religion resembles Hinduism in a number of respects. Ancient Judaism employed similar fire offerings as the Vedic religion. Its emphasis on Torah or the law is similar to the Hindu emphasis on Dharma. It has actively promoted mysticism in its Kabbalistic tradition, which contains an honoring of the Goddess. In fact some Jewish mystics teach karma and rebirth and promote yogic like teachings and practices, including non-violence.

In terms of social practices, the Jews like the Hindus are a tolerant religion, not promoting conversion, and a culture, not merely a belief system. They have never sent armies on crusades and holy wars or sought to impose their religion on others by the force of arms or propaganda, like Christians and Muslims. The Jews respect other religions, even those who follow very different practices, and do not claim that their's is the only true religion.

Historically there was trade between ancient Israel and India, via the Phoenicians, particularly during the reign of King Solomon, the most famous Jewish king. During the second millennium BC Syria was under the rule of the Mittani, an Indo-European people worshipping Vedic Gods, so some exchange of ideas even at that time might have been possible. Later some Jewish communities went to India where they found protection. There has been a long interchange between Hinduism and Judaism.

The main difference between Hinduism and Judaism is theological, with the Jews being opposed to the use of images that most Hindus use. However there are Hindu groups, like the Arya Samaj, who also oppose the use of images. In this respect Hinduism can include traditions like the Jewish as one line of approach. Hinduism as a religion has no real quarrel with Judaism, though unfortunately modern India under leftist and Islamic influence has not properly supported Israel, though the two countries have many common causes.

CHRISTIANITY

Christ exhibited not only mysticism but a practice of non-violence that may derive from a yogic influence. There are stories that Christ came to India to study during his lost years, or that he came to India after the crucifixion and died in Kashmir at a very old age. There is an additional story that St. Thomas, one of the twelve disciples, and in some Gnostic literature, the brother of Jesus, died in India (though this is highly speculative). Yet for certain we know that Hindus admitted Christian refugees into India as early as the fourth century AD, giving them a land to practice their religion without persecution.

Hindu and Buddhist ideas spread to some degree into Greece and Rome. Many of the early mystical traditions of Christianity, and some which were outside of it, reflect a knowledge of karma and rebirth and the seeking of mystical experiences. The Desert Fathers were ascetics much like those of India. However the development of Christianity as a social institution through the Roman Empire opposed and restricted these more yogic like elements in the early church and most were forgotten, like its rejection of the doctrine of rebirth as heresy. Catholic Christianity alone of the main Western religions developed monastic orders like the Hindu and Buddhist, which had mystical traditions as well (though subordinated to the authority of the church).

Trade between India and Europe continued throughout the Middle Ages up to the time of the Turkish invasion of Europe (the fifteenth century), which was why Columbus originally journeyed to America seeking India. Not surprisingly many of the great Christian mystics like Meister Eckhart or Hildegard of

Bingen arose in the Rhineland region, noted for its trade with the East. No doubt spiritual ideas came along with this trade. There is a possible Hindu and Vedantic influence on Christianity through the Middle Ages and into the Renaissance, where great thinkers like Marsilio Ficino mention Hindu practices with great respect. The practices of Christian mystics often have more in common with Hindu yogic practices of mantra and meditation, than with what is ordinarily regarded as Christianity.

Otherwise Hinduism and Christianity are very different in both their teachings and practices, particularly the Protestant form, which like orthodox Islam is against all images and generally anti-mystical. Catholicism, though having a mystical and devotional side like the Hindu, has an authoritarian structure and missionary militancy quite different than the diversity of Hinduism. Naturally as long as such missionary activity is directed against Hindus, it is difficult for Hindus to respect Christianity as a spiritual path, however much they may appreciate some Christian mystics or Christ himself.

ISLAM AND SUFISM

Early Islam had a considerable influence from Hinduism and Buddhism. Hindu traders lived in Mecca and contributed to the culture of the city. The Pre-Islamic religion of Arabia, like the Pre-Christian religions of the Middle East and Europe, was much like the Hindu, using a multiplicity of names and forms for the Divine and not formulated as a belief system. Mecca was a site wherein the Goddess was worshipped and contained 360 icons, much like those used in Hindu temples. The stone at Mecca was an ancient sacred stone much like the Shiva lingas or Shiva stones of Hindu worship.

The first part of India to come under Islamic influence was the province of Sind, by the mouth of the Indus river. Mathematics, astronomy, medicine, and other arts and sciences better developed in India were taken in part back to the Middle East.

Hindu Vedantic teachings were taken by the Sufis, the mystics of Islam, who are defined even today by the Dictionary of Islam in India as Muslims following Vedantic ideas.

Afghanistan and Central Asia came under Islamic influence from 700-1000 AD. They were originally regions of Buddhist and Hindu predominance and preserved aspects of these teachings. Even today many Sufis look to this region as their holy land, particularly eastern Afghanistan and its portion of the Himalayas, which links them back further to the greater Himalayan tradition that is more typically yogic in nature. Hence Hinduism has strongly influenced the mystical side of Islam.

However Hinduism and Islam are otherwise almost opposite religions, with Hinduism presenting all the diversity and creativity of the tropical jungle and Islam the stern absolutism of the desert. Islam is more of a social-political movement than a spiritual teaching. Otherwise it would not be so intolerant of yogic traditions like the Hindu (and to its own Sufi tradition) that emphasize the inner quest more than any outer religious identity. Hinduism has more affinity with the Sufis as with Western mystics but finds that they often do not understand the full range of yogic practices or the ultimate truth of Self-realization.

NATIVE, TRIBAL AND INDIGENOUS RELIGIONS

There are two general types of religions that exist in the world. The first is organized and belief-oriented religions which are centered around a particular teacher or formulation of the Divine. Most typical in this respect are Christianity and Islam. They usually have an historical revelation, a time bound vision of their mission, and insist upon the same belief structure for all human beings. They are strongly monotheistic and generally recognize only one life for the soul followed by heaven or hell. They tend to be aggressive, proselytizing or militant. These belief systems are imposed upon existent cultures as a kind of religious superstructure which often denigrates the value of any native cultures that predates them.

The second are non-organized, indigenous, tribal and native beliefs. They have many names and forms of the Divine, with no set dogma or seeking of converts. These religions include the native and tribal beliefs of Africa, Asia and America, and the pagan religions of Europe. These religions are connected to Nature and to the Earth, and thereby are peaceful and passive. They are part of an organic unfoldment of life, and not the imposition of an ideology or dogma. They breathe the cycles of eternity and are not historical revelations. They are interwoven with the culture of the people and must be taken up as part of the whole way of life. They aim at spiritual experience, a greater awareness of both the cosmos and oneself, which they would never reduce to a series of beliefs, and they generally believe in rebirth or reincarnation. They contain similar traditions of Yoga, shamanism, dance and chanting as the Hindu, and a knowledge of higher states of consciousness, both occult and spiritual, though not always to the same degree.

Buddhism and Jainism primarily belong to this category, as they have an organic basis and emphasize meditational experience rather than belief (which cultural base is largely Hindu), and have a great respect for Nature and the sacredness of all life. Taoism and Shinto are entirely of the second group. Judaism contains aspects of the second group as well, as it is an organic tradition, rooted in a people and a culture, and not seeking world domination. Yet rejecting the image worship and the multiple deities of native religions, it has aspects of the first group as well.

Of the native traditions Hinduism, which integrates the indigenous religions of Southeast Asia, is the largest, the most organized and the best preserved. Therefore Hinduism provides the key to these organic religions and can show us their relevance as part of a universal tradition and global spirituality.

Today, with a new interest in mythology and shamanism, we

are rediscovering the validity of native religions and their spiritual practices. We are discovering in the native religions of Africa and America much psychological sophistication and a greater connection with Nature that we all need in this ecological age. Unfortunately most of these native cultures have been overrun if not destroyed, particularly by the conversion efforts of belief-oriented religions, and those few which are left are fighting for their lives.

Christianity and Islam spread mainly by converting people from their indigenous beliefs, teaching them that their indigenous religions, and the culture on which they are based, were wrong, inferior or evil. Hinduism, on the contrary, teaches people to preserve their indigenous beliefs, to cherish their native heritages. Hindus are seeking to help such indigenous cultures and spiritual traditions revive themselves and flourish in the modern world. Those following such native traditions should examine Hinduism and form a common alliance with it. Those seeking to preserve the religious and spiritual heritage of humanity contained in these native beliefs will find a common cause with the Hindus.

Hinduism and Religion

Though Hinduism finds an affinity (though not identity) with the mystical traditions of Christianity and Islam, it cannot accept the exclusivism and intolerance that has occurred in the outer side of these religions, and which to some degree has occurred even in dharmic traditions (even in Hinduism). Hinduism can be critical of these and other religions on a number of points, particularly where they fail to understand the higher levels of consciousness and universal laws like karma.

Yet Hinduism is not afraid of criticism by other religions. It is not restricted to a particular revelation and so can grow and develop where it finds itself to be wrong. It is willing to listen to those of other religious beliefs, and change itself if such criticism is found to be correct. Its religion is ever renewing itself through time and not confined to any historical doctrine.

Hinduism has no one book, teacher or event that everything has to be harmonized to. It accepts an evolution of religion as well as one of life, with the ability of people today to improve upon their religion, make it more relevant to themselves, or to invent new religions that may be better, or at least more useful, than the old. Hinduism views past religion as the ground on which to build our own unique spiritual realization. The past should neither be ignored or discarded, nor should we limit ourselves to it, but use it carefully as a resource for our own development today. Above all, Hinduism cannot accept various religious divisions as real. Truth, after all is One. This means that there are no separate religious compartments that we belong to, Hinduism for the Hindus, Christianity for the Christians, and so on.

In Sanatana Dharma, like science, Truth is a matter of reason and perception. Truth is a universal fact that each objective observer can discover by probing to the depths of his or her own mind. We must question and examine all that we call religion in the fire of inquiry. Otherwise we are not searching out the Truth but merely attempting to uphold various identities, which have no real value except as tools of self-discovery. This means that people of all religions must come together and question what religion and spirituality really are, even if it requires, as it must, questioning our own traditions, and abandoning those aspects of them which fail to hold to the Truth.

There may be those who feel hurt or offended if their religion is questioned, but no true scientist feels offended if his theories or experiments are scrutinized. Nor is questioning in itself offensive. On the contrary, it can be a courtesy and a help. Those who follow Sanatana Dharma are open to having their views questioned, particularly those on the nature of consciousness, which is the real issue of all true inquiry.

There is no reason for us to feel offended if our religious beliefs are questioned. If they are true, like the heat of fire, any objective examination will affirm them, and such questioning will only make them stronger. If they are not true, like fire being wet, we have lost nothing in discarding a false belief. In this respect the universal tradition must include deep questioning. Let all doubts be brought out. But let us question in order to find out what is true, not merely to refute or uphold one particular belief or another. The ultimate Truth is beyond all beliefs, theories, names and forms. It is our own nature divested of limiting concepts and conditioned thoughts.

Hinduism does not regard it important or wise for any religion to insist upon a separate identity for itself — that human beings should consider themselves to be in one religious camp or another as Hindu, Buddhist, Christian, Muslim or whatever. To do so removes a teaching from the universal and turns it into something restrictive. Yet there is nothing wrong with the idea that our path is best, if it is accompanied by openness, tolerance and respect for the views of others who might not agree with us. It becomes a problem when it is associated with militancy and the attempt to impose one view upon others, in short when it becomes self-righteous.

Though Sanatana Dharma may not accept any exclusivity it does state that we should not reject anything. Let us accept all great teachers and teachings and integrate them together into a universal science of Self-realization. Let nothing of any real spiritual aspiration in humanity be rejected wherever it might occur. Let no real spiritual aspiration be destroyed in the name of conformity to a belief. As human beings we should all come together and share our spiritual knowledge, not out of trying to convert others, but out of seeking to unite with the Infinite.

We should have more religions, not less. Each one of us should have his or her own religion, and it should agree with our inner perception, not be the product of social regimentation. The important thing is that our religion is a seeking to connect to the Divine within, that it is part of a path to Self-realization, not merely trying to conform to a social image of what is supposed to be holy or pious.

Hinduism does not see it as a sign of greatness that all people in a country belong to the same religion, follow the same prophet, read the same holy book, or perform the same prayers. Hindus would consider it a sign of spiritual poverty. It would be like if the people in a country all wore the same style of clothes, produced the same style of art, ate the same food, and all tried to look like each other. Diversity, through freedom, leads to true Oneness. We discover the unity of the tree by tracing back the creative current from each leaf to the trunk, not by reducing the tree to one branch only, which is only to stifle if not kill it.

Hinduism states the more the sects the better, as each sect will allow different people to find a connection with the Divine. It says that the religions we know are not separate or self-contained entities. They are merely sects of the universal religion and to the extent they think they alone represent that universal truth, they lose their value. What is important is that all the different religions come to recognize each other as subgroups within a greater or universal tradition that transcends any person, book or historical revelation. Then alone will there be peace in the world and in the hearts of human beings.

From non-being lead us to Being, from darkness lead us to Light, from death lead us to Immortality.
Brihadaranyaka Upanishad I.3.28

I was the father of the human race and I became the Sun.
Vamadeva, Rig Veda, IV.27.1

All this in the beginning was God. It knew itself as "I am God." Therefore it became all. Whoever among the Gods, seers or men has awakened to That, he also became That.
Brihadaranyaka Upanishad I.IV.10

1.7
Idolatry and Dogmatism: The Veils of Maya

The greatest charge that predominant Western religions of Christianity, Islam and Judaism have made against other religions, particularly Hinduism, is that of idolatry — that they worship a God other than the One God and are therefore committing a great sin or error. The greatest charge that people make against these religions in turn is that of dogmatism — that self-created religious authorities are trying to impose an arbitrary set of beliefs upon all people, which favors one group over another and leads to oppression and exploitation.

There is no doubt that religion should question our attachment to the outer world and the missing of our true connection with the Divine. Yet when religion mistakes that inner reality for a particular code of belief, it becomes guilty of the same outwardness it is criticizing. It becomes dogmatic, which is another form of idolatry, or trying to limit truth to a particular fixed form.

To insist that God should be given only one name or worshipped in only one way indicates ignorance of the unlimited nature of Truth. True religion shows us the limitations of our outward seeking but without imposing an outer standard on our inner search. The inner search for the infinite and eternal cannot be limited by any social, emotional or intellectual formulation. There can be no outer group which owns or dispenses the inner Truth as if it were a material or intellectual commodity. Such so-called religion is not a seeking of the Universal and Eternal, but the assertion of a personal point of view which divides humanity into hostile camps.

Idolatry charges people with regarding as Divine some material thing like a stone, a piece of wood, or a picture. Yet even the so-called primitive savage knows that his idol is not the deity he worships but merely a means of communication with it. Idolatry properly understood consists of regarding something other than the Divine as reality — valuing money, sex, power, or any outer object over the Spiritual Being or Pure Consciousness underlying the universe. In Hinduism this belief in the reality of something other than God or the Self, is called ignorance or illusion (*avidyā* or Maya).

Sanatana Dharma teaches that we should regard the Divine as the reality and our true Self. We should not grant reality to anything apart from Consciousness. This, however, is a matter of profound discrimination, not a simple banning of the use of images, and insisting upon a particular outward code of conduct and worship for all people.

Hinduism and Idolatry

As a universal tradition, Hinduism contains within itself a place for all forms of worship from the most basic ritual to the highest meditation. This includes worship with and without form — whatever may be valid for different human temperaments and stages of development. Therefore Hinduism employs abundant forms of all types, as well as every sort of formless meditational approach. Most Hindus use images in their religious worship and most Hindu temples contain many of them.

This abundance of forms has been criticized by aniconic (anti-idolatry) traditions not as a universal approach, but as the idol worship of primitive people. They associate Hindu images with the idolatry and perversion that was charged against the Pagans by the Christians, Jews and Muslims. The idea is that whoever uses images in religious worship is somehow immoral, perhaps a worshipper of the devil, and does not know there is only One God. Image worshippers may be lumped together with criminals, perverts, or whoever at the moment is regarded as representing deviant behavior in society, as if the use of images led to moral depravity.

Such ideas are prejudice, if not bigotry, and are akin to racism and its negative stereotypes. People who hold them never take the time to communicate with so-called idolaters and find out what they are really doing (and discover that they are also human beings, often with more love and tolerance than the religious zealots who attack them). Not surprisingly the charge of idolatry is often leveled as part of a campaign of conversion, invasion and conquest. It has been used as an excuse for smashing statues, robbing and demolishing temples, for plunder and genocide, all conveniently done in the name of God. Such a God is but a personification of intolerance and his worship is built on the blood of innocent people.

Anti-idolatry religions have not only been opposed to the use of images, they have often regarded it as a virtue to take offense at the use of images by those outside their religion. They have at times made it their divine right to interfere with the religious practices of others, if such practices involves the use of images, and to force others to worship God in the correct (their) way. They often spend more time criticizing the idolaters than seeking God.

Western missionaries through time, and Christian fundamentalists today, have used a charge of idolatry to misrepresent Hinduism and other Pagan religions. Such people are passing on superficial distortions which are intellectually misinformed, if not dishonest. They never mention that the images are looked upon only as vehicles or communication devices, not as real in themselves. Their statements would be equivalent to Hindus calling Christianity a religion of human sacrifice for the holy communion ritual of drinking the blood and eating the body of Christ.

Hindus use various images in their religious worship — which may include statues and pictures, anthropomorphic forms of deities, and great teachers and avatars who may be regarded as the Divine in human form. Hindu worship consists of burning incense, lighting lamps, reciting prayers and singing devotional songs around these sacred images. Some of these objects of worship are representational. Others are symbolic and geometric, like yantras and mandalas. Some are places like sacred mountains and lakes, where Gods or sages project their influence. All things in the universe are objects of worship once we recognize the sacred presence which pervades all things.

Hindu images of Gods and Goddesses have supernatural characteristics to show their higher reality. Deities may be depicted with several heads, many arms, and various unusual weapons and adornments. Occasionally they may have animal characteristics, like an animal head or body. Some in fact are depicted as animals. Sometimes they are shown with frightening features like fangs, adorned with serpents, or standing on corpses. Such forms may appear strange to anyone who is ignorant of mythic symbols or the imagistic vision of the higher mind. Yet to a deeper vision — which anyone can come to by a little open-minded study — these images are the great archetypes of life, the embodiment in form of the great truths of the Eternal and the Infinite, in which our ordinary mental constructs must be broken down. Those who make the charge of idolatry against such use of images only demonstrate their ignorance of symbolic language and mythology. Not surprisingly, strongly aniconic traditions are usually opposed to mysticism altogether, and have stifled art as well.

Such a worshipper of images was Paramahansa Ramakrishna, whom many Westerners have been inspired by. Ramakrishna was a priest at a Hindu temple and worshipped the Divine Mother in the form of Kali, who has a terrible form replete with fangs and a garland of skulls. Let those who are opposed to the use of images show among their members a being of such spiritual realization of Ramakrishna.

We should note that religions that use images have not historically been more violent or sensual than those who deny them. Hindu and Buddhist communities contain a strong ascetic tradition, as well as an emphasis on non-violence, even though these traditions use images. Image-denying religions, on the other hand, have been guilty of violence and destruction perpetuated in the name of destroying idols and converting heathens and infidels through various crusades and holy wars. The non-use of images has obviously not increased our human sensitivity or respect for other cultures.

Icons and Idols

All religions use images and forms to some degree. Catholic and Greek Orthodox Christianity use images, icons and statues, as an examination of most churches will reveal. Hindu, Buddhist, Taoist and Shinto groups use them as well. Native American, African and Asian religions abound with them. The ancient religions of the entire world from Mexico to Greece, Egypt, Babylonia, Persia, India and China used images, as archeology so clearly reveals. The use of images therefore appears as an integral part of human religious practices and no universal religion could be regarded as complete without them.

Most Protestants and Muslims deny the use of all images as idolatry and accuse the Catholics of idolatry for their use of images. No statues or images adorn their churches or mosques.

Yet we do find that many Protestants have a picture of Christ, or at least wear a cross, which is still a usage of images and symbols. Muslims worship Mecca and a special rock placed there. They pray only in the direction of Mecca, which is the limitation of the Divine to a place. They similarly regard mosques as sacred places. Many Muslims pray at the tombs of their saints. Muslims often have pictures of their religious or political leaders (note the worship of Ayatollah Khomeni in Iran), sometimes those of Mohammed, perhaps with his face veiled. This is also a use of symbols. Both Protestants and Muslims regard their holy books, the Bible and Koran, as literally the Word of God. This is also a worship of objects.

However, there is a strange dichotomy in how religious images are judged. When they are part of the Christian tradition they are called "icons" and classified as works of art and sacred in nature. When they are part of non-Christian or Pagan traditions they are called "idols," which is a derogatory term that indicates not the sacred but mere superstition. In the case of native American and African images, even when done by a culture as advanced as the Mayas of Central America — which built great pyramids and had many great cities — they are lumped along with so-called "primitive" art.

By this logic what makes for idolatry is not the use of representational forms in worship, but only the use of non-Christian images, which is obviously a prejudice. An image of Krishna as the good cowherd is on par with that of Christ as the good shepherd, the Divine as the caretaker of souls. To make one into a superstitious idol and the other into a sacred image is hypocritical and intolerant. It is like saying that only spices used in American cooking are legitimate spices, while those used in Indian cooking are food adulterants!

What Christian would accept a depiction of Christ being called an idol? Would Christian religious leaders approve of it in the press of Christian countries? Yet Hindus and other non-Christians routinely accept that depictions of their deities — who represent such high truths as Self-realization — are demeaned as idols.

To call such images idols implies that those who worship them practice idolatry or take the image itself as a God. This adds yet more prejudice and error to the judgement. The use of an image — whether we call it an icon or an idol — does not imply belief in the reality of the image. That we keep a photograph of our wife and children at our work desk does not mean that we think our wife and children are the photograph.

The use of the term idol inflames the sentiments of anti-idolatry religions like Christianity and Islam, as both the Bible and the Koran instruct their followers to destroy idolaters and their temples. The use of the term idol is thus careless, insensitive, and potentially inflammatory. It should be removed in an effort to promote greater understanding and good will between religious groups.

Idolatry and the Book

One may confuse Truth which is unlimited with any number of limited things, not merely graven images. Books, names, personalities, and institutions can be invested with the illusion that they are the Truth. To identify any statement with Truth is idolatry. Truth is more a matter of how something is said than simply what is said. To insist that any statement is literally true does not even work in ordinary communication, much less deeper levels of poetic and religious discourse. In fact literalism itself is nothing but idolatry, the identification of Truth with a limited object.

The written word itself is the first of all idols because as the most evident form used in human communication, it is the foundation of all other dogmatic constructs. To make any statement literally true is to invest words, which are inherently limited and capable of a number of interpretations, with Absolute Truth. The idolatry of the word, idea, name or book, is perhaps the worst of all idolatries. It confuses reality with the most empty of things, a mere verbal representation.

Verbal constructs are less real than ordinary realities. For example, the word tree is far less real than an actual tree. So too, the word God is not only less real than God, but less real than any actual object. It is certainly far less real than even one human being. To sacrifice even one living human being for such a mere concept is not only a sin against God, it is a sin against life. To identify God or Truth with a particular name or statement is to fall not only from spiritual reality but to alienate ourselves from the world of Nature. For this reason Vedic texts emphasize that Truth is found where all speech turns back, and that it is different than anything in this world which people can perceive as an object.

Many religious groups insist that their book is literally the Word of God. They have identified God's word with a material thing, a mere book, which is words printed on paper. How can the Infinite and Eternal Reality have speech or words? God is not a physical person who has a mouth. His Word is merely a metaphor for his creative intelligence. This Word is a vibratory state of awareness, not something that can be found in any dictionary or made into any dialect. The Word of God cannot be captured on a piece of paper. Even the words of a great person cannot be reduced to a single book.

To regard an actual book as the word of God is a form of idolatry. This worship of a book creates literalism, or taking all statements, however metaphorical, as actual facts: like the Christian belief that the world was created 6000 years ago because this is the age of the lineages of the prophets given in the Bible since the time of creation. It creates dogma — the idea that something is true merely because it is in a book that is said to be the Word of God.

A book itself does not say anything. It has to be read and interpreted. Usually any book is capable of various interpretations.

Scriptures, which are written in archaic and symbolic languages, as well as being the diverse works of many authors, time periods, and points of view, are capable of any number of interpretations as is obvious by the disagreement of Biblical scholars.

A book is a passive object which if used properly can yield knowledge, but if used improperly can yield half-truth or even falsehood. We could compare a book to a musical instrument. The person who plays it is more important than the instrument itself. The worship of books is the product of a period of illiteracy when a book was something rare and valuable, and when people could often afford to have only one book. After the modern information revolution, this worship of books appears quite regressive and can no longer be sustained by any thoughtful person.

The Idolatry of a Name

The foundation of all material things is the naming process. Through names we discriminate forms. The name creates the idea of external reality. It divides us off from the Divine or nameless Truth. The Divine transcends all names. To insist that only one set of names for God is correct is another form of idolatry or materialism.

Hindus do not mind if Brahman, their main term for the Divine, is called God, a Western and generally Christian term. However, Christians object if Hindu terms like Brahman or Ishvara are used for God, even though they mean much the same thing, the Supreme Being. Muslims do not allow Sanskrit names for God, though such things are not fundamentally different in meaning than Allah, or Persian Khuda. Those who refuse to accept God called by the same type of name in another language are only demonstrating their ignorance of what the Divine really is, the Unlimited. They are showing that they have never really experienced God but are content with a mere word as indicating that Absolute Truth.

Emotion in the Depiction of God

The Biblical and Koranic God, even though regarded as beyond representation, is often portrayed as having human emotions. He is said to be jealous, vindictive, wrathful or vengeful. He has his favorite or chosen prophets and people, as well as his enemies whom he punishes with natural disasters like plagues, floods and earthquakes. He talks with people and even interferes with human affairs and political matters, functioning as a judge noting the good and evil of people, giving them rewards and punishments of an often tyrannical order.

Such a God appears as a person with some common, and not entirely noble human feelings. He appears as a personification of anger and wrath, or as representing the ego of certain people. Such a God appears to be the confusion of the Divine with a particular mental or emotional formation, which is material and transient. It is very convenient to put God on our side and make those who think differently than us followers of the Devil, but there is nothing particularly spiritual, sensitive or even humane about it.

The Divine as a transcendent reality no more possesses anger and jealousy and is no more a judge, than he is a person with hands and feet. If one rejects the idea that God can have any image or human representation, then certainly God cannot have any human emotions or partialities either. Therefore he can have no only Son, final prophet, or one scripture, as these are all material limitations which no Spiritual Reality can be attributed with.

Yet if God can metaphorically be described in symbols and images, his traits can be metaphorically described through emotions. Saying that God is jealous can be a metaphor for indicating that only the eternal endures and whatever transient thing we are attached to must be taken away from us by the force of time. To say that God is a stern judge can be a metaphor for saying that the law of karma, which is a product of Divine wisdom and natural law, is the real giver of good or bad results, which cannot be altered by human wishes. Such metaphors should never be taken literally or we destroy their real meaning. Hindu deities like Shiva and his wife Parvati have such terrible forms and emotional expressions to express their transcendence of the human condition and its dualities of high and low, good and evil, but these are never taken literally. And they are never made the basis of holy wars and ethnic cleansings in the name of religion.

Idolatry and Art

The use of images is part of an artistic approach and rendering of our relationship to the Divine. For this sculpture uses statues, painting uses colored surfaces, music uses sound, and poetry uses verbal images. To deny these things as idolatry is only to banish art from our relationship with the Divine. For this reason aniconic traditions have generally remained artistically sterile. Where for example can we find great religious sculpture or painting among orthodox Muslims or Protestants? Both the Bible and the Koran, though they reject graven images, abound with poetic images, which are responsible for much of the beauty of these books. If a poetic image is acceptable, why not a formal image? Is not a picture worth a thousand words? Why is a poetic form of art allowed as religious but not a plastic form like painting and sculpture? In fact it could be argued that the literalism of certain religious traditions in worshipping their books has only occurred because they deny the use of images. The book becomes a substitute image to fill that aspect of universal aspiration which requires an object to worship.

Traditions that reject art and the use of images, which are used in most spiritual approaches, are limited and incapable of representing the full aspirations of humanity. Hinduism as Sanatana Dharma or a universal tradition includes all forms of art as valid approaches to the Divine or truth. It has music, dance, poetry, drama, sculpture, painting, architecture, not as ends-in-themselves but as different languages of worship. Yet this has not prevented it from developing formless approaches as well, which it has developed through formless meditation methods to a degree largely unparalleled in aniconic traditions.

The Idolatry of a Person

There are many great teachers and Truth cannot be limited to a single person, however great he or she may be. To insist that God has only one Son or that he has a final prophet is itself a form of idolatry — an attempt to limit ultimate Reality to what is only an appearance in time and space. We are all sons of God and we are all potentially God-realized sages. Whatever good or evil that has existed in any human being exists in each one of us. Whatever potential of greatness that has existed in any human being belongs to us. To set up limitations around our inner potential is not only to limit humanity but to deny the immanent Godhead.

Hinduism holds that the individual, you or I, is the most important thing. The teacher is only an aid and a guide to our own Self-realization. Hinduism does not sacrifice the sacred nature of the individual for any prophet or savior, however great, but directs each one of us to our own Self-realization as the highest goal.

Idolatry and Dogmatism

The very religious groups who have most condemned other beliefs as idolaters have themselves been the most guilty of dogmatism, an authoritarian insistence upon the sole truth of a belief that does not allow any objective examination, much less any other point of view. For this reason they have tended to suppress any criticism against them. Dogmatic beliefs use the specter of idolatry to condemn those who think differently. But idolatry and dogmatism are actually the same thing, the limitation of truth to a particular form, person, judgement or idea.

Exclusivism in religious belief — that our God, savior or holy book alone is true — is itself idolatry, the limitation of truth to a form or construct in the realm of time and space. Unless we transcend the idolatry of dogmatism and exclusivism in religion, it is not spirituality we are following but some divisive creed which breeds conflict and can never lead us to peace.

To do this we must recognize all the various ways human beings have used to approach the Divine, the Infinite and Eternal, and allow for their free exploration, which must overflow the boundaries of any particular religion, whether they use images or not. We are not children that religion must threaten or cajole to keep in line. We are intelligent beings, centers of cosmic awareness, with the potential of all the universe. If we treat ourselves like children or animals to be herded in a particular way we only stifle our deeper consciousness. However, if we recognize our true Self and provide it a rich field in which to grow and the freedom to discover, then there is no limit as to how much each individual can flower in Truth, even those considered to be ignorant or evil. This requires faith in God as dwelling in human beings, not in God as apart from ourselves, who being separate from us can never uplift us.

Part II

Questions And Answers

A single wheel revolves with a single rim, with an unlimited number of spokes moving both before and behind. With half of itself it generated the universe. Where has its other half gone?

Atharva Veda X.9.7

Encompassing all beings, all worlds, and all directions of space, approaching the original being of Truth, with the Self he entered into the Self.
Going around Heaven and Earth in an instant, going around all the worlds, the directions, and the enlightened realms, breaking the extended line of karma, he saw That, he became That, he was That.

Shukla Yajur Veda XXXII.11-12

The infinite Mother is Heaven. The infinite Mother is the Earth. She is the Mother, the Father and the Son. The Infinite Mother is all the Gods and the five peoples of humanity. She is all that has been born and all that will be born.

Rig Veda I.89.10

Questions 1.
The Basis of The Eternal Tradition

A universal tradition integrates all valid ways of knowledge from ordinary sense perception to the highest samadhi or spiritual absorption. It cannot be limited to the partialities of any particular system or ideology, yet it must contain teachings for people of all levels and temperaments. In this section, we will examine the main issues of religion and spirituality and how they appear from a universal perspective, as provided by the tradition of Sanatana Dharma.

A. Religion, Spirituality and the Modern World

WHAT IS GOD?

God is the term most often used in Western religious thought to describe the Supreme Being or spiritual reality behind the universe. The term God is originally a Germanic word and relates to the idea of the good, the summum bonum, what is supremely beneficial in life. God in the Jewish, Christian and Islamic sense stands for the Creator of the universe, who has a personal nature, and is generally conceived of as a father who resides in Heaven.

Sanatana Dharma teaches that there is an ultimate spiritual reality, which one can call God, but that this reality transcends all names, forms and actions. Its highest Truth is one of monism — not that there is only One God but that there is nothing but God, who includes all creatures within a greater Being. Such a Divine being is not merely creator. He is the creation itself as well as the Uncreate which transcends time, space and causation as pure consciousness, called Brahman or the Absolute. All creatures and all the universe are in essence God. Our soul is one with God and can experience God in consciousness.

Brahman is the very Self of all beings. It is neither male nor female. It is beyond emotion and expression. It has no only sons, favorite prophets or chosen people. It transcends time, space and person. All of creation consists of merely the surface waves on its infinite sea. It is a unity of Truth, not of belief, and a Truth that has many forms and functions in its manifestation.

Brahman is not apart from the world. It is the very being and presence underlying all things. It is equally present in an ant as well as in a human being. There is nothing apart from it. Yet it is not tainted by anything. Like space it pervades everything but assumes no form. While one can call Brahman God, one should realize that Brahman is a universal principle of Being transcending both the Creator and the creation and is not the same as the God of monotheistic beliefs (which Hindus call Ishvara or the Lord).

WHAT IS NON-DUALITY (*ADVAITA*)?

Non-duality is the understanding that there is only One Truth or Reality, and therefore only One Self in all beings. This One

Truth is Being-Consciousness-Bliss Absolute. It exists equally in the Creator, the soul and in creation and transcends all three. It is not merely a theory but is the experiential unity of the perceiver, the action of seeing, and the object perceived.

Without knowing the One, we remain trapped in duality, ignorance and sorrow. To know the One is to become it, which is to recognize its Self-existent reality. This requires profound meditation, which in turn is only possible if we have first purified our minds of egoism and learned to live our daily lives in harmony with universal law.

Sanatana Dharma bases itself on non-duality. For this reason it cannot set up one religious identity against another. It recognizes the same Self in all beings. Its various practices help us merge into the One, which transcends all human limitations.

IS ATHEISM WRONG?

Atheism, the idea that there is no God or Creator, is a conception of the human mind which occurs at various stages of mental and spiritual development. It appears in undeveloped minds who are unable to perceive any deeper reality than what is evident through the physical senses. Atheism also appears in more developed minds who see through the limitations of organized religion and its dogmas and can no longer accept them as true.

Some Dharmic teachings, like Sankhya philosophy or Buddhism, are atheistic in the sense that they do not regard God or a cosmic Lord as the ultimate reality. They may recognize the Creator as a secondary reality, however, and see Pure Consciousness as the ultimate truth of being. Such systems are atheistic only in the sense of not regarding theism as the ultimate truth. Such non-theists are not materialists but have a trans-theistic spiritual view of Reality.

It is wrong to say that atheists are bad, whereas those who believe in One God are good. The important thing is our inquiry into Truth. If this inquiry is more alive in an atheist than in the dogmatic follower of a particular religion, such an atheist is a better seeker of Truth and therefore closer to God who is Truth than the so-called religious person. Actually most of us are atheists, including those who regard themselves as religious. What we believe in is not spiritual reality but in money, sex, power, converts and ideologies, all of which are material. Seeing reality as other than Divine is the root of all of our problems.

IS GOD PERSONAL OR IMPERSONAL?

A universal tradition recognizes the full range of personalities of the Godhead. Yet the Divine is impersonal as well as personal, the formless Absolute of Being-Consciousness-Bliss as well as the cosmic Lord and Creator. The impersonal is a higher reality because the personal implies limitation. Beyond creation there cannot be any person, even a Divine Person.

There is no contradiction between the personal and impersonal aspects of the Godhead. The Impersonal Divine in its creative play assumes various personalities as the Creator, Preserver, and Destroyer of the universe. These personalities may be either male or female, through the great forms of the Divine Father and Divine Mother. Yet the Divine is beyond self and other as the sole and Self-existent Reality. In that impersonal and uncreate Existence is true immorality and perfect peace.

WHAT IS OUR RELATIONSHIP WITH GOD?

With God or the Universal Being is our only enduring (eternal) relationship. God is our true origin and goal, our ultimate friend and companion. God is our father, mother, son, daughter, brother, sister, friend, and master. Whatever we are related to in essence is God or Brahman as the true Being of all. God is the Self, the Divine Presence which dwells in the hearts of all beings. We are not merely related to God, God or the Supreme Being is our true nature. In the highest truth, we don't have a relationship with God, we are God.

All that we experience is related to us, part of our own eternal and infinite consciousness and its creative capacity. The love we feel with others is only a portion of the love that is eternal, which is our own immortal Self. All relationship is an attempt to see ourselves in the other and the other in our self. There is only One Self in all beings seeking to rediscover its universal wholeness. All our relationships are in the Self and of the Self, which is neither you nor me but all.

WHY DO RELIGIONS CALL GOD HE?

God is both male and female, and beyond both male and female. One can call the Divine "He" relative to the masculine qualities of the Cosmic Being like strength, justice, will or discernment. One can call it "She" in reference to its feminine qualities like love, devotion and receptivity. One can call God "It" relative to its neutral qualities like infinity or pure existence.

If one only calls God "He" then such a God is not the Supreme Being but a personification of a male centered view of reality. As our culture is dominated by male energy, not of a higher but a lower order, naturally we project this idea upon God as well. Such a one-sided conception of God is reflected in exclusivist religions, which claim that they alone have the truth and thereby lead us to various extreme or even violent actions. Therefore while we can call God "He" we should not limit how we can conceive his reality. He is all beings and all relationships. He-she-it, you-me-them, whatever entity we conceive is our very own Self.

WHAT IS THE IMPORTANCE OF THE DIVINE MOTHER?

In predominant Western religions the Divine is worshipped as Father but not as Mother. This heavenly Father is often portrayed as a stern, angry or jealous God — a strict judge and giver of punishment to those of his children who violate his seemingly arbitrary laws. Protestant Christianity and Islam have banished the Divine as Mother from their religions. Catholic and Greek Orthodox Christianity have accepted the feminine only as the mother of Jesus, not as God in her own right — even though it appears that devotion to the Madonna has been the strongest living mystical tradition within Christianity and its greatest sustaining force.

Sanatana Dharma as a universal tradition has always recognized the importance of the Divine Mother. According to Hinduism the deepest relationship that we can have with God is that of the Mother. No human relationship is closer than that of the mother and child. It best mirrors our relationship with God. India itself is looked upon as the Mother. The Hindu religion itself is seen regarded a mother and its teachings are her milk.

In the modern world wherein we are recognizing the equality of the sexes we can no longer reject the feminine aspect of Divinity. The rejection of the feminine aspect of the Divine — which is loving kindness, tolerance and caring nurturence — and the promotion of the stern male-only father-sky God, has led to the religious animosity and holy wars which have devastated humanity over the last two thousand years.

What religion has aggressively promoted a belief in the Divine Mother? What form of religious fundamentalism or exclusivism has ever been made in the name of the Goddess? Who could ever kill people in the name of a God named Mother? What Mother would ever allow her children to be killed or hurt, no matter how much they may have fallen? What Mother would condemn her own children as sinners? Who could say "believe in the Divine Mother or you must be killed or go to an eternal hell?" Not surprisingly Hinduism, the world's major religion that has honored the Goddess, has seldom promoted religious hostility, and has never created such ideas as eternal damnation.

The female is the form side of the Divine. Woman represents the Divine embodied. Her worship requires the creation of appropriate forms in which to revere her. We must once again create images of the Divine Mother to allow her healing grace, which is essential for world peace, to descend. Without acknowledging the forms of the Divine Mother our religions must be imbalanced and lead to various excesses in human behavior.

WHAT IS THE RELATIONSHIP BETWEEN GOD AND NATURE?

Some religions place God and Nature apart or in conflict with one another. Others see Nature as God's creation, which he owns and rules from on high and for which the glory belongs only to him. The Hindu view is a little different.

According to Hinduism Nature is the manifestation of God who is our very Self. Nature is our own body. The entire universe is our manifestation, the reflection in form of the Truth of who we really are. We not only exist in Nature, Nature exists in us. We are the Cosmic Being that expresses itself through all the forms of creation. God has not merely created Nature, Nature exists in God. Nature is the expression of the Word of God. It is the Divine Message and teaching vehicle through which we can come to know our True Self.

What Hinduism teaches is not pantheism, the idea that Nature is God, but monism, the Truth that there is only One Reality which includes the world and is not apart from anything. Hindu saints and sages have always reveled in the world of Nature, communicating through her with the Divine Existence. Nature is the Divine Mother who, if we are open to not only her beauty but her wisdom, will unfold all the mysteries of consciousness to us. Besides the outer Nature is her inner form, the power of yogic knowledge, the intelligence that directs the evolution of consciousness, which ultimately reveals all the universe within us.

WHY DO PEOPLE WORSHIP GOD IN DIFFERENT FORMS?

The Divine though formless in essence assumes various

forms in its cosmic creative play. We ourselves have a form and are used to relating to life through various forms. To move from the limitations of form to the unlimited formless Divinity, it helps to first conceive God as having a form. There is nothing wrong with such forms as long as they are used as vehicles. If we take them to be literally true and dismiss other possible forms for the Divine as wrong, then such forms become an obstruction and a cause of conflict.

Different people worship God in different ways because the minds of human beings are different. The ultimate way to God is to worship the Divine as the Self of all beings. This means that God can be found in the rocks, mountains, rivers and stars, as well as beyond the world. Actually every form is a form of the Divine worthy of worship. What is important is to allow the free use of all forms so that all the doors to the Infinite are open to all beings. We must not only see God beyond the world but God in the world, in every form, to really know the omnipresent reality.

CAN GOD BE PORTRAYED IN ANIMAL FORMS?

God dwells in all creation. Animals are manifestations of the same Divine spirit as human beings. We should therefore honor the Divine presence in animals, which is not to worship their outer forms. No one, even the so-called primitive savage, considers that the animal state is the highest condition for the soul. No one thinks that God is no more than an animal. Those who honor animals do so from seeing the Divine Being expressing through them, not through look up to the animal state.

Hinduism respects the Divine presence in animals. It recognizes that animals project certain cosmic energies through the Divine Self present within them. Animal images appear in Hinduism for their archetypal and poetic value, not as a mere worship of lower forms of life. Respect for the God in animals, which includes picturing the God in animals, is part of any universal teaching. It is not a sign of lack of spirituality but of a greater sensitivity to the sacred nature of all life. If we refuse to recognize God in animals, it only shows that we have not yet come into contact with the real Divinity, that our God is a human prejudice, not a universal Truth. It indicates that we will abuse and exploit animals for our own personal pleasure, which is exactly the case in the world today.

Animals also have a soul, a mind and a personality. Unless we can see the Conscious Being in all creation, we do not really see. We do not know ourselves, nor will we function as a humane and compassionate presence in the universe.

WHERE DO PEOPLE GO WHO WORSHIP GOD IN DIFFERENT FORMS?

We gain that which we set our hearts upon in life. We go to that to which we are most devoted. This may be different than the names and forms we subscribe to, or the beliefs that we hold. What we are most devoted to is that which we give most of our attention to, the most constant object of our thoughts.

Those who worship God go to God in the way in which they worship that Reality. We develop in ourselves the qualities we most honor. If the God we worship is a God of anger, then we go to anger, we develop more anger in ourselves, and we go to worlds and incarnations dominated by anger once we have left this transient life. If the God we worship is a God of love, than we develop more love in ourselves. We go to worlds and incarnations dominated by love.

To see where we will go we must look at the qualities we admire and focus on. There is a science to this that can be observed and understood, just as the plant we grow must be of the same nature as the seed we put into the ground. This is why it is important that we are cognizant of what we worship or honor in life.

However only if we know the Supreme Being as the Self do we know the Truth and are liberated. Otherwise we are trapped in ignorance, whatever we may worship, because worship implies a duality between the worshipper and the object worshipped. The highest worship is meditation which cognizes the Self-existent Reality. While worship in the ordinary sense means honoring an external being, in Sanatana Dharma it stands for meditation practices to realize our true Self.

WHAT IS THE NAME OF GOD?

There is only One Divine Reality or Supreme Being, which is both beyond all names and forms and has an unlimited number of names and forms. One can call it Shiva, Vishnu, Divine Mother, the Creator, Buddha, Allah or whatever one likes. All the names and forms of the Divine which human beings have developed through time have their validity. But we must transcend names and forms, even the name of God, to find That Reality which is beyond all material and mental limitation.

We don't think that the English word for grapes is the only legitimate word for grapes and those who call grapes by any other name know nothing about this particular fruit. Yet in religion some groups may insist that the name for God belonging to their particular community is the only true name and should other people call upon that spiritual reality by another name, they must be calling upon something else or even worshipping something undivine. The name is not the thing. Even a person cannot be reduced to a single name. How much less so the Infinite Being? God has all names and transcends all names. What is important is to know that Reality, not to try to impose one name or one idea about it on all humanity.

A name for God enables us to establish a relationship with that transcendent Reality. Generally the name reflects various Divine qualities — like love, peace, or truth — which allow us a means of access to that higher Truth. Repetition of Divine names is perhaps the easiest method of directing the mind to Truth. But when we limit that transcendent Reality to a mere name, which is a collection of letters, then the name itself becomes the factor of illusion and separation. We must use the name as a messenger to contact the Being, not merely worship the name itself. Ultimately we are that Being and his name is our name, which our every breath and heartbeat proclaims.

HOW SHOULD RELIGION BE PROPAGATED?

True religion spreads itself by the force of Truth. It does not rest upon overt efforts and transcends all organizational endeavors, which should only aim at disseminating information, not promoting any dogma. True religion (unity) is reflected in universal interdependence. It is spread by promoting unity consciousness in thought, word and deed. Without recognizing this universal Truth to seek to promote a particular religion is only to promote a separative and warring creed.

Religion is the recognition of the Eternal and the Infinite. To cause it to grow is to honor its Self-existent Reality. This religion of Truth is inherent in nature. The wind blows it. The sun shines it. The rivers make it flow. Flowers bloom through it. What is important is that we take it up and let it spread and develop our own greater awareness, as we ourselves by its power learn to transcend all the petty identities and opinions of the mind.

In promoting religion we must avoid all propaganda, which as an effort to influence the mind through emotions and slogans, not through the force of truth, calm thinking and meditation, is itself a form of violence. Religious propaganda is a contradiction in terms. Religion is a means of connecting us with a higher reality. This cannot be done through appeal to the lower aspects of the human mind — agitated emotions, suspicions, and clever thinking, which propaganda aims at.

HOW SHOULD RELIGION BE ORGANIZED?

According to Hindus there should not be one religion, one church, one pope or religious leader, or one religious institution for the entire planet. Religion should not be organized as a dogma, belief system, or social institution. It should not be standardized or stereotyped or it loses its spirit and creativity and becomes rigid and artificial.

Religion should aim at spiritual knowledge, through inner practices like Yoga and meditation. It should not be a vested interest to gain an external following but have its reality on the inner planes of consciousness. Otherwise religion, like any vested interest, becomes corrupt. The larger the institution the greater the corruption is likely to be.

The Hindu model is of many smaller spiritual groups and organizations in a general alliance or federation, respecting a unity of Truth but a diversity of approaches to it. In this way religion can grow in a natural and organic way and one in which the individual, the real bearer of the sacred flame of consciousness, is honored and nurtured, not scaled down according to a belief or system.

WHAT IS THE IMPORTANCE OF SCRIPTURES?

Scripture in the Western religious sense means the Word of God as revealed in a particular book like the Bible or Koran. Scripture can also stand for an inspired book or source teaching that a particular religion honors as very important. The books of various religions, like the Bhagavad Gita of Hinduism or the Tao Teh Ching of Taoism, may be called scriptures even though they may not literally be regarded by their followers as the Word of God, nor may the religion itself be theistic. In this vast universe, any number of scriptures or inspired religious books are possible. Hindus have many scriptures like the Vedas, Agamas and Puranas but none is regarded as the only Word of God or as literally true.

The supreme scripture, the real Word of God or the Supreme Reality, can never really be put in human language, which is inherently limited by time, place and culture. The Divine Word is a state of consciousness, best revealed in silence of mind. It is not a mere book that can be pulled off a shelf and quoted. It is best represented by mantra, particularly the mantra OM, which is the essence of the Vedas.

Different scriptures come into being relative to the varying needs of people according to time, place, culture, and individual temperament. This is the same as the differences required in food and clothing, though there are universal human needs for food and shelter. Some scriptures have much spiritual truth in them, others have very little. There is no standardized teaching or level of discourse in the various so-called scriptures of the world. The idea that only one scripture is true would be like saying that only one type of food is good. The idea that all scriptures are equally true is like saying that all food is equally good. For this reason the Hindu tradition contains many works that have been given a scriptural status. These include the Four Vedas (particularly the Upanishads), Puranas (of which there are about twenty), Ramayana, Mahabharata (including the Bhagavad Gita), and Agamas.

The highest truth is to contact the Word of God within the heart and discover God within oneself. Hence if a teaching does not point out a path of Self-realization, though it be called the Word of God, it cannot represent the highest truth. Higher than the Word of God is to know oneself.

WHAT IS THE ORIGIN OF SANATANA DHARMA?

Sanatana Dharma as a formulation of the eternal tradition has no specific origin in time. Its origin coincides with the beginning of creation itself. Sanatana Dharma as the universal religion arises anew with each cycle of creation, being inherent in the very laws of the universe.

Because it has been formulated in terms of Sanatana Dharma there is no specific point in history when we can say that Hinduism began. Nor can we rigidly delineate the forms of Hinduism from those of other religions, which being products of time must rest on the eternal. As not having an ,origin, Hinduism has no end.

Sanatana Dharma is based upon universal principles, like the law of karma, which are true in all worlds and all cycles of creation. Though its names and forms may vary, its principles or dharmas are unchanging and must be rediscovered by all creatures in every world. The origin of the True Dharma is within us. It is the very root of our deepest thoughts.

WHAT IS THE GOAL OF SANATANA DHARMA?

The goal of the universal tradition is Self-realization, the realization that the universe exists within us — that the universe is the embodiment of our deepest consciousness which transcends time and space. The goal of Universal Truth is to become one with it, which is to become one with all. This is liberation from all bondage based upon fear and desire and the various dualities of attraction and repulsion. For indeed, if we are all, what else could exist for us to fear or to desire?

Actually the goal of Sanatana Dharma is ever realized because the universe is inherently one with consciousness. To reach this goal is to recognize its Self-existent Reality. This is to merge in the ocean of unlimited Being-Consciousness-Bliss. It is liberation from all bondage and sorrow.

Yet beside its ultimate goal Sanatana Dharma recognizes all the other goals of the universal manifestation, which is the organic unfoldment of all the levels, layers and different types of worlds and creatures. While this leads to the ultimate goal, each stage has its appropriate secondary goals, manifesting the full beauty and glory of creation.

IS EVOLUTION ENDLESS?

Evolution is a process of development in time. Time has no end. Therefore there must always be an evolution within the field of time. Though one universe may come to an end, another must come into being. Evolution of form, life and mind is eternal, though no particular thing that evolves is itself unending.

However there is a part of our nature that is unchanging, which has never been limited to the field of time. This Timeless Being can never evolve because it does not exist within the domain of action. Pure Consciousness is not a material thing or a product of time that can grow or decline. What evolves is the mind and its ability to reflect consciousness.

What is necessary is to know our true Self — the immutable constant of our being. Then we transcend time and circumstance. Then evolution, on whatever level it may occur, cannot limit us, though the forms of our outer expression may change and develop in ways that we may not be able to presently conceive. We must learn to view the unending changes of evolution from the standpoint of the Immutable Self. This is Divine delight.

WHAT IS KARMA AND REBIRTH?

Those who follow yogic traditions, as well as many Nature-oriented religions, teach that the soul takes many births in its evolution toward universality, Divinity or enlightenment. The soul must reap the fruits of its actions, must experience the consequences of the energies it has put forth. Just as there is an evolution of form (the body) through the world of Nature, so there is a corresponding evolution of consciousness (the mind) through repeated births of the soul, which itself is the underlying manifest or conditioned consciousness behind the body. The soul is Nature's vehicle for the evolution of intelligence, which occurs through its experiences in repeated births.

The law of karma is very scientific. The effects of our actions must be of the same nature and extent as the original actions themselves. It is not a question of reward and punishment but a law of energetics. Our actions set in motion a subtle or occult force that pushes us along in life. If we act in a violent way towards others, for example, that violence becomes embedded in our psyche and reflects upon us, causing us to act and to be acted upon in a similar way. If we act in a loving and compassionate manner that energy carries us along the stream of love and brings the forces of love into our life to the same degree and manner as the love we have put forth. Whatever we set in motion through action, even if that action is directed toward others, we must come to experience within ourselves. When we die we take with us the essence of our actions and the will that has caused them, which becomes the basis of our next life.

Karma is the residue of past actions that follows the soul along its journey until it is able to transcend action which, based on desire, is always limited. The goal for Dharmic traditions is liberation or union with Truth, the Self. This arises from knowledge, not action, because action which occurs in the realm of time cannot bring us to that which transcends time. We must learn to look beyond action and give up the sense of being the doer. Then the fluctuations of action and its result cannot disturb us, and whatever we do, being detached, will be inherently good.

IS LIFE PREDESTINED?

There is a destiny or karmic pattern to our lives. Whatever exists in the realm of time must follow the rhythms of time and the law of cause and effect. The present fruit must be of the same nature as the previous seed. Whatever we are in body and mind must be the result of our previous physical and mental patterns. This destiny for some people is very fixed. For others it is capable of modification, though its basic features cannot be changed. For example, we cannot change our parents, nor can we alter the country or time in which we are born. Some people have such a developed nature along a particular line that we can say that they were destined to be great or destined to be a criminal, almost regardless of circumstances.

This is not to say that our Being is predestined but only the outer pattern of our actions, which themselves can be modified for the future. Our consciousness, not being a product of time, is inherently free. Karma and destiny belong only to the body-mind complex, which is not really our's anyway but belongs to the world of Nature. Our ultimate destiny, which is inherent, is to realize our immortal Self. Everything else is an accident or illusion.

ARE WE PUNISHED FOR WRONG ACTIONS?

Reward and punishment are concepts of an undeveloped mind. The Divine Being is not some great parent or judge in Heaven dealing out rewards and punishments. There is a natural law (*dharma*) and its consequences according to the law of cause and effect (*karma*).

If you put your hand into a fire you,get burned. God is not punishing you for the sin of putting your hand in a fire by burning you. It is not a sin but a matter of ignorance of natural law and consequent experience of pain or limitation. Just as there are physical laws, like fire's capacity to burn, so there are mental and spiritual laws. Violence, for example, brings eventual destruction upon its perpetrator. But one is not punished for violence, violence as a negative state of mind with negative consequences creates its own punishment.

The problem is that the long term effects of our actions are not as obvious as their immediate results. For example, if we eat food, like too much sugar, which tastes good but is bad for us its negative effect will not manifest immediately, like fire burning us, but will take time, causing eventual disease through poor digestion which may manifest as arthritis, heart disease or any number of problems. Because of the time lap involved between the cause and effect of our actions we may not recognize the connection between the wrong food and the disease.

On the level of behavior, anger is destructive to our finer sensitivities and prevents us from developing higher consciousness. However, if our minds are not properly evolved we may not recognize this pain, we may indulge in anger and find pleasure in it. But eventually we must experience the consequences of the forces we set in motion, both on a short term and a long term level. Our anger, fear and attachment must lead us into situations that make us suffer. Wrong action itself is its own punishment because it causes the constriction of our consciousness into the outer realm of life, which always results in unhappiness.

DO HEAVEN AND HELL EXIST?

Sanatana Dharma recognizes that the soul or reincarnating consciousness is one with the Divine and Eternal Reality. The soul is immortal and by its very nature ever blissful, free and happy. However, veiled by ignorance, it falls into darkness and confusion and through misconceptions about the nature of Reality makes various mistakes about life which lead to suffering in different incarnations.

Souls by their karma, the power of their own actions, create their own destiny, which leads to various happy or unhappy states of existence. A very happy state could be called heaven and a very unhappy state, hell. Yet there is no eternal or absolute heaven or hell. Any embodied state being bound by time must be transient and come to an end after a certain period of time. Nor does any realm contain such extremes of pleasure and pain that the ordinary idea of heaven and hell portrays. All embodied states must bring some degree of both pleasure and pain, joy and sorrow.

Moreover an unlimited result cannot arise from a limited action, any more than a limited seed can produce an unlimited plant. Therefore an unlimited or eternal heaven or hell can never result from limited creaturely actions, such as occur in an ordinary human life, which must lead to repeated incarnations, not to any final heaven or hell. The actions that we do in one life do not have eternal ramifications but only those into a corresponding field of time. Wrong actions lead to suffering but such suffering is equal to the nature of the action. There cannot be an eternal result through transient action. The idea of an eternal heaven or hell is irrational and shows an ignorance of the basic nature and laws of the universe. Hindus believe in a loving God who would never condemn any creature to an everlasting hell. To them, such a God would be the worst of tyrants and unworthy of worship.

Heaven and hell have been used by various priests to entice or frighten people into certain beliefs. Such heavens and hells do not exist. This heaven and hell idea appeals to the basic reward-punishment conditioning mechanism of the undeveloped mind. It does not promote real ethical behavior so much as creating emotional imbalance and sometimes religious fanaticism. It is important to recognize that our actions have their consequences in both this and future lives, but to hang the specter of an eternal heaven or hell over people is only to promote fear and ignorance.

DOES EVIL EXIST?

There is an Absolute Good but there cannot be any absolute evil. Evil being a form of ignorance and limitation can never be absolute, though it can be a powerful force in this realm of the ignorance. All souls are inherently good and can only temporarily become evil owing to ignorance. This evil consists in doing actions which harm other creatures and thereby also harm oneself.

Various negative forces exist in the universe which could be called, in some sense, evil. Just as there are toxins and pollutants in the physical environment, which can be called bad, so there are negative forces in our psychic and mental environment. Wrong actions create a negative force, which like mob action, can appear almost demonic. Yet however strong evil appears it can never win in the realm of Truth and Eternity. Only in the outer realm of appearances can evil appear to have any real power. Inwardly in consciousness it does not really exist.

The idea of a Devil or that of an entirely evil being is wrong. No creature exists who is inherently evil or who can act in an entirely evil manner. However, the evil or harmful actions of people can create a negative force that appears to have an existence of its own and can be almost overwhelming. Such negative powers and entities do exist and must be reckoned with but can be transcended.

These negative forces are not the product of religious unbelief but of willful egoism. The way to transcend evil is to transcend the ego, which is to go beyond the barriers of belief and identity. Unfortunately, the specter of evil has been used to dominate or destroy people who think differently than a particular group. Such an idea of evil is itself one of the most evil things the human mind has ever invented, as the violence perpetrated in its wake throughout history has demonstrated. It turns other human beings, who are also God, into demons who have to be destroyed and who are not even worthy of human consideration.

DO ANGELS EXIST?

There are many different worlds, levels and layers of the universe beyond the physical, each with its corresponding types of creatures or entities. Such beings more subtle than humans could be called angels. Hindus call them gods or devas, though again there are many different levels of such entities, with the highest Gods being powers of the Supreme Knowledge. There are also different classes of sages and seers who exist on different levels of consciousness and their particular worlds and are angelic, celestial or divine in their function.

Angelic beings may serve to guide or help human beings and aid in natural evolution. Yet these beings may not themselves be enlightened, though their consciousness may be far beyond what is ordinarily human. They may have powers of creativity or perception, like the ability to see the future, which they can relay to human beings to various degrees. However they are no substitute for our own meditation or for human spiritual guides.

Also, Divine forces take various appearances relative to the human mind. Coming into contact with an influx of spiritual energy the human mind may imagine that it is contacting an angel or some higher entity. All such Gods, angels and devils dwell within us as various formations of the power of consciousness. We should not come under their power but contact the Divine within us. We should ourselves return to our true nature as the Master of the Universe, the ruler of all Gods, angels and spirits.

CAN HUMAN BEINGS BE REBORN AS ANIMALS?

Human and animal evolutions are generally distinct. Once a soul has advanced to the human level, which affords easier access to higher states of consciousness than the animal state, it seldom falls back into animal births. Yet souls who are in the transitional phase between animal and human births may go back and forth for several incarnations. Human beings who have done much evil may also temporarily sink into some animal birth owing to the density of their karma.

However, while the general rule is that animal and plant evolution is lower than human evolution, there are exceptions. Sometimes even great sages can take animal births like that of a bird, monkey or deer, or plant births, like that of a great tree. Such births allow the sage to devote more time to meditation as they are less likely to be bothered by other people. Realizing the same Self in all beings they can experience these lower forms of life as part of the same Divine existence. For example, Ramana Maharshi brought his cow to a state of liberation or Self-realization, demonstrating that spiritual practice is not achievable only for human beings.

Liberated sages can also manifest or communicate to us through plants and animals, and through the whole world of

Nature. This is because they themselves have become the entire universe. In this case the forces of nature become their vehicles, though they might not actually take birth within them.

B. Religious and Spiritual Practices

WHAT IS YOGA?

Yoga arose as a Hindu system of spiritual practice to enable us to realize the unity of the individual soul (*Jīvātman*) with the Supreme Self or Supreme Reality (*Paramātman*). There are many different yogic approaches in the Hindu tradition including the Yoga of Knowledge (*Jñāna Yoga*), the Yoga of Devotion (*Bhakti Yoga*), the Yoga of Service (*Karma Yoga*), and the Yoga of Technique (*Kriyā Yoga*). The latter can be divided fourfold as Mantra Yoga, Laya Yoga (the Yoga of the Sound Current), Hatha Yoga (the Physical Yoga) and Raja Yoga (the Yoga of Meditation Techniques). All the systems of Hinduism, Buddhism and Jainism employ yogic methods to some degree.

The most specific Yoga system is the Raja Yoga of Patanjali which is explained in his Yoga Sutras. The main traditional teachings of Jnana Yoga are those of the great sage Shankaracharya. The main text of Bhakti Yoga is the Bhakti Sutras of Narada. Jnana, Bhakti and Karma Yogas are all dealt with in the Bhagavad Gita of Sri Krishna. Yoga therefore is a complete and integral science of spiritual development with methods and approaches for all temperaments and levels of aspirants. The main yogic method is meditation.

WHAT IS VEDANTA?

Vedanta is the portion of the Vedas or the scriptures of Hinduism that deals with the ultimate truth of Self-realization, which is the true goal of life. It teaches the great truth that the Self is God, that our inner being is one with the supreme reality. There are several schools of Vedanta but all seek realization of

God or Truth. Vedantic schools discuss the nature of the Absolute (*Brahman*), the Creator (God), the soul (*Ātman*) and Nature, as well as the nature of karma, rebirth, bondage and liberation. Vedanta contains philosophy, theology and various yogic approaches. It is a vast treasure house of wisdom which explains all the mysteries of life and comprehends all worlds and all states of consciousness.

Yoga is the practical side of Vedanta. Without yogic practices Vedanta remains a mere theory. Without Vedantic knowledge yogic practices remain superficial. Vedanta is the real essence of Hinduism and Yoga is its practice. The great teachings of Yoga-Vedanta are the core of Sanatana Dharma or the Eternal Tradition and should be spread all over the world.

ISN'T THIS A DIFFERENT VIEW THAN YOGA IN THE WEST?

Yoga in the West has come to emphasize asana or yogic postures, which is just a small and preliminary part of the yogic system as the Western world is very physically oriented. As such it is Hatha Yoga or the Yoga of physical culture that has become most popular. But even traditional Hatha Yoga includes pranayama and meditation, as well as various internal purification practices. It is a part of Sadhana or spiritual practice and is meant to lead one to Raja Yoga or the deeper meditational practices. However the deeper aspects of Yoga are recognized by many people, even in the West, particularly those who want to go deeper into the tradition.

WHAT IS MEDITATION?

Meditation, like religion or spirituality, is a word that today can be used to mean any number of things, several of which have little to do with what meditation really is. The word meditation may be used for prayer, contemplation, visualization, affirmations, pranayama, mantra and so on. So too the goal of meditation has taken on many meanings. Meditation may be used for stress relief, for fulfilling one's personal desires and any other limited objective.

Meditation (*Dhyāna*) in the true sense refers to the ability to unite the mind with the object of our perception. Its goal is liberation from the dualistic condition and unification with the Divine which is the ultimate ground of Being in all objects. Meditation occurs when we empty our minds of extraneous thoughts and focus on the Divine Presence that is the True Reality behind all things. This is the main method of the Yoga of Knowledge (*Jñāna Yoga*), but a similar meditation merging into the Divine Beloved is the basis of the Yoga of Devotion (*Bhakti Yoga*).

HOW IMPORTANT ARE MEDITATION TECHNIQUES?

Meditation techniques, however necessary, are themselves aids to meditation but not meditation itself which is beyond all techniques. True meditation occurs when the mind is empty of its concerns and filled only with awareness of the Divine and Universal, which pervades all the forms that it sees.

Techniques work to harmonize the mind and body to allow for meditation to proceed without obstruction. Yogic postures (*āsanas*) help calm and relax the body. Yogic breathing practices (*prāṇāyāma*) help deepen and calm the breath. Mantra, visualization and concentration techniques help control and focus the mind and draw it within. Then meditation, which is the natural state of the mind, can flow more easily.

However if one merely does the techniques but does not create the time and space for meditation itself, one has only laid the foundation but not built the house. One has not yet gone far on the path of meditation. On the other hand, if one tries to directly meditate without having done the preliminary practices it is like trying to build a house without a foundation. It is unlikely to endure. The beauty of the Yoga system (*Rāja Yoga*) is that it provides all the appropriate techniques as well as showing their limitations and not encouraging us to make them ends-in-themselves.

DOES MEDITATION HAVE PREREQUISITES?

Meditation is not something that anyone can do at any time. Like any profound practice it requires a certain foundation and particular way of life. Meditation, which is directing the mind towards mergence in God or Ultimate Reality, cannot be done unless one's life is oriented properly.

To properly practice meditation requires first of all a foundation of ethical living. One should hold to the universal ethics of non-violence, truthfulness, non-stealing, control of sexual energy and non-attachment. One should practice a daily life of cleanliness, contentment, austerity, self-study and surrender to God. These are the preliminary practices of Yoga (*Yamas* and *Niyamas*) as defined by Patanjali in the Yoga Sutras, the classic text on Yoga. Naturally one cannot follow all these perfectly in the beginning but they should be the guiding principles of our behavior.

These prerequisites mean that we should live a clean, simple and quiet life, that we should not be pursuing name, fame or pleasure, that we should have emotional peace of mind, that we should have right relationship and be doing a vocation which is helpful to others. Sitting in a comfortable posture (*Āsana*), calm control of the breath (*Prāṇāyāma*), withdrawing the mind from sensory distractions (*Pratyāhāra*) and concentrated attention (*Dhāraṇā*) are the yogic practices on which meditation is built and these should also be done appropriately so as to facilitate meditation.

WHY IS MEDITATION IMPORTANT?

Meditation appears to be a useless act. It doesn't produce anything tangible, or help anyone in any visible way. To understand its importance we must understand the nature and role of the mind. The mind is our instrument for perceiving truth. It is like the mirror in a reflector telescope. If that mirror is tarnished or if its surface is uneven, we cannot perceive things correctly. If that mirror is clear and even then we can perceive things as they are, which is to see the Divine presence in all.

Meditation is important because it purifies the mind to allow us to perceive the Truth. Once we know the Truth we can act in harmony with it. The very knowledge of Truth is the greatest of all powers. Hence meditation is the greatest action that we can become involved in. It can gain all the worlds and all time.

WHAT IS SELF-INQUIRY?

Self-inquiry (*Ātma-vichāra*) is perhaps the most important meditation practice of the Yoga of Knowledge (*Jñāna Yoga*). It consists of tracing the I-thought back to its origin in Pure Consciousness. One casts aside the object portion of our thoughts, the this or that with which the I has been identified, which is ultimately the I-am-the-body idea, and strives to discover the pure I-in-itself devoid of all objectivity. This means to try to find out who we really are in our eternal Being as apart from the transient becoming in which we are involved. This system is perhaps best explained in the modern world in the teachings of Ramana Maharshi, though it is the essence of Vedanta as found in the Upanishads and Bhagavad Gita.

WHAT IS DEVOTION TO GOD (*BHAKTI YOGA*)?

Devotion to God is devotion to the Universal Being and the forms It takes to guide Its creation. It is not mere devotion to a religious leader or holy book, which is an external thing, but a recognition of the Divine Being as the inner Reality behind the universe.

Devotion may involve repeating the Name of God, chanting, singing, rituals and a deep meditation wherein we come into proximity to the Divine in our minds and merge into It. Devotion usually takes a form, which may be that of a particular Deity, avatar or teacher, though formless devotion exists as well. It usually establishes a relationship with God as father, mother or beloved. Devotional practices, however, are not formalities or technicalities but a spontaneous unfoldment of the heart in its love of God.

Devotion is the most basic and easiest of all spiritual paths because love of God is inherent in the soul. Even if we cannot think of knowing God, we can uncover this spontaneous love of the Eternal Lord. Devotion is also the basis of wisdom because only if we love Truth can we properly learn what it is. All of our human problems occur from seeking love apart from the Divine. Seeking love in the Divine, which is to recognize the Divine love in all creation, is the end to all human suffering.

WHAT IS THE IMPORTANCE OF SURRENDER?

Surrender is the main approach of the Yoga of Devotion (*Bhakti Yoga*). It consists in surrendering oneself completely to God or Truth. This requires offering all our thoughts and feelings, wishes and desires to the Divine to work with as is the Divine Will.

Surrender is the main capacity of the soul. It comes to us naturally when we give up personal seeking. By surrendering into the Divine presence in all things, we win the Divine grace inherent in everything. Surrender then is an acknowledgement of the Universal Truth and a perception of the Universal Being in all beings.

We suffer in life from an unwillingness to surrender. We as human beings try to do everything ourselves. We try to impose our limited personal will upon the unlimited universe, which leads to frustration. We even think that the burdens of the world belong to us and that we must try to save everyone. Surrender, which is recognizing the Divine rulership over all, is letting go of this personal will in which there is peace and happiness. We cannot change life, nor do we need to try to. The Divine power is ever at work and creating all that is necessary. If we look within and surrender we will find that all the imperfections of the world lose their significance.

WHAT IS TANTRA?

Tantra is a set of Hindu teachings generally giving various rituals and techniques to achieve the various goals of life, including liberation. Buddhist and Jain Tantras of a similar nature also exist.

The highest Tantras are spiritual texts providing worship of deities, mantras, and meditation to achieve union with God and Self-realization. They are great yogic teachings and imbued with the higher truths of Vedanta. Tantras of an intermediate level use rituals and mantras to gain personal goals like health, prosperity, marital happiness or children. Inferior Tantras use similar methods to gain control over the minds of other people or even inflict harm. Inferior Tantras are a kind of black magic that no spiritual person can really approve of.

In the West Tantra has mainly become known through various sexual Tantric practices. In fact to most Westerners Tantra means sex. Such sexual Tantras were usually part of the intermediate or inferior Tantras, not the higher Tantras. They make up only a small portion of Tantric teachings and should not be made to represent Tantra as a whole.

As the Goddess represents the Divine Word and the force of Nature, most Tantric approaches are based on worshipping Her. She controls all energies and gives mastery over all techniques. She is the power of Yoga, the Yoga Shakti, that leads us to our true Self.

WHY SHOULD ONE REPEAT MANTRAS?

Sound makes up the mind. It determines the field in which

we think, feel and perceive. You can observe this for yourself. Note the kinds of sounds you repeat and take in during the day and see how these affect you. A harmonious sound pattern in the mind facilitates a deeper awareness. A disturbed sound pattern in the mind prevents the mind from going deeper.

Mantras are spiritually energized sound patterns designed to link us up to the Divine Word or cosmic creative vibration. They help purify and silence the mind to allow for deep meditation. Mantras, which are usually also Divine Names, set up a different kind of energy in the mind, an intentional energization of the mind toward spiritual practice and realization.

Mantras are simple and easy to do as they only require that we recite a word audibly or mentally. Mantras can be done anywhere or anytime as they do not depend upon any external substances. Mantra is thereby the most practical tool of the spiritual life. All of us should do regular mantras to connect with the Divine. Then we will no longer have to struggle to meditate. Mantra should become the ground of our minds, then nothing that comes from the realm of the senses can imbalance us.

WHAT IS SERVICE (*KARMA YOGA*)?

True service is to serve the Divine and work to help the Divine Will unfold in the world. This requires devotion and surrender. Service is not mere charity and it is certainly not promoting one religious creed against another or fostering conversion to a belief.

Such service is only possible when our actions are not based upon personal or collective motivation, when we are not seeking special results for ourselves in what we do. Service may involve all manner of help whether charity, medical aid, teaching, establishing schools or hospitals, and so on. It may involve not only helping people but helping animals and the Earth itself. It may sometimes involve political action but this has to be approached with great care, sensitivity and selflessness. Yet whether these outer forms are helpful depends upon on if we are working in harmony with Divine Grace. This we can know by the peace of mind our service brings us and its ability to open us up to higher states of consciousness wherein we see the Divine in all beings.

Whatever we do in life should be a service to God. If it is not then our action is deficient and will not bring us all that we truly seek. Our spiritual practice itself, meditation done properly, is the highest service wherein we bring the Divine Power directly not only into our own minds but that of all the world with which we are connected.

WHAT IS THE ROLE OF COMPASSION?

Sanatana Dharma emphasizes compassion as the main attitude we should have toward other creatures, and charity or giving, as the main duty we need to perform in life. Compassion consists of offering prayers, blessings and good wishes to all beings, including animals, plants, departed ancestors and inhabitants of subtle worlds. Charity consists of actions done to benefit other people and the world, not merely material aid but service, including teaching.

Yet charity is part of the outer dimension of the teaching. In the Oneness of Reality there is really no one to give and no one to receive. True compassion must rest upon Self-knowledge or it is a separative act. True compassion is not helping those we consider to be weak, poor or deprived, but respecting and nurturing the Divine Self in all creatures. Compassion toward others should be balanced with devotion to the Divine. True compassion comes from the Divine and flows through us by the strength of our devotion. True compassion has no secret motive to gain, or to receive recognition as being a compassionate person. It is part of the movement of Oneness wherein we do not see any real difference between self and other.

WHAT IS THE PLACE OF PRAYER?

Since the ancient Vedas, Hindu teachings contain various prayers, praises and propitiations to the Supreme Reality in its different aspects. Prayers may be given on different levels. The lower level consists of praying to the Divine for ordinary goals of life like health, wealth, and family happiness. This lower level of prayer is essential for the right functioning of society. The higher level is to pray to God for spiritual knowledge and Divine love. This is necessary to bring us into the spiritual life. There is also a third form of prayer wherein we pray to the Divine for the benefit of others. The highest form of this is to pray to the Divine for the benefit of all creatures, with prayers for universal peace and understanding.

There is a science of prayer whereby we connect with the Divine energies in the universe to bring about the fulfillment of the desires of the soul. For this the use of the appropriate mantras and rituals becomes helpful.

Prayer can also be misapplied or part of a system of black magic. If our prayer is motivated by the wish to control or hurt others it is impure. Prayer to convert others to a belief, for example, is a lower form of prayer that is tinged with egoism and violence.

Yet all forms of prayer have their limitations. Praying to God for some personal reward is tainted with egoism. It is not wrong but it does not reflect a mature soul. Praying to the Divine for universal well-being, however useful, is also no substitute for meditation. Praying to the Divine to know him is also limited by the concept of duality, that God is apart from ourselves.

Prayer is preliminary to meditation through which alone there can be direct knowledge of the Divine. Real communion with the Divine comes through the silent mind, the mind that is not seeking anything for itself but is open to the bliss of Pure Existence. The receptive mind is the highest state of prayer, in which no thought occurs.

WHY SHOULD ONE PERFORM RITUALS?

Whatever action we do repeatedly is a kind of ritual and becomes very powerful in shaping our lives. If we jog every day or watch a certain television program every week then these things gain a certain force in our lives. Any routine or discipline is a kind of ritual. Religious rituals are special actions with spiritual meaning that we repeat in order to set in motion a higher power in our lives. Hinduism has many such rituals which employ all the essences of creation — flowers, fragrances, fruits, incense, lamps, and artistic forms — to help create a favorable environment to bring down spiritual vibrations into the world.

Yet when a religious ritual is done without knowledge or devotion, or when there is an intention to control others or further some vested interest through them, such rituals become negative. They become forms of hypnosis or black magic and can generate negative forces. It is important only to do rituals that are formulated to bring peace and understanding, which link us with the whole of life, and not merely place us with a particular community which may be opposed to others. Ritual, moreover, should be creative. It should not be standardized or stereotyped, though it does have its laws and processes that reflect the great creative forces of life.

Ritual is necessary for everyone. It purifies the mind and brings benefic forces into society. It changes our psychic field so that we become receptive to higher forces. We must also remember that the most important ritual or regular action we should do is meditation, which is the great ritual of awareness, offering the seen into the seer for the beauty of Reality.

WHAT IS THE IMPORTANCE OF TEMPLES?

Temples are places wherein a force of collective spiritual aspiration can be focused. They are like power stations for generating a higher consciousness in society. They are like communication centers to contact the Divine and the cosmic powers.

Thereby temples are the most important buildings in any community, more significant than any government building, news center or bank. They do all these functions but on an inner level. Temples serve to bring spiritual energies into the world and they work to purify our collective psyche of negative karmas.

But a real temple is a place of inner worship. It is not a church where preaching goes on, and where dogma and authority are imposed upon the minds of people, but a place of peace wherein meditation and devotional worship occurs to open our minds and hearts to the Divine.

WHY DO HINDU TEMPLES APPEAR NOT TO BE HOLY?

To the Hindu mind religion and life are not separate, just as God and Nature are one. A Hindu temple includes life and people along with the Gods and gurus. It is not an austere or puritanical monument to a belief, but an expression of life in all of its richness and abundance. Therefore it includes art work, paintings and sculptures of all kinds. It includes music and dance and the temple itself is a place where various festivals occur. It has a place for animals like elephants, monkeys, cows or peacocks. It has incense, lamps, flowers and generally a water tank for ritual bathing. Even food and sweets are there. It is a place not only for adults but also for children. It is a place not just for a Sunday service or prayer at a particular time of the day but a place one can come to at any time. The Hindu temple is a miniature universe. It includes everything and therefore it does not stand apart from anything like other places of worship may appear to.

WHAT IS THE IMPORTANCE OF PILGRIMAGE?

Pilgrimage consists of visiting various sacred sites generally to perform worship or meditation. These sacred places may be man made structures like temples or various power spots in

Nature like mountains or rivers. Such places in Nature may be made more holy by the practices various sages and yogis have performed there. Hindus recognize innumerable such places and find them wherever they live. They are not bound to any single holy center.

Each place has its own energy. Certain places have a greater spiritual energy than others, which we can benefit from by visiting them. Yet the pilgrimage to external holy places is no substitute for the inner pilgrimage which is mantra and meditation. Actually our entire life is a pilgrimage and all places are sacred sites. This is what we learn through going to holy places.

IS CONTROL OF SEXUAL ENERGY NECESSARY?

Sexual energy has a tremendous power, not only for creating new life but for bringing about a higher stage of evolution in humanity, for facilitating an inner or spiritual rebirth. For this reason, as also for ordinary ethical and hygienic reasons, Yoga advocates control of sexual energy.

Yet sex is not a sin or evil. It is a force of nature, like fire, that can be used in constructive or destructive ways. Sex is the ultimate energy reserve of the physical body, the subtle essence of all our bodily tissues, upon which its entire stamina and endurance depends. Unless some portion of that energy is preserved and directed inwardly, we will lack the power to develop a higher consciousness, just as a car, however well made, cannot take us very far without adequate gasoline to run it. For health, creativity and spirituality we must preserve a portion of our sexual energy so that we have the power to accomplish these goals.

This does not mean that we should fight with sex or regard it as evil but that we must recognize the limitation of our energies in life and decide what we really want to do with them. If we truly aspire to the higher life, we must set aside the proper energy to approach it or we are only deluding ourselves by thinking we are spiritual. Control of sexual energy must be aligned with yogic practices to transmute, however. It is not a question of suppressing the energy but of orienting it in another direction.

WHAT IS THE PLACE OF MONASTICISM?

Most religions have monastic orders, which therefore must be part of any universal teaching. Such orders, properly formulated, allow individuals to devote themselves exclusively to spiritual practices by not placing outer demands upon them.

There are various monastic orders within the Hindu tradition. Hindu monks do not always live at a particular monastic institution but may wander, either gaining food by begging, stopping temporarily at different ashrams, or taking residence in the mountains. They devote themselves to lives of Yoga and meditation and often become the greatest teachers.

True monasticism, however, should not be confused with missionaries, who are not devoted to spiritual practices but to converting others to a limited belief. If one is not doing spiritual practices, monasticism is no more than a devotion to a dogma or institution, and generally turns negative. Such militant or political monastic orders have done great damage in the world.

Nor does the value of monasticism exclude the value of the married or householder life. While the monastic path can be more direct, the householder life is generally more practical and can in time lead to the same goal.

WHAT IS THE IMPORTANCE OF NON-VIOLENCE?

Non-violence is the cardinal virtue recognized in Sanatana Dharma or any universal tradition. Non-violence is the supreme Dharma, the great law of life. To the extent that we fall from non-violence we cease to be truly religious and lose our connection with God.

Dharma means natural law and the most basic natural law is to remain in harmony with our fellow creatures. No creature likes to suffer. To attune ourselves with the nature of all beings, we should not seek suffering for any being. Non-violence, therefore, is the foundation of all true ethics of truthfulness, honesty and non-stealing. Non-violence in Hinduism is the universal great vow. Only if we have an attitude of non-violence toward all beings can we have true universality.

Non-violence means not to wish harm for any being in thought, word and deed. It is not merely a matter of refraining from physical violence. Nor is it just a matter of refraining from military action. It means non-violence in our own homes and families as well. Nor is it limited to human beings. It means to not be violent towards plants, animals or the Earth itself, which means to restrict our consumption of meat and our use of energy for personal pleasure. Non-violence is not only in regard to our own action, we should not support or condone violence by others, which is not to attack it but to withdraw any association that we might have with it.

Non-violence is the best way to Self-realization because if we see the Self in all beings and all beings in the Self, we cannot possibly wish harm to anyone. Violence is the denial of religion which, first of all, should be peace. To use violence to promote a religion — whether through thought, word or deed — is to deny the real spirit of religion. To try to make a religion spread through the use of force is not to spread religion but irreligion. This at least is the Hindu view.

DOES NON-VIOLENCE EXCLUDE SELF-DEFENSE?

True non-violence recognizes the right of people to defend themselves, their life and their property, including their family, community and country, from unprovoked violent attack. However monks and yogis who have renounced the world no longer have any attachments. They are not required to defend anything, though it is not wrong for them to defend themselves if they choose to.

Yet self-defense should never be an excuse for violence. Even if we have to defend ourselves we should not hate those who are attacking us. We should act only in such a way as to prevent more violence from occurring. Self-defense should not be a disguised form of self-assertion. It never requires that we attack others first or that we aggressively seek to promote our beliefs or expand our borders.

On the other hand, non-violence should not be an excuse for not defending the Truth, which requires that we hold to the Truth even when faced with opposition. Non-violence does not mean to passively and fearfully allow the forces of untruth to promote themselves unquestioned. True non-violence is not cowardice that flees from confrontation but Divine courage which faces all confrontations without running away or resorting to force. This means not responding to violence with violence but responding to it with Truth and fearlessness.

WHY IS THERE VIOLENCE IN HINDU STORIES?

The main violence that we observe in Hindu mythology is the destruction of various demons by the Gods, avatars or great sages, as in the story of Rama and Ravana. These are symbols for truth destroying falsehood and are far from ordinary depictions of human violence much less a glorification of it. Even in the Mahabharata war, violence is only resorted to as the last measure by people of the warrior class, after all else has failed, and is taken up only as a defensive battle. There is nowhere in Hinduism a glorification of violence to promote religion or the idea that violence can be good, though naturally Hindus, being people, have themselves been guilty of violence at times, but this has been to go against their religion.

WHAT IS THE IMPORTANCE OF VEGETARIANISM?

All religions strive to reduce the consumption of meat in one way or another. Some religions, particularly in ancient times, turned the eating of meat into a sacrifice, a religious ritual that requires special preparation. Even hunting cultures only consume meat after such rituals and make sure to use all parts of the animal and to ask for forgiveness for their action of harming the creature. Only meat that is appropriately sanctified is considered proper for eating. No tribal people eat meat quickly or carelessly, or accept situations, as today, wherein animals are raised in a brutal and mechanical way for meat production.

Other religions, like Judaism, Islam and Christianity, try to reduce aspects of meat-eating but not meat-eating itself. Judaic and Islamic law forbids certain animal foods, like pork and shell-fish, and has a special way of killing animals for consumption that was originally meant to reduce the negative effects of meat (like removing all the blood of the animal). Even Catholic Christianity has forbidden eating of meat on Fridays. While such measures fall short of vegetarianism, they do show the same direction of motivation. As these religions approve of restrictions on meat consumption, we must consider that it is yet better to eliminate it altogether. Hence it is clear that reduction of meat consumption is a common practice in all religions, the universality of which should be recognized. On the other hand, we do not find instances where any religious books restrict the consumption of vegetables in the same manner.

Hinduism is a vegetarian religion, though it has accepted the eating of meat for those who are not yet ready for the spiritual life. Buddhism and Jainism also emphasize vegetarianism, though Buddhism as it is practiced in many Buddhists countries today does not always do this. In Buddhist countries like China which don't emphasize vegetarianism for the common people, it is still stressed for the monks. Vegetarianism goes hand in hand with non-violence and helps promote a deeper sensitivity in life. Religions based upon non-violence have always emphasized vegetarianism.

Meat diet causes many diseases. Modern studies show that

cancer, heart disease, arthritis and other ailments occur more frequently in meat eaters, and that vegetarians have generally a better longevity. Above all, meat tends to dull our sensitivities, which is why most great thinkers tend to eat less meat. Hence, it is a scientific matter that meat-eating has many negative side-effects.

In addition we must consider the special crisis of the planet today, wherein meat consumption is one of the prime causes of pollution and the devastation of the natural environment. It also encourages a lack of respect for animal life that is behind the reduction of natural inhabitants in the world.

WHAT IS THE PLACE OF ART IN SPIRITUALITY?

The Western world has long suffered from a split between the sacred and the profane. Into the profane was placed not only business but art, science and philosophy. The sacred was limited to the realm of religious law and theology, in which creative expression was denigrated along with the idea that the world is evil and God or Allah has no image (and therefore is apart from Nature and humanity). This denial of images, as in Islam or Protestant Christianity, naturally stifles art, particularly of a sacred nature. When images were allowed as in Catholicism, their forms were restricted according to religious doctrines. Similarly music was sometimes banned as unholy or restricted in its forms or usage. When art did escape the shackles of religion, which began in Europe with the Renaissance, it developed apart from religion and has become largely a personal affair, not a way of connecting with the cosmic and with the Gods and Goddesses as it was among the ancient Greeks who lived prior to this split.

In India this split did not occur, though Hindus do discriminate outer or mundane from inner or spiritual knowledge. Yet in the Hindu view art can be part of a way of spiritual knowledge and theology part of the mundane. It is a question of attitude and approach. Art can bé a natural expression of devotion or love of

God, while theology may be no more than a sterile dogma. Hence the Hindu religion is filled with poetry, drama, sculpture, painting, music and dance as an integral part of worship, as part of the temple itself and its regular activities. The forms of Hindu art are filled with the beauty and variety of all life and Nature. The music is not somber or rarefied but full of vitality. The sculpture can be voluptuous. It is hard for people to tell the difference between Hindu religious art on one hand, and art of a folk or personal nature on the other. The two were never separate.

Art is one of the doors to the spiritual life. Creativity is step toward Divinity. Such art, however, should be done as an act of worship or as a means of seeking Truth, in which case it can embrace all the beauty of Nature and wisdom of Awareness. Art done out of selfish or commercial motives, or which comes from the intellect only, cannot take us to the real fountainhead of creativity that lies within us.

Today we need a creative renaissance in the world, in which art in all of its forms, abstract and representational, is once more taken up as part of the spiritual life. Art should be a form of worship, filled with devotion, and carrying the power of the Cosmic Being. Otherwise we have failed not only in the realm of art but in the realm of spirituality as well, and our culture will remain immature.

WHAT IS THE PLACE OF THE OCCULT?

Western religions have generally been opposed to the occult. They have been against divinatory methods like astrology and have oppressed or even executed occultists as witches. They often see occultism as the working of the Devil. The Pagan traditions that such religions originally supplanted used the occult, and discrediting the occult was part of the strategy for overcoming these older traditions.

Sanatana Dharma or the universal tradition accepts all valid forms of knowledge. It recognizes the occult as a subtler realm of Nature. Beyond the physical, the realm of gross form, it says that there exists the astral realm in which various spirits, gods and angels exist, and through which we can develop various extrasensory powers and experiences. Knowledge of this subtle realm is part of life and can be explored. It is nothing either to fear or to be in awe of.

The occult is one of the doors to the spiritual life as it takes us beyond the limitations of the senses and the materialistic idea of reality. Yet occult knowledge, though it can help direct us toward spiritual knowledge should not be confused with it. Spiritual knowledge is knowledge of the Self, who is the Supreme Divinity beyond all worlds. Occult knowledge is subtler than the physical science but still limited to the manifest realm. The occult planes include subtle realms of illusion and magic. We must be careful in our examination of them just as we have to be careful in dealing with chemistry, nuclear physics or other subtle aspects of science. We should explore them with the help of devotion to the Divine and awareness of the higher Consciousness and not lose sight of the fact that they are only another aspect of who we really are. Such an examination of subtle realms was an integral part of the Raja Yoga system of Patanjali.

WHAT IS THE ROLE OF ASTROLOGY?

Astrology is the most important of the occult sciences because it shows how the subtle forces of the universe affect us throughout our lives, both individual and collective. Any universal spiritual tradition requires a sound system of astrology for a complete understanding of the workings of universe.

Vedic or Hindu astrology (*Jyotisha*) is such a well-developed system of astrology imbued with the wisdom of innumerable sages and self-realized yogis. It is a complete science with many layers, reflecting the profound harmony of the universe. It can help us understand the pattern of our health, career, relationships and the development of our spiritual life. It provides the keys to the movement of our life on all levels.

Such a science of astrology should not be confused with crude fortune telling, however. It is not a matter of wishful thinking but of a profound study of how the stars and planets affect us, not only outwardly but inwardly. The true astrologer is the ultimate psychologist and sociologist who can help us build the foundation for the spiritual life. He or she unfolds the hidden pattern and meaning behind our lives so that we can take the appropriate action at the appropriate time and thereby fully use our soul's potential in this incarnation.

WHAT IS THE PLACE OF AYURVEDIC MEDICINE?

Health is the foundation of all that we do. Without adequate health we will not have the energy to pursue any of the goals of life. Yet true health is not merely physical strength and stamina but purity of body and mind, which is necessary for spiritual practice. As a spiritual form of healing Ayurveda directs us to Self-understanding as the ultimate means of health and harmony. It does not stop short with feeling good physically but shows us how to use the healthy body to pursue a higher life.

Ayurveda is the medical part of the universal tradition of Sanatana Dharma. It shows us how the great forces of Nature work to sustain our body-mind functioning and how they can be consciously used to maintain the harmony and health of our entire being. It promotes health through the use of diet, herbs, specially prepared mineral formulations, and profound therapies of detoxification and rejuvenation, along with recommending a life-style based upon the ascertainment of our particular psycho-physical constitution according to the balance of the elements within us.

Ayurveda is the medicine of Nature, the medicine of life, which brings to us the healing forces of this great universe. Until we adapt the healing forces of Nature into society our planet must remain in crisis and our medical systems as much a curse as a blessing.

WHY SHOULD ONE LEARN SANSKRIT?

An essential part of the seeking for a universal tradition is the looking for a universal language. Such a universal language exists within Sanatana Dharma as Sanskrit, the ancient spiritual language of the great yogis and seers. Sanskrit is the oldest of the Indo-European languages and has been looked upon as the Mother of all languages.

Language is based upon sound and meaning. The meaning is the most important thing but the sound should be appropriate to it. This is why poetry, which blends sound and meaning, has so much power. Each sound has a certain energetic quality that can be useful for conveying certain meanings. Sanskrit is a purely spiritual language in which sound and meaning are united in the right way. Sanskrit reflects the laws and powers of cosmic intelligence. It patterns human speech after universal law. As such it is an extremely precise language for working with spiritual experiences. Not surprisingly we have had to import many Sanskrit words into English — like guru, mantra, prana, shakti, kundalini — to help understand this realm that our ordinary language and mentality has not had much experience with.

Learning Sanskrit can be an important tool for developing the mind, controlling thought, sharpening perception and increasing creativity. It also provides access to the largest literature of Self-knowledge and Yoga in the world, including Hindu, Buddhist and Jain teachings going back for many thousands of years. However we should not merely learn to read Sanskrit or approach it as a dead language. Much of the power of Sanskrit is in its sound. We should learn to speak and chant it or otherwise we really don't know the language.

Classical Sanskrit was codified by the great grammarian Panini (c. 500 BC), whose classic the Ashtadhyayi is still studied for a proper understanding of the language. His model of language was recently found to be the most scientific for use with computers. Sanskrit is thus both the language of the past and the future and through it we can communicate with all time.

The almighty power of the Supreme Divinities is only One.
Rig Veda III.55.1

Endless vast paths encircle Heaven and Earth.
Rig Veda V.45.2

May Heaven and the Atmosphere grant us peace. May the Earth give us peace along with the Waters. May the herbs and the forests be peaceful to us. May all the cosmic powers grant us peace. May the Divine Being grant us peace. May the entire universe be at peace. May there be the peace of peace. May that peace dwell within me.
Shukla Yajur Veda XXXVI.17

Questions 2.
Sanatana Dharma and the Modern World

In this section we will examine the issues of culture, religion, and spirituality to see not only what is relevant today, but what is truly universal and meaningful. In this way we will find much that is significant not only in the spirituality of Sanatana Dharma but in its cultural forms, regardless of whether we live in India or in the West.

A. Religion, Spirituality and the Modern World

SHOULD WE FOLLOW ANY RELIGION AT ALL?

If we look at what religions have done to humanity throughout history, it appears that it would be better not to be religious at all. It would save us from many wars, hostilities and misunderstandings, such as world history is mired with and which our newspapers proclaim almost daily. On the other hand, the record of materialist ideologies like communism, socialism and capitalism has not been better, and has similarly resulted in exploitation and violence often on a grand scale. And none of us appears to be content thinking that this is the only life that we possess.

All of us at some time or another seek an answer to the ultimate questions of life — Does God or any spiritual reality exist? How might we know it? How can we live in harmony with it? Is there some part of ourselves which is immortal and part of God?

Religion in the true sense is the seeking of such higher knowledge. It is a means of discovering that Divine reality within us, not a dogma defining what God is outside of ourselves. Such religion is not an organized belief system but a set of spiritual practices to be adapted on an individual basis. These practices include the full range of human approaches to the Divine, the paths of knowledge (*jñāna yoga*), devotion (*bhakti yoga*), service (*karma yoga*) and meditational techniques (*rāja yoga*). While we should discard religion in the outer sense as organized dogma and social conditioning, we should embrace religion in the inner sense as yogic and meditational practices. Otherwise our lives will have no enduring meaning and we will take nothing with us at death but frustration and delusion.

WHAT IS THE PURPOSE OF RELIGION?

Religion, as it occurs in the world, contains two aspects. First, within all religions can be found certain moral principles which reflect a greater universal ethics. Religion tells us not to be selfish, not to harm others, not to lie, steal, or cheat, to do good, to be helpful, compassionate and thoughtful. These are universal human values that all societies require to some degree in order to function at all. While the details of such principles vary in different religions, all religions contain them to some degree.

Second, religions contain an aspect of dogma. They brand certain actions wrong not because they violate any universal ethic but because they go against a particular belief which is limited to one group only. For example, if a religion tells us that it is a sin not to go to church on a particular day, that it is wrong to call upon God by another name than the one sanctioned by the religion, or that it is heretical to think that God is not limited to a particular prophet or incarnation, these are not statements of universal Truth but the tyranny of a belief. They are dogmas which are not universally true but reflect only the opinion of a particular group. These dogmas end up promoting actions that violate universal ethics, causing us to mistrust and mistreat those who do not subscribe to them, dividing humanity into the godly believers and the ungodly or demonic non-believers who must be converted or conquered.

The first aspect of religion, universal ethics, is preliminary to the spiritual path and is, in fact, the very foundation for it. The second side, theological dogma, is harmful to the spiritual path, and contradicts the first side of religion. It is spiritually unethical to insist that one is wrong or sins by questioning religious dogma, or that by not limiting oneself to the prescriptions of a particular religious belief one has done an act of the same negative nature as harming another person.

Organized religion combines the nectar of universal ethics with the poison of exclusive belief. Unless we can sift the nectar from the poison such religion will harm our spiritual potential. Following universal ethics completely, like the principles of truthfulness and non-violence, we can take what is good in religion and dispense with what is not.

WHAT IS THE DIFFERENCE BETWEEN RELIGION AND SPIRITUALITY?

Religion and spirituality are not the same thing, as many of us have discovered through seeing the harm perpetrated in the name of religion. Religion at best serves to provide ethical training and shows various outer ways of worshipping God through rituals and prayers, which can help maintain harmony in society. Spirituality consists of internal attitudes and practices which lead to Self-realization and transcends all external rules and rituals.

One who has truly entered the spiritual path goes beyond all outer religious identities.

Today the world needs not a new religion but a universal spirituality. A universal spirituality, a sense of Sanatana Dharma, will take what is of value in all religions and not circumscribe us within the field of any of them. It will emphasize spiritual practices over all dogma and ideology.

To achieve the real goal of life we should follow an enlightenment path, a path founded by Self-realized sages which leads to Self-realization. All that is called religion does not do this. The exoteric dimension of religion, which is belief and ritual, can never be equal but is at most preliminary to the esoteric dimension, which is meditation. We must recognize the value of the inner teachings and cease to emphasize outer differences of names and forms.

WHY TRADITION?

Religious tradition has often been a negative factor in the world. It sets up various authorities and conditioning patterns that stifle individual intelligence and creativity. It establishes vested interests who war with each other to control the minds of people. It appears that we would be better off without it. However, if we look deeply, we see that such criticisms do not apply to tradition itself, which is continuity in a field of knowledge, but to authoritarianism, which is not even beneficial for maintaining a living tradition.

It is not possible to avoid tradition. We must develop teachings that grow and continue with time. This development through time itself becomes tradition. As soon as a teaching endures beyond the lifetime of a teacher it becomes a tradition. Or as soon as it expands beyond the teachings of one person, it becomes a tradition. One person in isolation cannot accomplish much in any field. Without a tradition of science to work from, what can one person do in the name of science, for example? Just as we need continuity, which is tradition, in other branches of learning, so we must have it in the spiritual realm. Otherwise each person is compelled to start from the beginning.

Culture and intelligence are collectively developed phenomena. They are the product of many people working together over a long period of time. Tradition is important in all that we do. Language, for example, cannot be developed by one person alone. It is part of a great collective effort. A comprehensive and open spiritual tradition is the need of our times. Tradition provides a guideline of experience to help us grow. Yet tradition must be kept open and alive and not become rigid or authoritarian. For this it must base itself not on fixed forms but on living spiritual experience. Tradition should be a field of resources for all to benefit from, not a set of dogmas no one is allowed to question.

ARE ALL RELIGIONS ONE?

There is only One Truth behind all religions, whether the so-called world religions or primitive beliefs. The different arts and sciences also represent various attempts, though they may be indirect, to connect with the One Reality. Recognizing such a Universal Truth, we should strive to develop a universal religion which includes not only what is good in religion, but what is good in art and science, and in all human endeavors to know Reality. All ways of connecting with Truth — whether formulated as religions or not — are like various rivers that flow to the ocean of Truth. They all have a common goal, though not each singly can reach it.

Yet to reach that Truth we must follow a path that leads to Self-realization. Few religious teachings regard Self-realization as the goal of life. Therefore they cannot take us all the way to it, though they may be of preliminary benefit. And religion is sometimes a mask for adharmic activities, for attitudes that do not enlarge our minds and hearts but narrow them down to some dogma or opinion. Such religion cannot take us even part of the way to Truth, which is universal.

Sanatana Dharma is not meant as another one of these streams but as an attempt to portray the reality of the ocean, which accepts all streams without being limited to any of them. For this reason all the spiritual practices that can be found in other religions — like prayer, ritual, mantra and meditation whether devotional or knowledge-oriented — exist within the greater Hindu tradition.

AREN'T ALL RELIGIONS THE SAME?

Because there is a unity of Truth behind all religious seeking and, above all, because there is a commonality in the religious experience, some people have come to the conclusion that all religions are the same — that it doesn't matter if one goes to a temple, church or mosque, or whether one prays, fasts or meditates — that as long as one is doing something that can be called religious, one will get to the same goal only along a different route.

Let us compare this with the field of art. Because there is a unity of the human creative experience behind all art does not mean that all art is the same, and it certainly does not mean that all that is called art is good art. Similarly that there is a unity of scientific inquiry behind all scientific pursuits does not mean that all science is the same, that all scientific theories are correct and lead to the same conclusions, or that it does not matter what experimental procedures we employ.

There is a tremendous gap between organized religion, which divides people, and the religious experience, which unites them. And the religious experience itself has different stages, levels and variations. All religious experiences are not merely equal or the same. There are many gradations between ordinary human consciousness and Self-realization, which should not all be lumped together as the same thing. Religious experiences can also occur in an impure or untrained mind and be mixed with egoism and delusion. Moreover, there is a diversity of spiritual practices, like the Yogas of knowledge and devotion, which proceed by different lines and have their own characteristic experiences. While we should recognize the unity of the religious experience, we should also acknowledge its diversity and multilevelled nature.

That all religions are one is a statement similar to that all water is one. This does not mean that all water is the same or that all water is fit to drink. That all water is one does not mean that it is not necessary to carefully consider the quality of the water we drink. There are religious doctrines and practices, which are outward or of preliminary value and others which are limited or even wrong. To discover the real truth of religion requires a great deal of discrimination, a discerning of the essence, not merely an acceptance of all forms.

AREN'T ALL RELIGIONS MERELY ALTERNATIVE APPROACHES?

One may recognize the differences that exist between various religions but consider them to be merely different alternatives, just as different roads may all lead to the same goal. This is true of religious teachings that have inner values and practices of meditation and Self-realization, but differ only in outer factors of name and form, like different enlightenment or Self-realization traditions. We can consider these to be different approaches to the same Truth. But we also observe that there are religious teachings which differ in fundamental values, goals and practices, not merely in superficial names and forms. These cannot be merely different ways to the same reality.

For example, we can recognize that there are many different names for fire. Calling fire by a different name does not mean that one does not understand the nature of fire. But this is not to say that fire can differ in its essential nature and qualities, that for some people fire is hot and for other people it can be cold. While formal differences can be reconciled, substantial differences cannot. Truth must be the same. It cannot differ according to the different beliefs and opinions of human beings.

Where religious differences are merely a matter of words or forms, we can recognize a common truth behind them. If one religion calls the ultimate reality love, another calls it truth, another calls it the infinite, we can accept a common reality behind all these formulations. But when religious teachings have differences of a substantive nature we cannot accept their varying views as equally true. For example the law of karma and rebirth leading to bondage or liberation cannot be equally true as that of sin or salvation leading to heaven or hell, as the two views are substantially different. Such views may be reconciled into lower and higher, or outer and inner truths but they cannot be given equal validity. This does not mean that we must insist that only one religious belief is valid but that we must maintain an inquiry into Universal Truth and find out the real nature of things. The goal is to discover the Truth of things, not merely to uphold religion as we know it, which is a very mixed affair, as Truth. Religion, after all, is an expedient measure to aid us in the pursuit of truth. It should never be made an end-in-itself.

ISN'T IT WRONG FOR RELIGIOUS PEOPLE TO DISAGREE?

Each one of us sees the world differently. The very beauty of life is that each being is unique and has his or her own unique perspective. Such differences need not be a problem. We should honor and respect them. Through them each person provides a new vision of the universe. Such differences only become a problem when we insist that one perspective is correct for everyone. For example, there is an underlying unity of all human beings but we all have different faces. To arrive at human unity it is not to make all people have the same face, but to see the common humanity behind and through all different human forms.

It is not wrong for us to disagree with one another. After all, no opinion of any human being can be regarded as the absolute truth that no one can question, and no verbal formulation is final or incapable of being distorted. We must hold to the truth that we perceive, even if no one in the world agrees with us. To find truth we must express how we see things and compare it with how other people see them, and try to find out what is really there. This clash of inquiry leads us to discovery. But we should not promote disagreements or refuse to recognize common truths merely to uphold a particular identity or belief as opposed to others.

We must recognize the right of others to see things differently than we do. We must create a culture that honors many different points of view. This does not mean that we should create a culture in which all things are permitted. We must base our lives on higher universal values, like non-violence, truthfulness, compassion, and self-discipline. But this should allow any number of names and forms for the spiritual life and its activities. Universality is not a matter of agreement, which may be no more than a social consensus or blind uniformity, but of integration in which one goes beyond all dualities.

SHOULD WE NOT COMBINE ALL SPIRITUAL TRADITIONS?

All true spiritual teachings have an inherent unity, which is the recognition of the spirit or Self as the highest Reality. Such a universal tradition is intrinsic in Universal Truth. All true teachings are always part of it. Yet such a universal tradition cannot be arrived by putting together the fragments which may exist in different teachings, any more than the moon can be put together by collecting its reflections that exist in various pools of water. To discover the universal tradition it is necessary to discover the Self-existent reality behind the universe. Without knowing ourselves, to try to put together a universal tradition through what we have learned from books or from other people, however great, remains second hand and artificial and cannot possibly endure.

The beauty of Sanatana Dharma is that it is already based upon a universal understanding which uses all aspects of the spiritual life including theistic and non-theistic approaches, Yogas of knowledge, devotion, service and technique, and both imagistic and non-imagistic approaches. Yet without awareness of the inner Self such aids remain limited in value, like tools without the proper person to employ them. Sanatana Dharma provides the basis for a universal tradition but it needs the enkindling factor of our own Self-knowledge to truly manifest it.

CAN I BE A FOLLOWER OF ALL SPIRITUAL PATHS?

One should recognize the validity of all true spiritual paths, though only a part of what is called religion is a spiritual path. There are a number of spiritual paths which provide meditation practices that can, if applied with the proper background and guidance, lead to union with the Divine or the inner Self. Moreover, it is good to know something about a number of the world's spiritual traditions in order to broaden one's mental horizon, just as it is good to know something of the different cultures and customs of various lands and peoples.

However, life is limited. One does not have the time to follow out in depth the practices of all teachings, which require a certain period to work properly. For one's actual meditation practice one has to choose a certain line of approach, and a connection with specific teachers, generally within the same tradition.

We can compare this with any field of learning. One can recognize the validity of all true artistic approaches, but one cannot practice all techniques of art. One cannot be simultaneously a sculptor, painter, musician and dancer, in ancient, medieval and modern styles. In one's actual practice one will have to make a choice and follow it out. Moreover, the goal of a spiritual practice is not to learn various traditions but to know oneself, and for this the teaching is a guideline, not the end. To be a true artist one does not need to study all forms of art but to discover one's own creativity. If we spend our time exploring different teachings and traditions, rather than looking into who we really are, we have missed the point. The different teachings are aids to Self-realization. The important thing is to reach the goal, not to explore the different paths.

WHAT DO ALL HINDUS BELIEVE?

Hinduism as a universal tradition does not emphasize a particular code of beliefs that divides humanity into believers and non-believers. It does not begin with the assertion "I believe in God" but with the recognition "God or Truth and myself are one." It does not state that only those of our faith can find God but that God or Truth is the nature of all beings. It does not have articles of faith, like the belief in various miracles or special revelations, but directs us to discover the nature of Truth, which we can experience in our own consciousness as clearly as we can see the sun rise in the morning.

Hinduism is not centered in a particular name or form but on Truth which lies behind all names and forms. It is an open tradition that encourages a diversity of approaches, not a monolithic religion consisting of a standard creed. Its emphasis is Dharma or Universal Truth that one can perceive, not belief, which appears contrary to the nature of things. Hinduism recognizes not only the unity of the Divine but the infinity of Truth.

The principles which all Hindus accept are not articles of faith but dharmas or natural laws. Such are the law of karma, rebirth, the existence of a cosmic Lord (*Ishvara*) and universal intelligence, the beneficence of the world of Nature, and

Self-realization as the ultimate goal of life. Hindus similarly share common practices like ritual, prayer, pilgrimage, charity, Yoga and meditation but there is no prescribed system of activities that all Hindus must follow. There are common Hindu values and attitudes like non-violence, truthfulness, self-discipline and control of sexual energy, which are even more important than these practices.

These approaches are employed as ways of finding Truth, not as dogmas that tell us what that truth is supposed to be. Sanatana Dharma tells us that it is more important to give people the means to find Truth, than it is to tell people what Truth is supposed to be, which becomes a dogma. As Truth is our own nature, we need only let it come forth by no longer trying to impose any external influences upon it.

We see therefore that many people, who may not formally regard themselves as Hindus, may have a Hindu view of reality. This is because the Hindu view is not a sectarian view but the view of the whole, which is that One Self is All.

ISN'T THE UNIVERSAL TRADITION MORE THAN HINDUISM?

The question assumes that Hinduism is a limiting factor for a universal tradition which it does not have to be. Hinduism or Sanatana Dharma does not separate itself off from the universal tradition. It is not seeking an identity apart from or within the universal tradition. It is simply asking us to recognize the universal tradition, so that we don't have to invent names like Hinduism to scale down its formulation.

Hinduism welcomes the search for a universal tradition and the inclusion in it of all spiritual aspiration. But it says that such a tradition must be created through spiritual experience, through following the teachings of Self-realized sages. It cannot be put together merely on an intellectual level, nor simply built up as an organization. It is not a matter of merely combining all the spiritual traditions of humanity together in the same place or same book but of having the realization of Universal Truth. This only occurs within the individual who himself or herself has transcended all outer seeking. It cannot be accomplished by any group or organization.

If Hinduism is seen in its true light as Sanatana Dharma or the universal tradition, then whoever realizes that Universal Truth is also a true Hindu, regardless of the names and forms of their religious life. Hinduism includes not only the religions of this world but those of the different planes of consciousness up to the Absolute. It is not only the religion of one incarnation but of all our births whether in this world or another.

SHOULD NOT WESTERNERS FOLLOW A WESTERN RELIGION?

Some people in the Western world believe that Eastern religions, like Hinduism and Buddhism, have no place in the West, which should follow Western religions like Christianity and Islam. Such people do not understand that Eastern dharmic traditions are not religious belief systems but universal ways of spiritual knowledge.

We note a curious cultural prejudice. Those born in the West do not mind if Western religions like Christianity and Islam are adopted by peoples in Eastern countries. Westerners are not asking Christian missionaries to be recalled from Asia because the Western Christian religion is not appropriate for Eastern people. Nor have Muslims limited the spread of their Western religion to only the Western part of the world. Westerners do not think that it is wrong for Western religions or for Western art and science to go to the East. Yet they call their systems "Western" and want to maintain their geographical purity when so-called "Eastern" teachings gain recognition in regions where they have traditionally predominated.

If Western religions are going to be exported to the Eastern world, Eastern religions must be imported to the West, just as the movement of trade must go in both directions. What is important is to take the best in human culture whatever its origin. We don't refuse a peach because it comes from what was originally a Chinese tree. So too, we should not refuse meditation teachings because other cultures have developed them better than we have.

And why should it be a problem for us if anyone finds spiritual benefit from a teaching that arises outside of their given cultural context? After all spiritual knowledge transcends limitations of time and space. Western culture has not traditionally given emphasis to spiritual knowledge such as has occurred in the East. That many Westerners have found benefit from Eastern spiritual teachings is a fact which should be honored. It would be cultural chauvinism to deny it.

True religion, whether it predominates in the Eastern or Western parts of the world, is not a matter of geography. All the religions of the world are followed in areas far beyond the geographical locale of their origin. Religion speaks of the ultimate issues of life and death and should orient us to the Eternal and the Universal. In this respect Hinduism with its universal view has greater relevance for all human beings than any belief system which divides humanity into believers and non-believers.

DON'T WESTERNERS REQUIRE A SCIENTIFIC APPROACH TO SPIRITUALITY?

We all need a rational and scientific approach to the spiritual life. Otherwise the spiritual life becomes dogma or superstition. Yet to scientifically approach the spiritual life is different than to scientifically approach a material object. Spiritual Reality, being the infinite and eternal, cannot be observed in a laboratory, dissected on a table, or seen in a telescope or microscope. It requires a super-scientific approach which is to be capable of directly observing the workings of our own minds. It requires the ability to reason between the Eternal and the transient and to focus one's awareness on the Eternal.

The beauty of dharmic and meditation traditions is that they have maintained a scientific approach to the spiritual life which can be used by people all over the world. Yet the spiritual life is not merely a science, it is also an art, and must be approached with sensitivity and creativity. The spiritual aspect of life being the most subtle portion of our nature, requires the appropriate subtlety of mind to discover. It cannot, like an object on the table, be obvious to our outer vision. The science of Yoga is such a scientific approach to spirituality that we must develop on a global basis.

WHAT IS THE ANCIENT WESTERN VEDIC HERITAGE?

The Western world has had many connections with the Vedic and Hindu tradition through history. At an ancient period, mainly the pre-Christian era, we see a commonality of language, culture and religion between the European and the Hindu. For example, there are many terms in common between English and Sanskrit: mother-matar, father-pitar, brother-bhratar, sister-svasar. There are many European and Vedic equivalent names for God: Divine-Deva, Zeus-Dyaus, Jupiter-Dyaus Pitar, Uranus-Varuna. The Greek and Roman reverence for the Gods and Goddesses through temple worship is of the same order as the kind of worship that goes on in temples in India today. At the original core of any indigenous European culture is a Vedic affinity or perhaps even a Vedic identity.

Westerners need not regard the Vedic heritage as simply Eastern, it is universal and also part of an older European heritage that can again be reclaimed, now that the hold of the exclusive religions of the Middle Ages, which suppressed mysticism and spirituality, is coming to an end. The study of the ancient Western Vedic heritage is one of the most important areas of historical research to be embarked upon today and will be very important in reclaiming the spiritual foundations of Western culture.

DON'T WE NEED PRACTICES DESIGNED FOR US TODAY?

We must have spiritual teachings appropriate for our changing circumstances, wherever we may live. For this it is essential that we follow a living spiritual tradition, not a dead and stereotyped belief which ties us to some by-gone era. Yet as the goal of the spiritual life is the Eternal, the teaching must be grounded in the Timeless Reality and not merely be a fad of the moment. The forms we follow should be based on the Eternal Truth but adjusted according to the needs of the times.

The universal teaching is a science of Self-realization. We are first of all who we are. To know ourselves is the most important thing, whatever our cultural or geographical background. That Self transcends time, space and objectivity. It is the Eternal Presence. Yet it is important to connect with a tradition of Self-knowledge, as a tradition allows a broad approach so that we can find a teacher and teaching suitable for our temperament.

Moreover, Self-knowledge creates a certain culture and way of life. It creates an awareness of our posture, from which the science of asana or yogic postures arose. It creates an awareness of breath, from which the science of pranayama arose. It creates an awareness of speech, from which the Sanskrit language arose. It creates a science of health, from which Ayurveda arose. It creates an understanding of symbol and ritual, from which the science of puja (Hindu ritual) arose. A culture of Self-knowledge is useful and this is the essence of Sanatana Dharma. Naturally it has to be continually adjusted individually and collectively, but it has always done this.

What the West, and each part of the world for that matter, needs is a living spiritual tradition, which goes back to enlightened and Self-realized teachers. Since the West has not preserved such a tradition in its culture, it must connect up with traditions from the parts of the world which are still alive. Hinduism or Sanatana Dharma, offering such enlightened traditions, without insisting upon the adaptation of an exclusive religious identity, is a good basis for this.

WHAT IS THE IMPORTANCE OF A YOGIC TRADITION?

Spiritual traditions exist to various degrees and for various purposes. What is necessary is a comprehensive spiritual tradition that contains a complete and practical science of Self-realization. Fragmentary, broken or incomplete spiritual and occult traditions have some benefit but they may not be sufficient for full realization.

A comprehensive spiritual tradition must contain all the different paths of knowledge, devotion, yogic technique and service and in the proper proportion. It must recognize the importance of posture, breath, mantra and meditation. It must employ the use of ritual, form and image, as well as direct, formless and imageless approaches. It must be based upon an understanding of the law of karma and the process of rebirth. Yet it must be free of fixation upon any particular personality, book, name or idea. And it must be connected to teachers who have realized this truth. The advantage of the yogic tradition is that it is such a tradition applied to all human temperaments, and through thousands of years of experience.

CAN I KEEP MY EXISTING RELIGIOUS BELIEF AND STILL PRACTICE YOGA?

Yogic practices are designed to lead us to the Universal Truth, which is Pure Consciousness. However, to do so they must cause us to question dogmas and limited beliefs of all kinds which are not universal. If the goal of one's religion is Self-realization than one can freely follow that religion along with yogic paths to Self-realization. However, if the goal of one's religion is less than that, then one's religion is at best a preliminary step.

To know one's Self one must eventually go beyond all theories, beliefs, names and forms, all the movements of the conditioned mind. We need not depend upon any belief. Rather we should learn to believe in ourselves, in our nature as Pure Consciousness that does not require any external support. Only when we are no longer dependent upon any external support can we know our True Nature.

IS YOGA HINDU?

Yoga is the science of meditation that appears in Hinduism, which is a broad tradition, as the essence of its spiritual practices. Yoga is not merely yogic postures but includes pranayama, mantra and various meditation approaches. Yoga is an integral part of Sanatana Dharma or the eternal tradition.

Yet whether we regard Yoga as Hindu depends upon what we understand Hinduism to be. If we follow the superficial and stereotypal view that Hinduism is an ethnic religion, then Yoga, which is a universal science, goes far beyond Hinduism, however intimately it may be related to it. We see Buddhist and Jain systems of Yoga and practices in many different mystical traditions that resemble Yoga.

However, if we understand Hinduism as Sanatana Dharma or the universal tradition, which is its true reality, then we see that Yoga and Sanatana Dharma must always go together. Yoga or union with universal consciousness is the practice of Sanatana Dharma or the universal path. Just as Sanatana Dharma leads us to universality, so does Yoga. Sanatana Dharma is the greater science and culture of Yoga, its application to all aspects of life.

IS NOT YOGA ENOUGH, WHY SHOULD WE TALK OF HINDUISM?

Yoga and Vedanta, which are the ways of spiritual practice and Self-knowledge, are the most important aspects of Sanatana

Dharma, its inner dimension. If we have these we have the essence. Yet the outer dimension of Hinduism is relevant because it has been formulated in harmony with the inner dimension. Ayurveda, Vedic astrology, Sanskrit, Vedic and Tantric ritual, Hindu mythology, Hindu music and dance, and so on, are important factors in building a spiritual culture which encompasses the whole of life. They show us how a spiritual understanding can penetrate into all aspects of life and learning, so all that we do individually and collectively supports the spiritual quest. It is not enough just to have spiritual practices. We need a culture and way of life that allows them to flourish. Hinduism provides both in abundance and fully integrated.

IS HINDUISM OF VALUE FOR WESTERNERS?

Many Westerners are fed up with organized religions, churches and dogmas. What attracts them in Eastern religions is precisely that they aren't religions such as they have been accustomed to but offer spiritual practices outside of organized belief systems. Westerners may be happy to adapt aspects of Hinduism like systems of Yoga and meditation but may feel no need to become Hindus in the religious sense, which they may equate with various superstition and prejudice.

There is nothing wrong with this attitude, except that it fails to understand Hinduism and what it can offer. Hinduism is not a belief system seeking converts. It is not striving to narrow down our sense of who we are or what we can do. It is a set of spiritual resources, carefully gathered since the most ancient times, which is available, like a wonderful set of tools, to help us build our own inner life.

If we regard Hinduism as merely another religion, then it is not of much value, and we should discard it like the rest. But if we understand Hinduism as a universal tradition, which shows how spirituality can be integrated into the whole of life, then it can be of great value for reformulating a global spiritual culture today. Just as those born in the East have to recognize the validity of modern science for all humanity, so Westerners may have to recognize the validity or Yoga or spiritual science, which is the essence of Hinduism, for all the world.

AREN'T THERE MANY THINGS WRONG WITH MODERN HINDUISM?

There may be much wrong with modern India, but this generally has little to do with the religion as properly understood. It is not the yogic science of Self-realization that has caused problems in India but the same greed and superstition that has created problems in every country. In fact there is no country and perhaps no religion in the world today that is not facing tremendous problems if we are at all honest.

There is much that is wrong with the Hindu social system, like the oppression done in the name of caste, which is a distortion of the religion. To recognize the value of Sanatana Dharma we need not blind our eyes to social, moral or spiritual errors in any religion or culture. On the contrary, it becomes the responsibility of one who recognizes the universal Dharma to promote it in all possible ways which is, first of all, to live it oneself. Yet to reject the spiritual side of the tradition because of outer problems associated with a society to some degree based upon it only shows that one is still attached to the outer world and does not understand the inner truth of the teachings.

SHOULD ONE FORMALLY BECOME A HINDU?

As a universal approach, the teachings of the Hindu tradition do not require that one have any particular outer religious affiliation but only that we live a truthful life. One does not have to formally become a Hindu to receive the inner teachings of Yoga and meditation. All that we need is a sincere aspiration to discover God or Truth.

However, it can be very helpful to formally become a Hindu

because it provides one a formal connection to the world's oldest continually existing enlightenment tradition. It brings one into the family of the rishis and yogis and connects us directly with their grace and guidance. We grow in life relative to the associations we make. To enter into an association with the sages is the best thing, and to do so with a tradition that embraces spiritual knowledge of all types can only be helpful. But we must put these teachings into practice for this association to be really meaningful.

WON'T A PERSON LOSE THEIR WESTERN IDENTITY BY BECOMING A HINDU?

Becoming a Hindu is not taking on an exclusive religious belief that cuts one off from other points of view. It is a means of opening up to the universal and eternal tradition (Sanatana Dharma).

We should ask, are we really Westerners (or Easterners) for that matter? We are human beings first of all and the legacy of all humanity belongs to us. Identity is something that we are going to lose anyway. Identity is what blocks our understanding of the Eternal. Our true identity is in Consciousness, not in any cultural association.

We should adopt whatever furthers our spiritual life, not just meditation practices but all forms of culture, language and behavior, wherever we may find it. Whatever we take out of this attitude is not a divisive identity but a way of action in harmony with the universe. Should people recognize their connection with Sanatana Dharma and its great stream of teachers and teachings, it can only be good. It will strengthen our true identity in the Self and not cause us to lose anything that really belongs to us.

HOW CAN WE INTEGRATE EAST AND WEST?

We must seek to bring together what is best in both East and West, and not merely throw them together. The better part of the

Eastern world is its spirituality. The better part of the Western world is its science and humanitarianism.

The Western world, particularly the United States, has made many gains in the outer world, developing science and technology. The Eastern world, particularly India, has made similar gains in the inner world, developing the science of Yoga and meditation. For a complete human development both the inner and the outer sides of the human being must be developed. As long as the outer side of man is not developed — as long as we are living in poverty, disease and ignorance of the forces of Nature — the inner side of man, the cultivation of the spirit must be limited. On the other hand, as long as the inner side of man is not developed — as long as we have no means of developing our deeper consciousness — the outer side of man, however well-developed with science and technology, cannot bring true happiness to anyone.

This does not mean that there has been nothing of spiritual value in the Western world or nothing of scientific value in the East. It is a matter of proportion. The greatest integration will occur when we recognize that East and West are just the two sides of our own nature wherever we are born.

ARE GURUS NECESSARY?

Seeing the exploitation brought on by some so-called gurus (many of whom have been outside any real tradition), there has been a tendency to want to reject gurus altogether. Some people have thought that the New Age they see dawning today will allow people to teach themselves or follow inner guides and that gurus are a thing of the past.

However, if we examine the matter deeply we see that teachers are as important in the spiritual field as in other domains of life. We have many different teachers during the education we receive in life and attend many schools. If teachers are not necessary, why don't we just leave our babes out in the woods, to teach themselves? Are teachers dispensable in other walks of life? Can a person learn the piano, or learn modern physics without a teacher? If teachers can be dispensed with in other fields of life, then perhaps they are dispensable in the spiritual realm, but not otherwise.

Inner guides can be important sources of wisdom and inspiration but they do not eliminate the necessity for living teachers. The mind can easily invent an inner guide according to its desire or prejudice. Such an inner guide cannot question us or challenge our preconceptions the way a living teacher can.

If we are honest we see that we all have spiritual teachers, that we all benefit from some sort of external guidance be it in the form of books, talks or one-to-one dialogue. Some of us may require prolonged personal contact with a teacher. For others a short contact may be enough (if it is accompanied by a long term practice of the teaching). What we don't need is personality cults of gurus, whereby we turn the teacher not into a guide of our practice but some external hero figure on whom we develop an emotional dependency.

The real role of a guru is to help us understand ourselves. The real teacher is merely an instrument along the path of Self-knowledge and does not make him or herself important as a separate entity. To respect and benefit from spiritual teachers does not mean to become dependent upon them, to imitate them, but to strive to discover truth for ourselves.

DOES ONE REQUIRE A LIVING GURU?

Naturally in any field of learning it helps to have living teachers. Living gurus are preferable to those who have passed away and we all require them to some degree. However, we may not all be able to meet supremely great gurus and world teachers, like Ramakrishna or Ramana Maharshi. What is most important is to follow a living enlightenment tradition connected to modern Self-realized teachers. Not all the teachers in such a tradition need be figures of the highest order, nor can we always tell if they are.

Many Dharmic teachings have maintained a living tradition up to the present era, like the various approaches of Vedanta. Certain more specific teaching lines have been established in modern times with a global approach such as those of Ramakrishna, Vivekananda, Ramana Maharshi, Sri Aurobindo, Swami Shivananda, Paramahansa Yogananda and many others. The great spiritual approaches they established are not for their lifetimes only. We can follow them with faith and confidence should they appeal to us but must integrate them into the greater goal of Self-realization, in which we must go beyond their formal and organizational differences.

Someone who lived hundreds or thousands of years ago cannot — like Krishna, Christ or Buddha — be a guru for a person living today, though they may have been a guru for people at the time in which they lived. Yet modern representatives of older Self-realized teachers can function as gurus, providing they are connected with the living reality of the teaching.

In seeking a teacher we must look to learn from the place where we are. If we do so we will find that there is always the appropriate guidance available for us. However if we have an inflated idea of our spiritual potential, then we might not find anyone good enough to teach us. In seeking gurus, moreover, we must not be caught by the net of name and fame. A true teacher is not necessarily going to be famous or charismatic in terms of this modern materialistic and sensate society. The greatest teachers are often unknown and have very few disciples. They may not even formally function as gurus at all. But all that they do serves to teach and demonstrate the higher Truth.

SHOULD ONE FOLLOW A TRADITIONAL GURU?

One should follow a teacher who gives us peace and who connects us with the Universal Truth. The place of their birth is a secondary matter, particularly in the modern world of global travel and mass communication. But connection with a tradition can be important.

There is a built in safety in following teachers who are part of greater and older enlightenment traditions. Human personalities are always limited. What one person has done, however right, may not be an appropriate model for another person to follow. Whatever the limitations of the person, the strength of the tradition and its many teachers protects us. The tradition offers proven teachings and various examples how to apply them which transcend the traits of any particular personality.

There is a danger in following self-proclaimed gurus who are not part of any tradition because the support of the greater tradition does not exist behind them. There is a danger in following one person traditions who have the same basic teaching for everyone, because the limitations of the person must imprint themselves on the teaching. There is a danger in following one person's synthesis of many traditions because even though the synthesis may appear broad, it must still reflect the limitations of the person.

Most of the problems people have had with gurus today have occurred by emphasizing the personality of a particular teacher over the greater universal teaching. This naturally occurs more with teachers who are outside of any greater tradition. The teacher is just an exponent of the universal tradition of Truth. We should never lose sight of this in our following the teaching.

CAN ONE CHANGE GURUS?

We have many teachers in the different fields of learning we may take up. We don't have only one grade school teacher, nor only one science teacher. Being exposed to a variety of teachers allows us a wider horizon of learning and we cease to identify the teaching with a person.

Yet it is possible to have a special close relationship with a particular teacher, like that of an apprentice, which we cannot have with many different teachers. We can and should have many different teachers, but we may also have a primary teacher whose teaching serves as the central focus for our practice, just as an artist or a doctor may have a primary mentor or tutor. In the spiritual life we should be connected to a greater teacher and teaching which expresses the realization of the Absolute Truth and provides a model for it. Such a Self-realized guru or Sadguru may be central to our practice, though they may not be a person who is still alive or whom we may contact intimately.

It is also important to maintain connection with the same basic tradition and approach. If we mix teachers of different traditions, and jumble different practices it can cause confusion. If we first ground ourselves in an enlightenment tradition then we can maintain a continuity of teachers and practices within it.

The important thing is to be serious about our practice not merely to run after external personalities. If we lose faith in our teacher after they leave the physical plane it only indicates that we did not connect to them at a deep level.

B. Civilization and Social Issues

WHAT IS SANATANA DHARMA'S VIEW OF CIVILIZATION?

According to Sanatana Dharma, or the universal tradition, civilization should be the progressive unfoldment of the capacities of the soul toward the ultimate goal of Self-realization. The soul through evolution gradually develops the powers of the senses, emotion, mind and intelligence until discovering its nature as Pure Consciousness. All of the universe is thereby a development of civilization, which should be the culture of consciousness.

Plants and animals also have their societies and their communication. Civilization is not unique to human beings or to this planet but occurs everywhere in the universe. Yet human civilization has its particular role. Human civilization should be the culture of spiritual aspiration whereby we seek to embody the universal consciousness in creaturely existence. This is neither the culture of religious belief nor that of materialistic science. It is the seeking of the Infinite in a rational, sensitive and experiential manner, not the promotion of an institution, nor the cultivation of the finite. True civilization begins with the spiritual life and it is based upon honoring the sages, those who have realized truth, and looking to them as our social role models and ideals.

HOW DOES HINDUISM VIEW WESTERN CIVILIZATION?

Western civilization is a comparatively recent phenomenon compared to older spiritual cultures like the Hindu which go back over five thousand years and recognize previous world ages going back far into what Western historical accounts describe as the pre-historic era. For Hindus the modern era began with the Buddha some 2500 years ago, when what was for them the ancient era ended. Hindus view Christianity and Islam as new religions also, which have therefore yet to develop the proper depth and tolerance that experience teaches.

According to Hindu thinkers Western civilization is still immature and at an adolescent phase wherein personal pleasure and sensory indulgence (*kāma*) are the most important values. Western civilization, except in areas dominated by fundamentalist religions, has advanced beyond the childhood phase, represented by the Middle Ages, when people were like frightened children dominated by religious authority (externally projected parental images). But it has not developed any real spiritual tradition. It produced a few mystics in the Middle Ages but no enduring science of Self-realization and yogic practices. Western art has also floundered without any spiritual roots and become mere personal expression leading either to anarchy or nihilism but not at all connecting us up with the cosmic powers which true art is meant to.

To the Hindu mind Western civilization and its adolescent values is destroying the planet and its deeper cultural traditions. However Western civilization at least has a freedom of inquiry and curiosity about the world that must lead it toward deeper knowledge in time, but as a cultural phenomenon on any large scale, this may take decades, if not centuries to develop, which is not surprising as the life of civilization is measured in thousands of years, not centuries. Western thinkers should remain humble and not get trapped in the arrogance of the intellect, then this development can occur quicker and with less suffering.

ISN'T THIS VIEW OF WESTERN CIVILIZATION INSENSITIVE?

Actually it is the Western account of history that is insensitive. Look at any book on world history coming from the West and you will see that it is mainly a history of modern Europe with spiritual cultures like the Hindu dismissed as of little importance, and ancient spiritual cultures like the Egyptians regarded as merely primitive. Similarly Western books on the history of philosophy give little credit to the great experiential spiritual systems of the Hindus and Buddhists. Their history of art has little regard for the monumental spiritual traditions of countries like India, Egypt or Mexico but is mainly concerned with the personal style art of modern Europe and America which is lacking in any sense of the Eternal and the Infinite.

Western civilization itself is arrogant and does not understand the rest of civilization, which has been its largest portion historically, or the great spiritual traditions of humanity, which are the essence of civilization. Western civilization pretends that it represents civilization as a whole, when it only represents one recent trend.

ISN'T WESTERN CIVILIZATION MORE HUMANE?

Western civilization through technology has succeeded better in giving material benefits to a larger number of people, though it remains to be seen whether this is an enduring phenomenon or will lead to some collapse owing to the exhaustion of the planet's resources. Western civilization has been better at recognizing the political rights of people, which are generally personal and materialistic rights to happiness in the outer world. Yet at the same time Western civilization has not provided any real spiritual benefit to people. It has fed the body better, perhaps, but it has starved the soul. This is like giving a person a better car to drive but starving their body. It is improving the vehicle but not the person who uses it.

True humaneness consists not of merely providing better food, clothing, shelter, medicine or human company to people, or giving them greater freedom to get these things — however necessary they may be — but of making us aware of our greater humanity, which is universal intelligence. To be humane means to treat others as we ourselves would like to be treated. This means not only to treat other people like we would treat ourselves but also treat animals and all of nature as we would treat ourselves. Otherwise our humanity itself is a curse upon Nature and will eventually undermine the natural basis of our own life, such as is happening today with the destruction of our natural environment, which is generally done in the name of progress and human advancement.

We should strive to be humane but unless we recognize the Divine Self as the true reality our humanity is a partial view that must exploit some other part of the world as less than ourselves, as well as failing to discover our true human potential, which is in universal awareness, not in material, social or intellectual gains.

ARE WESTERN RELIGIONS PART OF WESTERN MATERIALIST CULTURE?

In a broader sense yes. Western religions, including Islam, generally have the same basic outward view of life as Western science. This is evidenced by their emphasis on conversion and the formation of institutions, and their frequent hostility towards spiritual traditions, which is why orthodox Islam has oppressed the Sufis, just as orthodox Christianity oppressed its mystics, and why modern science dismisses mysticism itself as a delusion. Western religion — with some notable exceptions — has generally presented itself as a worldly institution seeking to grow in numbers, force, wealth and territory, not as a spiritual path requiring going beyond worldly seeking. Its discipline has been an outer one of loyalty to the faith, the church or the book, not an inner discipline of seeking liberation and Self-realization. For this reason the spiritual dimension that is found in meditational traditions is largely lacking in Western religions.

HOW DOES HINDUISM VIEW THE WOMEN'S MOVEMENT?

The Women's movement or feminism is largely a political and intellectual movement to provide women with the same social rights, education and intellectual expression that have been given to men. It is part of various political movements that have occurred in the world for providing social justice to different groups that have been historically oppressed or discriminated against. It is a well-justified movement that can hopefully help rectify some of the mistakes of human culture today.

Hinduism has presented the world with a well-developed tradition of Goddess worship and with many great female saints, sages and yoginis, which tradition is still flourishing today. This tradition is not merely an intellectual or religious belief but based on a direct experience of the Divine Mother and her cosmic powers by various practitioners. It is a matter of the heart (devotion), not an intellectual or political view, though it does have its philosophies.

However Hindus have also oppressed women and not allowed them to develop their intelligence as freely as men, keeping them subordinate socially. This is a fall from Sanatana Dharma and has been one of the causes for the decline in Hinduism that has occurred through the centuries. In this regard the Women's movement can help reform Hinduism in a more universal light.

The modern feminist movement has been helpful in upholding the material and intellectual rights of women. It also needs to reclaim a true women's spirituality or path of Self-realization, which its political and materialistic values may not always support. Unfortunately the feminist movement may still define women according to outer values, in which personal pleasure and egoistic achievement are the main goals of life. To the extent that women do this they are not upholding real spiritual values, though this might improve the state of society. Fortunately many women are looking in a spiritual direction and for this taking interest in the experiential forms of spirituality, such as Hinduism, in which the Goddess still lives and communicates to us.

WHAT IS WOMAN'S SPIRITUALITY?

Spirituality is universal, the movement toward Self-realization inherent in all beings, which is the understanding of our true nature as Infinite Awareness. Women are included in this, and if they are not such spirituality is not real. Women have the same Divine Self and spiritual potential as men. Unfortunately there has been little done to help them develop this, particularly over the last two thousand years. In fact there has been little to help men develop their spiritual potential either, particularly in the Western world.

There are somewhat different approaches and issues in regard the spiritual life for women than for men, which should be respected, but the same basic truths and teachings exist for both. There is no women's spirituality as opposed to men's spirituality, or vice versa. True women's spirituality does not merely consist of women following female gurus or worshipping female

Divinities, but of women following a path of Self-realization. This requires connecting up with teachers and traditions that are based upon a real understanding of the Infinite and are not just projecting their own speculations and opinions.

Our political views should not determine or create our religion but our spiritual understanding should shape our social activity. Ultimately our true identity is not as men or women or even as human beings but as the Self of all beings. Our true happiness does not lie in material, social or political benefits — however necessary these may be in our outer lives — but in contacting our true nature which transcends time and space.

HOW DOES HINDUISM VIEW THE ECOLOGICAL MOVEMENT?

True ecology means to recognize the Divine Self everywhere in the universe and allow its full unfoldment on all levels and in all creatures. The ecological movement is at least moving in the direction of respecting the sacred nature of all life and reconnecting us with the unity of life. Presently it represents one of the most idealistic and progressive side of the modern psyche. However it is still often lacking in a spiritual perspective and while promoting a better ethical treatment of our environment, it does not always promote a higher standard of spiritual discipline for people and may follow amoral political values. Yet still Hinduism sees in it a great ally and an important trend of thought and awareness for the future.

WHAT IS THE HINDU VIEW OF THE NEW AGE?

Various cycles of civilization and different ages of humanity have come and gone through the great movement of time. Our current civilization is neither the first nor the last, nor the highest nor the lowest. Hinduism as Sanatana Dharma has witnessed the rise and fall of the civilizations of the world since ancient Egypt and Sumeria, and has an awareness of previous world ages thousands of years before the present cycle of civilization that began at the end of the last Ice Age. It both understands these cyclical changes and remains grounded in the Eternal Truth which transcends them.

Many people today, particularly with the change of the millennium, are looking for the dawn of a New Age of spiritual knowledge or global civilization. More specifically, the New Age movement is a name for much of the new thinking in spirituality, religion, and healing that has emerged in the Western world over the past few decades. It includes a number of strands with Eastern enlightenment traditions, Western occult approaches and various new ideas in health, psychology, sociology and ecology. It has a prophetic trend and strongly futuristic vision.

We are definitely entering into a new global age made possible outwardly by science, technology and rapid advances in communication, the so-called information revolution. Yet the spiritual side of this new age has yet to fully emerge. What is called the New Age is a mixed affair containing important new spiritual teachings and connections with venerable old traditions but along with the same old commercialism, fantasy, and exploitation applied to the spiritual life, often projected high tech or via a commercial mass media approach.

Hinduism generally finds an ally in the New Age because it also is looking for a planetary spirituality to reemerge. Hinduism encourages freedom of thought and exploration of both occult and spiritual realms such as is occurring in the New Age movement. Yet as an older tradition Hinduism sees the dangers of wishful thinking and of getting trapped in the occult, which many New Age groups are caught in. While we should endeavor to create a New Age it must be based upon the Eternal Truth and not upon transient desires or ungrounded speculations without any true realization. We should not overlook the older proven spiritual teachings of humanity and their practices and disciplines, though they may be difficult and laborious, in our attempt to be modern and to find quick and easy ways of achieving our goals. We must adopt them in a realistic way to our situation today. Then a real New Age will be not only possible but inevitable.

WHAT IS THE CURRENT TREND OF WORLD CIVILIZATION?

We live in an age dominated by economic development via technology. This movement began in Europe and America in the nineteenth and early twentieth century with the industrial revolution and the development of rapid transportation and communication. In Asia this movement emerged mainly after World War II. The downfall of communism has given it an added impetus, though there are parts of the world it has still not reached. The world must develop itself economically and technologically along global lines. There is no doubt about this, but it should do so in an humane and ecological manner. Those groups which promote a healthy and liberal economic development, which is yet considerate of human needs and protective of the Earth, are bound to be the most successful in the coming decades.

Unfortunately this economic age has severe excesses and imbalances, with the destruction of our environment and other forms of exploitation, which must lead to great problems for the world. Those who prosper economically not only dominate the world politically but promote their intellectual and religious views, which may be quite backwards or unenlightened, over those less affluent. Unless these excesses are dealt with properly we can expect major global difficulties through environmental changes and new diseases, not to mention the same old war, crime and terrorism.

People of spiritual insight must learn to adjust to this economic age, neither compromising their insights, nor failing to communicate with the world at large. A truly spiritual age for humanity is still far in the future, though a global economy will foster greater religious tolerance, and the development of science beyond a mechanistic and materialistic model will gradually move us in a spiritual direction. Those truly interested in the spiritual life must focus on individual realization and look beyond the limitations of the age, while yet fulfilling their social responsibility to share the spiritual teaching with the growing number who are becoming truly interested in it.

WHAT WILL THE FUTURE HUMANITY BE LIKE?

We must first shift to a clean form of technology, relying on solar and other renewable resources, and discarding oil and other "dirty" forms of power that damage and pollute the Earth who is our Mother. We must gradually reintegrate our cities into Nature by reducing their size and creating more parks and a greater space between houses. We must restore the quality of our food, air and water by reducing our reliance on chemicals and fostering organic methods of agriculture. We must place larger regions of the planet into Nature reserves where plants and animals can live without human interference or exploitation. We must reduce our consumption of meat and establish a more vegetarian diet.

We must return to natural forms of healing using herbs, diet, and body work such as is found in Ayurveda. We must develop a new psychology that considers the yogic knowledge of the higher levels of the mind and the role of karma. We must recognize our connection with the universe through occult sciences like astrology. We must gradually move in the direction of a global language, for which Sanskrit will probably be the best prototype. We must create an educational approach that encourages creativity and deep inquiry, rather than the mere memorizing of information or gaining of mechanical skills.

We must move away from sectarian and exclusivist religions and return to universal ethical values of non-violence and human unity. We must develop internal approaches to the spiritual life through yogic practices and meditation, and cease to rely on external forms of churches, books, and rituals. We must learn to see the universe not as matter or energy but as Consciousness. We must promote self-discipline, self-control and the building of character in order to create real leaders, giving up the culture of sensation, entertainment and instant gratification. We must restore the family system and community life, not as a rigid formation promoting narrow beliefs, but as an open and organic unfoldment of human and universal interconnectedness.

If we do not do these things voluntarily Nature will bring us shocks through our wrong behavior to impel us in this direction. But certainly it will be done and future generations, after making these changes, will be inclined to look back upon the twentieth century as a dark age of dirty technology, genocide, and global exploitation, which unfortunately it has been if we look at it honestly.

DOES HINDUISM FORESEE A GREAT GLOBAL CATASTROPHE?

Many groups, including not only Christian fundamentalists but New Age thinkers, are predicting great and sudden global calamities like massive earthquakes, the sinking of continents, great new plagues, nuclear war, and so on, generally scheduled to occur during the next few years around the turn of the century. Some Hindus have similar ideas but usually not to the same extent.

Unfortunately even without unprecedented Earth changes normal global fluctuations — including the kinds of earthquakes, floods and climate changes which occur regularly every few centuries — may be strong enough to cause severe problems. Today there are more people all over the world, including in marginal regions like flood plains and deserts, and a more precarious centralized economy making us more vulnerable to such changes. Yet beyond these regular fluctuations additional changes brought about by pollution and by our interference with our environment must have their effect. This means that certain shocks may occur globally for the world in the next decade or two, though this will likely be far short of the more dramatic predictions.

Such a period of shock, however, will not bring about the magical destruction of our enemies or usher the fortunate survivors immediately into a new golden or spiritual age. It will not happen overnight but last for a number of years. It will serve to force us to look at what we have been doing as a species, to face our karma, and get to work cleaning up the mess we have created through our own ignorance, greed, intolerance and selfishness. It will take decades of hard work by all countries to counter the side effects of our wrong actions as a species. This attitude of hard selfless work is what we need even today, not belief in wild speculations and magical solutions that paralyze our ability to act and usually cause us to blame someone else for what is going on. Each one of us individually must take karmic responsibility for the situation and be willing to spend the rest of our lives working to change it. With such an attitude we can indeed restore the world to a spiritual paradise, such as the ancient seers first saw it, and which is the real vision of humanity in Sanatana Dharma.

The future of humanity can be quite wonderful if we all work together. All of our problems can and will be solved. There is no need for pessimism, but there is need for much work and concerted effort and, above all, the seeking of Divine grace.

Truth, knowledge, infinite Brahman — He who knows That hidden in the supreme ether of the heart attains all desires.

Taittiriya Upanishad II.1

Bliss is the supreme reality. From bliss all beings are born, by bliss they live, into bliss they return.

Taittiriya Upanishad III.6

Surrender is powerful. In surrender I take refuge. Surrender upholds Heaven and Earth. Surrender to the Gods, surrender is their ruler. Through surrender even great sins we have committed are removed.

Rig Veda VI.51.8

Questions 3.
Common Questions About Hinduism

Close to a billion of the over five billion people in the world are Hindus by religion. India with its vast river system and subtropical climate has always contained a relatively large proportion of the human population. The Hindu religion has been going on for more than five thousand years, long before the other world religions came into being. In this respect perhaps more people have been Hindus through the course of history than have belonged to any other religion. All of us, during the course of our many births, have been Hindus during one life or another, particularly those of us who have had lives on the spiritual path, which has generally been a greater concern in India than in other countries. The Hindu Dharma is therefore ingrained within our samskaras, the deeper impressions of our souls which we can all access if we look within.

There now exists a significant Hindu minority in the Western world, particularly the United States, Canada and Great Britain, but also such peripheral areas as Trinidad and Guyana. This Hindu minority consists both of immigrants from India, many from the past few decades, and Westerners who have adopted Hindu teachings (who may not all formally call themselves Hindus). There are nearly a million Indo-Americans and a larger number in Great Britain.

What does a modern Hindu say, particularly when questioned by those who may know little about their religious tradition, to explain what Hinduism is? A Hindu in the West is often confronted with simplistic and derogatory ideas about Hinduism — that it is pagan, polytheistic, idolatrous, unscientific, socially backward or merely no more than a cult. Though more educated people in the West may not accept these opinions they may still be influenced by them, and may not have consistent alternative views. Modern Hindus are often not educated in their own tradition. They may not have any real understanding of it or its global relevance as Sanatana Dharma, a universal teaching. They may not know how to present it to others under any circumstances.

As Hindus are generally tolerant and retiring, they may say nothing or even apologize for their religion rather than try to correct wrong ideas about it. The thoughtful among them have sought to communicate their tradition better, particularly seeing the popularity of Hindu practices in the West, like Yoga and meditation, once presented in a universal light. But many Hindus have so diluted their tradition with statements like "all religions are the same," that they have failed to give Hinduism any character of its own. Instead of telling others what Hinduism is in its own right, they use Hinduism to give credit to other religions, whose beliefs and practices may not be regarded as the highest by the great Hindu sages of history. On the other hand, they may tolerate or even accept negative judgements against Hinduism by other religious groups, and not offer any Hindu critique of other religions so as not to appear offensive to anyone. They think that making Hinduism accepting of everything done in the name of religion is the best way to communicate its universality. This, however, does not lead to a better understanding of Hinduism but gives the impression that Hindus have no clear teaching like the other religions of the world.

Hindus in India — under the domination of Western culture in education and communication — may have encounters with missionaries or with Christian and Muslim minorities in India, similar to those that Indo-Americans have with Christian religious groups in America. They tend to feel that their culture is inferior to that of the West which is more modern and affluent, and therefore their religion must be inferior to those of the West (as if spirituality were a function of material abundance). Young Hindus trying to answer questions put to them about their tradition face these problems more keenly as they are as yet unsure as how to communicate what they think and are more under the influence of Western culture than their parents.

However, a revival in Hindu consciousness is now occurring throughout the world. Hindus are no longer willing to stand silent when faced with misrepresentations of their venerable tradition. A pride in being Hindu is arising, not as a religious arrogance, but as a recognition of the value of this vast and ancient spiritual heritage for the whole world. Such new Hindus are willing not only to affirm their tradition but to express its teachings, even when it may call into question other belief systems. They are willing to give a Hindu point of view on religious and social issues, which is not simply to agree with everyone but to point out the deeper wisdom that the Hindu sages have gathered through millennia of yogic practices. Along similar lines, a number of Westerners are beginning to recognize that there is a greater spiritual tradition — including such teachings as Ayurveda, Vedic astrology, and Sanskrit — behind the yogic and meditational practices they have adapted and that the entire system has relevance.

The following section has been devised to deal with the problems of expressing Hinduism in the modern age, which requires affirming its universality without losing its character. It requires fostering a pride in Hinduism without making it into another sectarian belief. It requires redefining what Hindu means and connotes to people, above all for so-called Hindus themselves, so that hearing the word Hindu evokes the Himalayan majesty of the great yogis, not the timidity of a kind but defeated people.

A. What is Hinduism?

HOW DOES HINDUISM DEFINE ITSELF?

Hinduism defines itself in terms of Sanatana Dharma, which means the "universal tradition." Such a comprehensive teaching is evident in the many-sided yogic and meditational practices of Hinduism, the vast culture of Hinduism including art, medicine and science, and in the Hindu recognition of the importance of all systems of knowledge, material, occult and spiritual. The social customs of Hinduism, with their emphasis on spiritual practices, are also based upon such universal truth, though some of them have departed from it through the long course of time. Hence they require adjustment in light of changing times.

For this reason it is important to redefine Hinduism in terms of Sanatana Dharma, to look at its universal perspective. Yet it is also important to redefine Sanatana Dharma or the universal tradition in terms of Hinduism because Hinduism has maintained a living universal tradition through the millennia, which is of benefit to all who want to become part of such a tradition today.

SHOULD THE TERM SANATANA DHARMA REPLACE HINDUISM?

The term Hinduism is subject to many misunderstandings, while Sanatana Dharma communicates the real meaning of the tradition. If Hindus use this term more they will have a greater understanding of the real tradition they follow and better allow those of other cultural backgrounds to appreciate it. To gain recognition for the term Sanatana Dharma, we must first understand the meaning of Dharma as natural law and one's inherent nature, which is radically different than the idea of religion as a code of beliefs.

However, owing to the familiarity and convenience of its usage, we cannot simply dismiss the term Hinduism. We must define it differently, which is as Sanatana Dharma, not as the religion of a particular country. Hinduism should come to connote Sanatana Dharma. This requires looking at Hinduism with new eyes.

HOW HAVE THE GREAT TEACHERS OF HINDUISM RELATED TO RELIGION?

The many great sages of India — the ancient Vedic seers from Manu to Krishna, the teachers of classical India like Patanjali or Shankara, and modern yogis like Vivekananda, Ramana Maharshi, Sri Aurobindo or Anandamayi Ma to mention a few — speak of themselves as part of a great universal tradition of Truth relevant to all beings. They have not promoted themselves as Hindus opposed to some other group, nor have they failed to honor the Hindu tradition in its depth and diversity. However they have been conscious of themselves as part of a tradition. They have not seen themselves as unique or entirely new in their knowledge, but expressions of an eternal tradition and its stream of sages that we can call Hindu, Sanatana Dharma or whatever we wish, if we understand its timeless nature.

If we want to see what Hinduism is really like we should look to the lives and teachings of the great sages, men and women, who have arisen from its background. In them we see the essence of universal spirituality, fully developed in form and expression through a particular tradition and manifold teachings, which yet has no limiting boundaries. Their only link is to God and eternity and they have not set up any religion as a factor of division within the realm of time and space.

SHOULD HINDUS BE PROUD OF THEIR TRADITION?

Hindus should be proud of their spiritual tradition, which is the oldest and most comprehensive in the world. They should be proud of the many great sages and yogis it has consistently produced through the centuries, in both periods of material abundance and those of poverty and foreign domination. They should be proud of their great modern teachers who show that the experience of God is not the rare gift of a prophet or single savior but the birthright of all human beings.

What other religion of this century has produced such figures as Ramana Maharshi, Sri Aurobindo, Paramahansa Ramakrishna, Anandamayi Ma, Paramahansa Yogananda, and Mahatma Gandhi? Yet look at how few modern Hindus have put their teachings into practice. While Hindus should be proud of their spiritual tradition, they should not be proud of themselves if they don't follow this tradition in their daily lives.

Hindus should not be proud of the backwardness and illiteracy of many Hindus. Nor should they be proud of modern Hindus who have abandoned their spiritual tradition for modern materialism, for leftist ideologies, or for some sort of religious dogma. Above all, Hindus should be proud of Hinduism's basis in Sanatana Dharma or the universal tradition and its refusal to cast itself into the mold of exclusive, particularized, and therefore divisive religious identities. But to do this Hindus must also manifest the universality of their tradition by how they live.

IS IT NOT ARROGANT TO BE PROUD ABOUT ONE'S RELIGION?

The pride of the ego, which is a separative pride is always divisive, as it insists that only its point of view is correct. Yet the soul, our inner being, has its pride, which is a recognition of the value of Spiritual Reality over material appearances.

One should be proud in a spiritual sense about the universal element in oneself and in one's Dharma. We are the Divine itself in manifestation. All time and space is but our shadow. The mentality of a slave or a sinner does not suit our Infinite Being. The soul should be proud of the Eternal Truth of its nature which states that "I am all." We need not bow down to any religious belief system or external religious authority. We need only recognize the Divine Presence within ourselves. This is Sanatana Dharma, the enduring Truth of all that is.

WHY ARE HINDUS APOLOGETIC ABOUT BEING HINDUS?

First, Hinduism as the formulation of a universal tradition is not an aggressive system. It encourages humility and respect for all peoples and all religions. It promotes itself through peace and love, not through preaching and condemnation. In the modern world, which has little of spirituality in it, many Hindus find that their tradition appears out of place. This has caused them to feel apologetic about their practices as part of an attempt to accommodate others. On the second level, the Hindu social system contains various regressive social customs, like untouchability, which Hindus feel ashamed of in the face of modern humanitarian political values.

Only those Hindus who don't understand the real meaning of their tradition as Sanatana Dharma and the centrality of its yogic approaches to world spirituality can be dominated by either of these views. In fact Hinduism, through Vedanta or the science of Self-realization is the teaching of lion-hearted souls. It is for the fearless and independent, for those who are willing to transcend the external view of reality.

Yet not all Hindus are apologetic about being Hindus. The apologetic Hindu may soon be a thing of the past, as the great value of Yoga, Vedanta, Ayurveda, Vedic knowledge and Sanatana Dharma spreads throughout the world.

CAN ONE BE A HINDU IN THE MODERN WORLD?

If we rephrase this question in terms of Sanatana Dharma it is easy to answer. Can one follow the universal tradition in the modern world? Obviously we must develop a universal view in order to be truly modern and global in outlook. If we don't follow the Universal Truth, we have fallen from Reality and live in illusion, whatever age we are born into. To be a Hindu in the modern world one must understand the basis of Hinduism in Sanatana Dharma. This is not just to be superficially universal in attitude or view but to learn to access the various practices of Hinduism for their universal relevance.

Sanatana Dharma, not being limited to a point in time or space, can be adapted to any time or place. As a perpetual or perennial tradition it demands names and forms appropriate to the time. Yet to follow the eternal tradition is not to be superficially modern — a creature of the moment, which is often no more than a fad, pursuing the latest social trend — but to live at the heart of creation. To be modern one is inclined to abandon religion and embrace the popular culture of entertainment, sensation and physical culture, or to take up modern intellectual culture, or modern politics which shuns religion. This however fails to answer the deeper issues of life.

The ultimate issue is not to be in harmony with the times but to discover That which transcends time. Then we become citizens of the universe and all time, and not just creatures of one age or another.

WHAT IS THE HINDU VIEW OF MODERN SCIENCE?

Hinduism as Sanatana Dharma, a universal way of knowledge does not require that we reject science or return to medieval superstitions. For example, Hinduism does not require that we believe that the world was created 6000 years ago, nor is it opposed to the theory of evolution, which it long ago formulated in a spiritual way as an evolution not merely of form but of consciousness.

Sanatana Dharma recognizes the validity of all forms of knowledge. Yet it says that knowledge is of two types. The lower knowledge — based on name, form and number — can only help us understand the outer world. It cannot reveal our True Nature or help us discover the Eternal. This lower knowledge is the realm of science, which is based upon measurement and observation of the external. It allows us to better understand and control the forces of nature. The higher knowledge, which is yogic spirituality, is based upon meditation and direct perception of the workings of the mind. This alone brings liberation and the attainment of immortality, whereby one goes beyond the realm of time and space.

Though science has its place it has its limitation, and where material science ends the spiritual science, which is Yoga, begins. To be truly scientific or objective, we must recognize both levels of truth and give each its respective place. The dialogue between these two forms of science is crucial for the future development of humanity and for developing a real and comprehensive understanding of the universe.

WILL SCIENCE AND YOGIC SPIRITUALITY BE RECONCILED?

While modern science has yet to recognize the higher yogic science, it has begun to move in that direction. The mechanistic or Newtonian view of the universe is now dead. The idea of the universe as energy which supplanted it, the Einsteinian view, is also coming in to question. The idea of the universe as consciousness is now being seriously considered by many scientists. It is only a matter of time, which could be as little as a few decades, for this idea to be validated in scientific experiments. Once this occurs modern scientists will have to again seriously consider the knowledge and practices of yogic scientists and their workings on the inner levels of the mind. The material and spiritual sciences will have to meet and create an integral science for all humanity including both in their proper place.

Sanatana Dharma is an eternal tradition. However much humanity may move away from its teachings, it must return to them in the course of time. Sanatana Dharma requires freedom of inquiry to discover it. This science has brought on a mundane level. Such freedom of examination must be brought into the workings of the mind, so that questioning our very ego itself we can discover our true Self which is beyond all sorrow. This is the ultimate scientific achievement for all people. It also requires the development of a spiritual psychology, a science of consciousness, including higher states of awareness, which alone can bridge the gap between science and religion.

HOW CAN HINDU CHILDREN BE RAISED?

Raising true Hindu children means following Sanatana Dharma or universal law, not merely imposing Hindu beliefs or rituals upon them. It means living in the Dharma and having a culture of the Dharma, which includes communities that maintain living traditions of ritual, Yoga and meditation.

Children are very impressionable to their environment. They want to be accepted and to be part of the society in which they live. They are most affected by sensation and their minds can easily be disturbed by wrong impressions. For this reason children must be provided a field of learning in which they can flower spiritually. This requires the right atmosphere at home and the right relationship between the parents. For this the parents themselves must have an active interest in some aspect of Sanatana Dharma and pass it to their children.

On top of this the right educational system must be created, or at least occasional camps for the children which immerse them in a higher form of life. Children must be brought into contact with real examples of the spiritual life, various gurus and teachers, so that they have an ideal which they can follow. They must be brought into the world of Nature so as to learn how to contact the immanent divinity. Without creating the proper environment and the right examples it will not be possible to get our children to become spiritual, just as a plant will not grow without water and light.

Hinduism contains many myths and stories that are helpful for teaching children like the Ramayana. Hindu children should be exposed to this literature, which can be quite entertaining for them, so that the seeds of spirituality can be planted in them.

HOW SHOULD HINDUS RELATE TO WESTERN CULTURE?

Western culture is primarily a secular and commercial culture. Its main benefit is its practical efficiency, scientific knowledge and humanitarianism. Its main limitation is its attachment to sensation and entertainment, which dull the mind. While the scientific and humanitarian side of Western culture can be helpful its lack of spiritual knowledge must be compensated for.

Western culture, though it has religion, is not a religious culture. On one hand, this largely frees Western culture from religious dogma, intolerance and bigotry that makes life difficult in countries dominated by a religious belief. On the other hand, it leaves Western culture in a spiritual vacuum, without any spiritual roots, which may deprive people of any deep connection with life or God.

Hindu culture is not a religious culture in the sense of an exclusive belief. It has a secular, universal and open minded approach. Yet it is not a materialistic culture. It is based upon spiritual and yogic values and practices, a tradition of Sadhana or spiritual practice. Therefore it does not have to clash with what is beneficial in Western culture but can afford the spiritual dimension that it needs. Hindus should take what is useful from Western culture but try to give it in return what they have to offer, which is a deeper approach to the spiritual life.

WHY DO HINDUS WORSHIP MANY GODS?

Human beings through history have formulated many different names and forms for the Divine or Eternal. Just as we have many names and forms for other things, whether it is foods, or types of art, so too, in religion a similar great diversity has been created.

The Western world has prided itself in monotheism, the idea that there is only One God as the highest truth. Western religions have said that only the names and forms which refer to this One God are valid but those which appear to worship another God, or a multiplicity of divinities, must be false. They have restricted the names and forms they use in religious worship, and insist that only one set, which is their's, is true and correct and others are wrong or unholy.

As a universal formulation Hinduism accepts all formulations of Truth. According to the universal view there is only One Truth or Reality, but this reality cannot be limited to a particular name or form. Though it is One it is also Universal, not an exclusive formulation. It is an inclusive, not an exclusive Oneness. It is a spiritual reality of Being-Consciousness-Bliss, which could be called God but which transcends all names. The different Gods and Goddesses of Hinduism represent various functions of this One Supreme Divinity, and are not separate Gods.

Having many names for something is not necessarily a sign of ignorance of its real nature. On the contrary, it may indicate an intimate knowledge of it. For example, Eskimos have forty-eight different names for snow in their language because they know snow intimately in its different variations, not because they are ignorant of the fact that all snow is only one. The many different deities of Hinduism reflect such an intimate realization of the Divine on various levels — which non-experiential belief-oriented religions seldom even approach. It is hardly a crude polytheism.

WHAT IS HINDU THEISM?

As a universal tradition Hinduism naturally includes theism or a recognition of the One Creator of the universe. However it does not regard theism as the only approach to the spiritual life, nor does it have only one formulation of theism that everyone must follow. Hindu theism may be formulated from the standpoint of any number of names and forms, like those of Brahma, Vishnu or Shiva, who stand for the Divine in its roles of creating, preserving and destroying the universe. It may emphasize the Divine as female rather than male in attributes, like Sarasvati, Lakshmi and Durga.

Hindu theism is an experiential system, not a mere code of belief. It says that it is not enough merely to believe in God; we must come to experience God through yogic practices. It emphasizes our inner relationship to God, not any mere outer formal identity.

Hindu theism includes monism or the idea that there is only One Reality. It recognizes that God as a personal reality rests upon God as the principle of existence or the Absolute. Like other systems of Hindu thought, Hindu theism recognizes karma and rebirth, and the practice of Yoga as the way to experience God. According to Hindu theism God has created us not to reward or punish us, but to know Him/Her and to become part of His/Her eternal and infinite delight, which is the ultimate destiny of all souls.

WHAT IS THE HINDU VIEW OF THEOLOGY?

Theology should set forth, both rationally and with proper consideration as to the role of faith, an understanding of God, the principles of cosmic creation and the way for the soul to return to its unity with God. Theology should link us up with the Divine Father/Mother of the universe in all its glory and through all of its forms and functions on the various levels of this manifold universe both inwardly and outwardly. Theology should not be a system of dogmas to follow outwardly, or ideas to limit our thoughts to, but should direct us inwardly to realization of God, and to Self-realization.

Most Western theology whether Christian or Islamic is of a dualistic nature. It stops short with an intellectual explanation of God or with the setting up of principles of faith, which are not to be questioned however arbitrary they might appear. It often appears more as an intellectual apologetic for religion rather than a deep inquiry into universal Truth. It mainly follows Aristotle, who was more of an intellectual than a spiritual person. Western theology does not understand the ultimate reality of the Self, which it does not mention, and is ignorant of the most important cosmic laws like that of karma. It has much to learn from Hindu theology. Hindus should seek to dialogue with Western theology to help raise the level of theological thinking in the world. In this way theology can be used to direct us to the spiritual path, not merely to uphold the dogma of one religion or another.

WHY DOES HINDUISM PORTRAY GOD AS A WOMAN?

Hinduism contains many feminine forms of the Divine like Kali, Durga, Lakshmi and Sarasvati. These represent different feminine qualities and functions of the Divine which contains both male and female energies. For example, Kali portrays the destructive energy, Lakshmi the nourishing, and Sarasvati the creative, while Durga is the Divine Mother in her protective role. Hinduism also has many dual male-female forms like Radha-Krishna, Sita-Rama, Uma-Mahesh, and Lakshmi-Narayan in which the female form is usually addressed first. The different masculine forms of the Divine in Hinduism have their feminine counterparts.

As Sanatana Dharma or a universal tradition Hinduism recognizes that the Divine contains both masculine and feminine attributes. Without giving proper honor to the feminine qualities a religion must be incomplete and one-sided, which must result in its teachings having negative consequences. Without recognizing the feminine aspect of Divinity one cannot claim to know God. To recognize the feminine is necessary to restore wholeness, completeness and universality.

WHY ARE HINDU DEITIES PORTRAYED IN WRATHFUL FORMS?

Hindu Gods and Goddesses often have fierce forms, including possessing fangs, wearing garlands of skulls, being adorned with snakes, and other frightening appearances. Even those that are benefic may carry various weapons. This may disturb people, particularly those who do not understand symbolic language and who may be opposed to the use of images in religious worship.

The Divine transcends our ordinary sensory perception of the world. It dwarfs our mind and ego. It includes death and goes beyond it. It consumes everything. Experiencing this Infinite Reality is very humbling, even frightening to us who are trapped in the world of limitation, as it takes away our ordinary identity and may make the world appear to be unreal. Spiritual realization is like death because it is the dissolution of our ego, or sense of separate self. Such apparently terrible Deities show these experiences of transcendence, in which even evil, death and suffering must be integrated into a Truth beyond all duality.

There is another way in which the Divine is frightening. It destroys all the forces of ignorance, illusion and negativity. It destroys all the demons that dwell in our minds. As such a destroyer of negativity it may appear fierce or as a warrior, but it is only something that those trapped in negativity need fear.

It is easy to see God in the beautiful and beneficent, but to enter into the Oneness we must also see God in the terrible and transformative. Without recognizing the Divine even in death we cannot go beyond death. Because of this Hindu and Buddhist traditions have always recognized the importance of wrathful Deities. They have never encouraged that we become wrathful and harm other people in the name of our God.

WHY ARE HINDU DEITIES PORTRAYED IN EROTIC FORMS?

Hindu deities and temple sculpture often appears erotic or voluptuous, so that Western missionaries thought these images were only a glorification of sexuality even though they were part of a tradition that has always valued asceticism.

God is the ultimate bliss and delight. Union with God is the supreme love, in which the male and female sides of our nature, the masculine and feminine aspects of consciousness must be united. To show this Hindu artists have traditionally employed graphic images. Such images are symbolic like Radha and Krishna, who represent the soul and its love of God. To the Hindu mind all of our passions should be directed to the Divine. For this reason it has not hesitated to portray them as part of a spiritual symbolism. But to confuse these with a glorification of sexuality is to completely misinterpret them.

WHAT ARE THE DIFFERENT BRANCHES OF HINDUISM?

Hinduism traditionally is divided into five main branches:

1) Vaishnava or worshippers of Vishnu
2) Shaiva or worshippers of Shiva
3) Shakta or worshippers of the Goddess (Devi or Shakti)
4) Ganapatya or worshippers of Ganapati (Ganesha)
5) Saura or worshippers of the Sun (Surya)

These groups generally coalesce into two, the Vaishnava and Shaiva. As Shakti is the consort of Shiva, her worship can be included with his. As Ganesha is the son of Shiva and Shakti, his worship usually goes along with his parents. As Surya, the Sun, is generally related to Vishnu, his worship usually goes along with that of Vishnu. There are many Hindus, however who accept all five of these approaches, which for most Hindus are intertwined anyway.

There is in addition the Vedic or Brahmanical tradition. This is usually divided up according to which of the four Vedas one follows:

1) Rig Vedis or followers of the Rig Veda
2) Sama Vedis or followers of the Sama Veda
3) Atharva Vedis or followers of the Atharva Veda
4) Yajur Vedis or followers of the Yajur Veda

Yajur Vedis are the largest group and divided into two main subgroups, the Shukla or White Yajur Veda school which prevails in the north of India, and the Krishna or Black Yajur Veda school which prevails in the south. Generally those following Vedic traditions also belong to one of the five or six divisions of Hinduism.

There are also Hindus of various philosophical views like Vedanta, Sankhya, Yoga and Tantra. All such divisions are only a convenient differentiation. Many other groups and subgroups exist, including various recent or modern groups like Arya Samaj or the Swami Narayan movement. In fact all religions can be considered as different branches of a universal religion or Sanatana Dharma.

HOW DO SHAIVAS AND VAISHNAVAS DIFFER?

The Shaivas and Vaishnavas, the followers of Shiva and Vishnu, differ mainly in name and in some forms. They share the same basic beliefs, like karma, and the same basic practices like puja (ritual), mantra and meditation. Shiva is considered to be the best devotee of Lord Vishnu and Vishnu is considered to be the best devotee of Lord Shiva.

Generally speaking, Vishnu represents the benign and approachable form of the Deity, who is worshipped more in the cities and plains of India, and Shiva portrays the more transcendent and transformative form of the Divine worshipped more in the mountains and villages. Dualistic and non-dualistic forms of philosophy can be found among both groups, as well as every form of yogic practice.

WHAT IS THE HINDU VIEW OF PHILOSOPHY?

India, and particularly Hinduism, has been the place of probably the greatest development of spiritual philosophy, which it has regarded as part of the spiritual path and the Yoga of knowledge. Hinduism has produced some of the world's most important philosophies, particularly the various schools of Vedanta. Yet its view of philosophy is very different than that of the West. The correct Hindu word for philosophy is darshana, which means "a way of perception." Each of the philosophies of Hinduism is a spiritual approach which requires following a certain life-style, ethical disciplines and practicing various yogic methods to arrive at this perception. Hindu philosophies are meant to help us realize the Truth beyond the world of the senses. They all have a view which transcends the ordinary mind-body complex.

According to the Hindu view there is little real philosophy in the Western world. Western philosophical thinking has gone down hill since the time of Plato, ever abandoning spiritual experience and a transcendent view of life for mere rational, speculative, and utilitarian considerations. It has come ever more increasingly under the domination of the senses, and is now little more than an apologist for a scientific-materialistic view that is unaware of higher dimensions of consciousness. Even Western religious philosophy, as in the case of Christian and Islamic theology, has largely been devoid of the kind of experiential spirituality and exploration of higher states of consciousness and samadhi found in all Hindu and Buddhist systems.

Philosophy in India, moreover, continues to be a living and experiential endeavor. Modern India has not only maintained its ancient philosophical traditions but has produced new philosophers like Sri Aurobindo who were also great yogis.

WHAT ARE THE DIFFERENT SCHOOLS OF VEDANTA?

The different schools of Vedanta vary around whether they consider the Divine Reality (*Brahman*) to be a pure unity, or whether there is some degree of duality between the soul and the Divine. All are spiritual philosophies emphasizing the Divine as the supreme reality. Advaita Vedanta or non-dualistic Vedanta, whose most important traditional teacher is Shankaracharya, teaches that the soul and God are absolutely one. Visishtadvaita, or qualified non-duality, based on the works of Ramanuja, teaches that the soul and God are both the same and different. Dvaita, or dualistic Vedanta of Madhva, teaches that God and the soul though deeply related are different, like lover and beloved. Lord Chaitanya's school of Acintyabhedabheda accepts both difference and non-difference and says Truth is indescribable. There are several other schools as well.

All these systems accept the law of karma, the importance of surrender to God, ethical disciplines like non-violence, and the practice of various yogic and meditational methods. Even dualistic Vedanta is not dualistic in the sense of Western religions, which in the case of Christianity may require the resurrection of the physical body and the soul living in that body in Heaven worshipping God in the distance. Dualistic Vedanta conceives the difference between God and the soul to be very subtle. All systems of Vedanta see the true relationship between God and the soul to occur only in Samadhi or a state of deep spiritual absorption which goes far beyond the limitations of the ordinary mind and senses, in which the physical body is all but forgotten. They all regard that we can experience God much more vividly than anything else we have ever known.

WHY DO HINDUS REVERE COWS?

It is curious how we approach the religion of others by reacting to what for us appear to be the lowest or most objectionable side of what they do. Predominant Western religions have conditioned people not to respect the so-called lower forms of life and to think that those who do so are somehow primitive or superstitious.

The cow is a symbol of Divine love and grace. With no thought of itself, but out of love, like the Divine Mother, it produces milk which nourishes other creatures. Respect for the cow is meant to instill the virtues of gentleness and receptivity into the human mind. Hindus do not worship cows. The cow to them is a great symbol of cosmic beneficence.

We can judge how a culture values the spiritual life by how it treats its cows. By this standard modern culture, which not only eats cows but raises them under artificial and cruel circumstances, is quite deficient in any deeper sensitivity. We should not only revere cows but respect all life, particularly those beings who function selflessly.

WHAT IS THE HINDU VIEW OF THE EARTH?

Hindus worship the Earth as a Goddess and form of the Divine Mother. They recognize that the Earth is not just a material thing but a cosmic power pervaded with a Divine Presence. They honor all creatures on Earth and the various beauties of the planet, the mountains, rivers, forests and oceans, which contain many sacred places for them wherever they live.

This worship of the Earth is not part of a primitive pantheism but part of a greater cosmic awareness which recognizes the Divine not only in Heaven but in the very ground on which we stand. Such a recognition of the Divine in the Earth is essential in the world today wherein we are destroying the planet. For Hindus ecology is not merely a social movement but part of religion, and for them religion is also ecological. If we view the Earth as a Goddess and as our Mother we will certainly use her resources correctly. If we fail to do this, we will abuse not only the Earth but all creatures on it.

DO HINDUS WORSHIP HUMAN BEINGS AS GODS?

Hindus may worship the Divine through the medium of great human beings who have realized the Truth. In such cases it is not the human personality or physical body of the person which is revered but the Divine qualities manifested through them. In fact, Hinduism holds that one of the best ways to worship the Divine is through honoring Self-realized sages because realized souls provide us with an example how to realize God in life, which can be more meaningful than a mere idea or image of God.

However if we literally worship a human being as God we fall from Truth as God is the Self, not a particular person. And if we consider that God can only manifest through one human being we fall into yet greater error because God manifests through all beings. Ultimately to know God we must see all beings in the Self and the Self in all beings.

WHAT IS THE PLACE OF PRIESTS IN HINDUISM?

Hinduism has various officiants who perform rituals and sacraments like marriage. These officiants are sometimes called priests. Their prime role is to aid in the performance of rituals. They do not take confession, preach, proselytize, or function as missionaries. Nor do they serve as intermediaries between the lay population and the Divine. These priests can be married and usually have families of their own.

Such priests are different from yogis or swamis and are generally regarded as fulfilling a lesser role. The yogis are the great teachers and gurus. The priests are helpers in the outer aspects of religion. Such priests are taught to bow down to the spiritual experience of the great sages and should never be made into a ruling class, either over religious or secular matters.

WHY ARE THERE SO MANY HINDU RITUALS?

Hindus worship everything, Gods and Goddesses, people, plants, animals, and different places in Nature. They may even perform ritual worship to inanimate objects like books, automobiles or computers. While this may appear as a superstition to those of us who are enlightened materialists, there is an important and universal meaning behind it.

To worship something in the Hindu sense is to recognize the Divine presence within it and to seek its grace. We need the grace, favor, communication and understanding of all that we are connected with in life, and nothing is really without consciousness or apart from the Divine. Hindu ritual-worship (*pūjā*) is both an art and science for accomplishing this. We need to honor the Divine in everything, particularly in the most simple and intimate things of our lives. If we only honor God in the distance, we are ignorant of his all-pervasive being, and our own ordinary actions will be ungodly. We have to have a strong and yet diverse culture of ritual aids to both the development of the human spirit and its proper interaction with the universe. While it may be difficult to understand for us today, it should not be devalued.

WHAT IS THE BASIS OF THE CASTE SYSTEM?

Caste is the most embarrassing part of Hinduism and the most difficult to explain to the modern mind. It appears as a religiously reinforced form of social oppression. Yet if we look deeply into the matter we see that caste is not something unique to Hindus, nor is caste as it exists in India today truly reflective of the great teachings of Hinduism as to how society should be structured.

Caste arose as part of the ancient world order, a division of society into priests (ritualists), nobility (warriors), merchants (and farmers), and servants, such as occurred throughout the ancient world. It has persisted more so in India and other parts of Asia because of conservative social attitudes. Yet it is no more essential to Hinduism today than it has been to other religions, including Christianity, that were once represented by the same type of social system. Most modern Hindu religious leaders have spoken against its limitations and many older teachers did as well. Traditional Hindu texts like the Vedas also portray a much more open society than what the caste system has become. So it is wrong to think that caste represents the original Hindu social order.

Behind the caste system was originally a great idea that became distorted. The Hindu social system (*varṇāshrama dharma*), which degenerated into caste, gave people who developed their minds, the learned, preeminence in society over the warrior and merchant classes. Unfortunately people became judged by their family of birth rather than by the real qualities of their character, which turned this great idea into a misleading appearance.

Sanatana Dharma is an eternal way of spiritual knowledge that may be associated with any number of social systems. Yet it does state that society should found itself on spiritual values or it cannot really serve the soul of man. Hinduism teaches that there is an organic structure to society, that certain types of people exist to fulfill the different functions of the social being, like his arms, feet or brain. Through this organic structure it regards all humanity, in fact all the universe as one great Being. Each one of us is not only part of that great being, each one of us is that great Being in its totality. This is the real meaning of our social interconnectedness.

In the modern world it is the merchant (commercial) class that rules the world, including dictating religion. The warrior class (those with the most guns or best weapons) also has much power. Spiritual people, the true Brahmins, generally have neither money, nor power, nor respect. In this regard we should not think that our modern social order is humanitarian but should look back to an ordering of society that reflects what is of highest value in each of us, which is not our property but our awareness.

WHO IS A TRUE BRAHMIN?

A true Brahmin is a person of spiritual knowledge grounded in cosmic intelligence, who understands the universal order, and works to further it in the world. To become a true Brahmin means to remain in a state of learning, ever seeking to open up to the Divine Reality. It requires a life of seeking truth and upholding firm ethical and spiritual principles like non-violence, non-attachment, humility and truthfulness. The pride of the Brahmin or the so-called priestly class, is a contradiction in terms as a true Brahmin is one who is without personal pride.

Such individuals become the teachers of society and should be respected, not for their position, but for the degree of connection with cosmic reality that they bring to all. All cultures have their learned people whom they revere, what could be called their Brahmins. These should be people of Self-realization for society to truly flourish. We should train at least a portion of society from birth to pursue the spiritual life. Otherwise our society's spiritual potential cannot truly grow. This is the basis of a real Brahmin class but it should not be based on birth alone. The individuals who belong to it must live the appropriate lifestyle or they should not be considered part of it.

CAN WE LOOK UP TO A RELIGION FROM AS BACKWARD A COUNTRY AS INDIA?

Many religions, including Judaism, Christianity and Islam, originated in cultures which were not materially affluent. Most of the great founders of important religious movements were poor or gave up their wealth. Note the examples in this regard of Buddha, Christ, and Gandhi.

Hinduism has been criticized as a religion because of the poverty of modern India. Such thinking equates the truth of religion with wealth, which is not a matter of religion at all. It also judges human spiritual aspiration and its social expression according to a particular period of human history. There were periods when Hindus were wealthier than Christians, as during the Middle Ages. Does this mean that Hinduism was then the true religion and then ceased to be so when Hindus lost their wealth? What kind of religion would that be?

No religion teaches that wealth and spirituality are the same, or that the spiritual development of a person is indicated by how much money or property he or she may possess. Yet this is what we do on a social level when we judge the religions of countries by their current economic status. Just as wealth in an individual is no necessary guarantee or indication of spirituality, so it is with countries. Such concepts only show how deeply we are attached to the outer world and its possessions. It is not surprising that our religions are more economic interests than spiritual paths. True religion is based upon renunciation, which is renunciation of attachment to name, fame and possession.

WHY IS INDIA SOCIALLY BACKWARD?

As Hinduism has been the main religion of India for thousands of years, there is a tendency to identify the backward social condition of India with Hinduism. However, we should note that modern India has not formulated itself according to the principles of Sanatana Dharma, but in its original constitution declared itself to be a socialist state. Not surprisingly, India is suffering from many of the same problems of other socialist and communist states and their stifling bureaucracies.

Moreover, India has been under foreign domination for many centuries. It was ruled by the Muslims from around 1200, then the British from 1757, and only independent since 1947. Though the majority of people in India are Hindus and its recent political leaders have been primarily of Hindu ancestry, there has been little of the Hindu religion and its spiritual values in the political or educational systems, particularly since Gandhi.

There are other problems in modern Hindu society like child marriage, and dowry deaths. These are social evils. To associate them with Hinduism as a religion would be like to associate the widespread use of drugs and sexual promiscuity with the predominant Christian religion of the West today. These evils are owing to lack of education, overpopulation, and a social inertia arising from centuries of foreign domination.

Poverty and related evils occur in Christian, Islamic and Buddhist, as well as Hindu countries. Yet because India is the only Hindu majority country (with the exception of Nepal), there is a greater tendency to identify its problems with the religion. We don't identify the poverty in the Philippines, for example, with its Catholic religion. Nor do we identify the success of Japan with its Buddhist-Shinto religion. We should address the real causes of poverty throughout the world, which are generally educational and economic, but not confuse them with the spiritual life, whose aim is not merely to improve society materially but to bring us into contact with the immeasurable.

WHAT IS THE HINDU VIEW OF ECONOMICS?

The economic problems in India today have largely been caused by the socialist policies of modern India, which are akin to the economic problems of the Soviet Union. Socialist countries make individuals dependent upon the state for their welfare, which suppresses initiative and independence in the economic life of the people.

Hinduism itself teaches independence (*svatantra*) in all domains of life and acknowledges the validity of the commercial (*vaishya*) class and its freedom to pursue prosperity as a valid goal of life. Hinduism teaches the individual to be self-sufficient and confident of his or her own Divinity. It does not make the individual subordinate to the state. Similarly it does not make the individual subordinate to big business but encourages an organic development of economic resources allowing all people dignity of work, and maintaining maximum economic independence for all communities.

The Hindu concept of Dharma contains an understanding of the proper role and limitation of the merchant class which should serve society, not rule it, following the guidance of the great sages and yogis. Commercial development is alright if it is based upon respect for the Earth, charity for all people, and respect for the spiritual life. Otherwise it becomes a curse, as it has over much of the world today.

IS YOUR'S NOT AN UNREALISTIC VIEW OF HINDUISM?

Very well, one could say, your view of Hinduism is universal, futuristic and beneficial for all to consider, but does the actual Hindu really think this way? Is not the average Hindu trapped in superstition and social backwardness? Are you not covering over this fact with a fantasy view of Hinduism?

The average Hindu may not be aware of the vastness of his or her own tradition. The person may not see beyond the particular sect he or she may belong to. But that is not to deny the underlying teaching. How many Westerners are aware of the beauty and profundity of European intellectual culture? How many of us today understand the formulas of modern physics? Does this mean that atomic power or computers don't work?

There is always a gap between a spiritual teaching and its social application because our planet is not yet very spiritually evolved. What is necessary is to raise people up to higher teachings, not to reject higher teachings for ordinary pursuits which are easier to do. It is not just a question of Hinduism. We all have a tremendous spiritual potential compared to which the other achievements of humanity — whether in art, science, business or religion — are mere trifles. Let us not demean ourselves. All time and space are but our shadow. If we follow the paths of Yoga and the traditions of meditation we can arrive at the Universal Self.

DO HINDUS NEED TO AWAKEN TODAY?

Hindus need to awaken today and once more reclaim and renovate their great spiritual heritage. This requires neither rejecting the tradition nor merely accepting it as it is. There is not only the Hinduism of the present to consider but that of the past, that of the future and, above all, that of all time. True Hinduism is this eternal tradition not its transient customs at any point in time.

Hinduism is not confined to its outer forms nor is it limited to its teachings at any particular point in history. It is always growing and developing. It is necessary for Hindus today to rewaken to their real spiritual heritage, which though not entirely obscured has been largely forgotten or misunderstood. It is important to revive Hinduism in its true sense, not merely to get Hindus to think that their religion as they practice it today is sufficient. Much of Hinduism today is something that the great Hindu sages would not be very happy about and some of it is contrary to the real spirit of the religion.

ARE YOU A HINDU?

I have studied various teachings originating in the Hindu tradition for over twenty years including Yoga, Vedanta, the Vedas, Ayurveda, and Vedic astrology and found immense benefit in all of them. I have also practiced these teachings and made them the basis of my spiritual life. Hinduism was something I discovered in myself through the pattern of my deeper aspirations and my search into the nature of consciousness itself. It was never imposed upon me from the outside. I did not become a Hindu so much as discover that I already was one.

I am happy to belong to this ancient and unending tradition of spiritual knowledge, whose impressions upon the soul cannot be removed even by death. Hinduism has a rich field of knowledge and culture, like the lap of the Divine Mother, in which the soul can freely unfold its infinite capacities. To enter into this teaching is a great blessing to all.

Yet becoming a Hindu is not a matter of taking on some divisive identity. It means recognizing Sanatana Dharma or the universal tradition. It does not require joining a church but recognizing the universal religion that comes from the Self of all. It is to embrace all human aspiration and all that has beauty in life, but centered on a path of Self-realization, not merely vaguely accepting everything as good.

However, I am sad that many Hindus today have little real appreciation or understanding of their tradition. To me it is a sign of ignorance to abandon such a profound spiritual system for modern political ideologies, like socialism and communism, to pursue material affluence, or to spiritually cripple oneself by following regressive religions traditions which are devoid of any real way for developing higher consciousness. Expressing the value of Hinduism as a Westerner, I hope I can get modern Hindus to reexamine their roots.

B. Hinduism and Other Religions

DO HINDUS HAVE PROPHETS AND MESSIAHS?

Hinduism does not look to prophets or messiahs who have a special relationship with God that other people cannot have and whom we must use as intermediaries, which is the Christian and Islamic view. It looks to great gurus or spiritual guides who set forth paths to Self-realization which must be adapted by each individual in his or her own way. From the Hindu view, which has seen the coming and going of many religious systems, a variety of great teachers and Divine incarnations comes into being periodically to guide human beings relative to changing circumstances. There is no beginning or end to such great teachers. We should take their message, the teaching, and put it into practice, and not merely revere them outwardly.

Hindu history records hundreds of such sages from ancient to modern times and says that we should honor what is great in all of them and need not restrict ourselves to one only, as if knowledge of God, which is infinite, was the property of one person. More important than any prophet, savior or guru is to contact the Truth within our own nature. An external guide, however necessary, is only an aid to Self-knowledge. We must discover the Divine presence within ourselves. Otherwise our religious practice is not yet mature.

WHAT ARE AVATARS?

Sanatana Dharma recognizes a perennial stream of various great teachers and sages, some of whose spiritual qualities are so pure that they could be called veritable incarnations of God. Certain special Divine incarnations can be called avatars, literally "Divine descents," though the term may be used loosely today for various great teachers, sometimes outside of its meaning in the Hindu tradition.

In the traditional Hindu sense, avatars appear to uphold and renovate Sanatana Dharma or the eternal teaching. They represent the manifestation of Lord Vishnu, the Divine power that preserves and protects the universe. Avatars do not come into being to found new religions in their own image or to establish different and contradictory religious identities and beliefs. Such great avatars of Vishnu were Rama and Krishna and, by some accounts, the Buddha. The lives of avatars, which often contain various mythic and legendary elements, are grand symbols of the spiritual search and go far beyond anything merely human. They thereby become models for others to study and emulate. The worship of avatars is an important part of Hindu devotional practice, but only one of its several streams and not all Hindu groups follow it.

Yet such avatars, however great, are symbols of our own inner Being which should be the real goal of our seeking. More important than any historical avatar is the Self-realized teacher who helps us understand who we really are. More important than the teacher is the student and his or her practice. Sanatana Dharma requires that each one of us realizes our inherent Divinity. An avatar helps teach us how to do that, but worship of an avatar as an external being is but a preliminary part of our own

Self-discovery.

ARE CHRIST AND MOHAMMED AVATARS?

Some groups have used the term avatar in a broad sense for anyone who has founded a major world religion. However, this is not the original Hindu meaning of the term which has nothing to do with organized religion but is part of a yogic symbolism. Christ and Mohammed are not part of the traditional Hindu scheme of avatars of Vishnu nor, we might add, are all the great saints and sages of Hinduism, including those who may have had equal realization to the accepted avatars. The avatar order reflects a certain teaching, which is one line of approach and is not meant to be inclusive of all the great teachers of humanity, many of the greatest of whom are unknown.

One can look to the Divine as manifesting through any number of great human beings. Such a great person becomes an avatar of sorts for those who worship him or her. Yet it is important that we truly honor the Divine in such great people, not merely our human attachments. Avatars should be part of a teaching that directs us to the inner quest, not to glorifying an outer religious institution.

Hindus respect all the great teachers of humanity, relative to the truth each one has taught. Yet this does not require that we turn all famous religious figures into Divine incarnations. We should honor each for the knowledge and virtue demonstrated in their life and teaching. More important than creating a cult around various famous religious personalities is to follow the way of spiritual knowledge and Self-realization that all truly great teachers direct us toward.

According to Muslims Mohammed is not an avatar but a prophet of God, a messenger, but not an incarnation. According to Christianity Christ was not an avatar or incarnation of God but the only Son of God. While Hindus may be inclined to redefine these teachers in light of Hinduism and yogic spirituality, they must also recognize that the great majority of the members of these religions would find such a redefinition to misunderstand what they really believe.

DO HINDUS BELIEVE IN REVELATION?

Hinduism is a timeless religion, a formulation of Sanatana Dharma, the Eternal Truth. Sanatana Dharma is not based upon any particular historical revelation — the message given to a particular person at a particular time and place. Nor is it looking toward some Armageddon, Day of Judgement, or end of the world. It recognizes the eternity of creation and the immortality of the soul. Its revelation is that of the Eternal in the here and now, in each individual soul, which is a matter of direct perception, not the message received from another.

According to Sanatana Dharma the revelation that we all need is Self-revelation, not that of an external deity. Self-revelation is enlightenment or Self-illumination which comes when the mind is silent. This revelation transcends all words and religious authorities and takes us beyond time. Great sages may bring important messages to humanity at different times but these are not the ultimate revelation which only comes through our own spiritual practice. Though we should honor the messages of the sages we should use these to understand the Eternal, not to trap ourselves in any temporal event, which must be limiting.

WHAT IS THE HINDU VIEW OF SIN?

Hinduism does not believe that human beings suffer from any original sin or inherent fault in their nature, which must be corrected by an external influence or special grace. On the contrary, Sanatana Dharma teaches that our original nature is pure goodness, Being-Consciousness-Bliss, and that we are all inherently one with God.

The Hindu concept of sin is one of uncleanliness, the accumulation of something extraneous that must be removed for us to return to our inherent purity. For example, the body naturally gets dirty everyday and one has to clean it. Such dirt is not a sin, though it is impure, if not sinful, not to keep oneself clean. There are similar emotional and mental impurities that we must cleanse ourselves from. In our natural activity we may pick up various wrong impressions, attitudes, and experiences. It is helpful to cleanse our minds regularly of them through ritual, mantra and meditation. Such mental impurities, if allowed to accumulate, can cause various emotional imbalances and lead to wrong actions that may result in harm for ourselves and others.

The Hindu view of sin is free of the ideas of guilt, fear and punishment. From its point of view the greatest sin is to call a person a sinner. There is not and never will be such an entity as a sinner. The same Divine Self exists in all beings who, through ignorance alone, commit various wrong actions. To call a person a sinner is to deny their Divine essence and make them identify themselves with the sin, which reinforces its hold on them. Whatever we think that we become. If we think that we are fallen, wretched, low sinners, that we become. If we think that we are God, we become God. We should not debase ourselves with thoughts that are not great. There are no sinners, though there are wrong actions. We should not condemn a person as a sinner but should try to understand what is right action. Right action is acting with respect for the sacred nature of all beings.

WHAT IS THE HINDU VIEW OF SALVATION?

Hinduism does not teach that we are sinners in need of salvation but that we are the Divine itself needing to awaken to its true nature. We are suffering from ignorance and the cure for this is knowledge. We have forgotten our true Self, which is eternal, and are caught in the outer world, which is transient. The Hindu concept is one of liberation, which is very different than the idea of salvation and should not be equated with it. Liberation is not from sin but from ignorance, which is the misconception that we are other than God. Even those who do good according to a particular religion, and are thereby said to be saved, are bound by ignorance if they do not know their true Self and are not liberated.

Hinduism does not look to salvation, or to a savior as anything ultimate. It looks to mergence in God who is the being of all. The only way to do this is through right meditation which clears the mind of the impressions that bind it to the external world. Liberation takes us beyond the cycle of rebirth, whereas salvation is just an emotional or mental state, which may bring some temporary peace or happiness, but no final release.

IS THERE A FINAL JUDGEMENT IN HINDUISM?

Hinduism is not a religion of judgement but of acceptance. It is not based upon the condemnation of anyone but upon the recognition of the sole reality of God. There is no final, absolute or irrevocable judgement about anything. As all actions are limited and relative, being bound to the realm of time and space, so must their results have an end. Can there be a final judgement about the sun, the wind or the rain? So too, human beings, who are replicas of the entire universe and its forces, can never be judged in any conclusive manner. In essence we are consciousness, which is one with God as the true Self. We can never be finally removed from it. However long we may appear to stay away from it, we must eventually return to it as our real home. Actions have their specific results which we must experience as long as we are bound to the realm of action. However action itself does not bind the soul but only the concept "I-am-the-doer." The ego or doer-sense causes us to identify with action, to seek gain externally, and thereby leads us to do wrong, self-aggrandizing, actions.

In reality there is no doer because consciousness transcends all material forms. If there is no doer, who is there to be judged? The soul is inherently free of action and its results. Once we realize this we go beyond cause and effect. But as long as we are attached to action owing to desire, seeking name and fame, we cannot experience this freedom and must suffer for what we have done.

God does not judge anyone, nor does a wise person judge others. The other person is God, who are we to judge God? Our actions speak for themselves and bring about their specific results. God does not punish a person for harming another. The very action of harm has its effect on the person who projects it. The only final judgement for all creatures is: "You are God, live according to your nature and be happy."

IS THERE HINDU FUNDAMENTALISM?

Fundamentalism in religion generally consists of literally believing in a single religion, prophet or savior, a particular scripture as literally the word of God and the insistence that all human beings accept it. Fundamentalism does not exist in Hinduism the way it can in belief-oriented religions because Hinduism does not insist upon One God, one savior, or one Bible for humanity, nor does it claim that its religion alone has the final or highest truth. There is no exclusivism in Hinduism that can sustain such religious fundamentalism. No true Hindu would say that only the Hindu scripture is true and those of other religions are false. No true Hindu would say that only Hindus can find God and non-Hindus must go to hell.

There are traditional Hindus who want to preserve Hindu values and the Hindu way of life, which is a culture of devotion and meditation. Such traditional Hindu values do not require the assertion of fundamentalism. There are also conservative and socially backward Hindus who may be trying to preserve regressive Hindu social customs like untouchability, which are unjust. This is the closest thing to Hindu fundamentalism, but to associate it with a monolithic religious fundamentalism is misleading. It is a social evil not a uniform fundamentalist belief system.

IS THERE MILITANCY IN HINDUISM?

Militancy has not existed in Hinduism to the extent that it has in belief-oriented religions. This is owing to the tolerant spirit of Hinduism and its emphasis on non-violence. Hindus have never invaded any country and tried to convert its people through force, propaganda, or economic pressure, the way Christian and Islamic countries have done through history. There is no Hindu history of holy wars, crusades, or foreign conquests, no Hindu church militant.

There are Hindu activists, but we seldom see the type of militancy in Hinduism that has existed in the name of belief-oriented religions. According to the Hindu view it is against Dharma or true religion to invade another country and try to convert it, to impose religious taxes on those of other beliefs, to promote missions that aim at conversion by misrepresenting other religions, or to denigrate the cultures of other people. Naturally there are exceptions to this even among Hindus in this militant age, but they are minor in their proportions. Most of what has been called Hindu fundamentalism is generally only a reaction against Islamic or Christian fundamentalism and militancy which has long made India its target.

WHAT IS THE HINDU VIEW OF CONVERSION?

There is only one real religion, the universal tradition of Truth. The different religions of the world are different formulations — or perhaps distortions — of that One Truth. Recognizing this universal tradition, true Hindus do not see the need to convert people to a particular belief. They recognize the Divine presence that exists already in all. If the other is God, what are we going to convert them to and why? What is important is to recognize the internal Divinity in all, not to convert others to our idea of religion.

There may be different religious and spiritual approaches that we can follow but this is at best to choose an angle of approach to the One Truth. Such different teachings are not different religions but different formulations of the one religion of Truth. Sanatana Dharma recognizes that many such approaches are possible and a diversity of them should always be encouraged, but that the underlying universality of Truth should never be forgotten. Such different teachings are Shaivism, Vaishnavism or Shaktism, which are different lines (*sampradāyas*) of Sanatana Dharma, not different religions. All the religions of the world can similarly be seen as different lines or approaches to the universal religion of Truth to the extent that such truth is their goal.

To get people to think that they have a particular religious identity and it should be replaced with another, is to confuse the Self with the body and is a sign of ignorance. God is our essential nature. The Divine is our Self. It is not something that we have to be converted to, a new identity to assume, but our own real Self that we have to discover.

CAN ONE BE CONVERTED TO HINDUISM?

As Sanatana Dharma or the universal tradition, Hinduism holds that we are all born in universal Truth. As immortal souls we can never be apart from it. We are always part of Sanatana Dharma. Even if we assume a specific religious identity we do not leave it. Can one ever be apart from the Divine whatever one's religious affiliation?

However, true Hindus do share their religion and welcome others to partake of it, not because they are seeking converts in order to dominate the world, but because they recognize that all beings are of one family. Such sharing is not trying to save others or give them a new identity but striving to connect all human beings to the universal family, which is the legacy of the sages.

One can formally become a Hindu by undergoing a ceremony called Shuddhi (purification), which is a short ritual lasting about two hours. Various Hindu groups provide this service. Yet becoming a Hindu is not converting to a belief that limits our freedom of inquiry. It does not require accepting a specific prophet, son of God, scripture or church. It gives one full freedom to follow whatever leads to Truth. One can be a Hindu and still follow Truth wherever one finds it. Joining Hinduism in the true sense is an inclusive, not exclusive process. It is a recognition of Sanatana Dharma, which requires that we live a dharmic life and respect all dharmic traditions and principles whatever their source. It requires that we begin a life of spiritual practices.

SHOULD MEMBERS OF OTHER RELIGIONS BECOME HINDUS?

The true purpose of religion is to know God, which is to know one's Self. The Hindu tradition as Sanatana Dharma contains the full range of meditational practices leading to Self-realization, which are not clearly understood in all religious traditions and are entirely absent in a number of them. If one is serious about the real purpose of religion, which is the inner quest, Hindu teachings are of great importance.

Hinduism, directing us to Self-realization, can be helpful to those of any religious background. It leads to a greater teaching that integrates religion into a spiritual view. Hinduism teaches cosmic laws like karma and rebirth that everyone should know. It emphasizes universal ethical practices like non-violence and principles of right living like vegetarian diet, which are essential to world peace. It contains a complete science of Yoga, including postures, breathing practices, mantra and meditation, which all people need to understand their True Nature.

Mystics of all types usually subscribe to Hindu type views and practices including rebirth, mantra, Yoga and meditation, even though the more orthodox in the religions may not. The advantage of Hinduism is that it is a religion which does not have a gulf between the mystics and the orthodox and which provides spiritual practices for people at all levels.

CAN IT BENEFIT A HINDU TO JOIN OTHER RELIGIONS?

A true Hindu recognizes the portion of universal Truth that is manifest in all religions. Great teachings and good values can be found among individuals of all backgrounds which should be honored, but this does not require formally joining any particular church, particularly those which promote exclusive beliefs and thereby divide humanity into hostile camps.

A true Hindu can never take upon one religious identity as opposed to another, just as one cannot leave the universe in which one lives. Hinduism recognizes the truth of religion as such and attempts to maintain that truth in an open tradition. It says that we should recognize all religions as different approaches to the universal religion, which recognizes the sacred nature and immortality of all beings.

SHOULD ONE NOT FOLLOW THE RELIGION ONE IS BORN INTO?

We are born into many things and with many different proclivities, some which may reflect our real nature, others which may be obstacles that we should strive to overcome. The religion of our birth may be one or the other.

Religion, properly understood, is an aid to Self-realization and not an end in itself. One should follow whatever religious teachings most aid in this realization, regardless of their origin. If the religion one is born into has a living Self-realization tradition that one can follow, one should certainly adapt it. If the religion of one's birth does not have such a tradition, then one should look to teachings that do. We must learn to use religion to further our inner understanding and cease letting religion use us to further the vested interests, which are usually of a worldly nature, that may sustain it. We do not belong to any particular religion, rather all religions belong to us.

In the global age that is dawning we no longer are restricted to the culture or religion of our area of birth but have access to that of all humanity. We should strive to benefit from the spiritual legacy of the human race, just as we are learning to benefit from the scientific knowledge and culture of all areas of the world.

IS HINDUISM A CULT?

Cults are temporary religious movements wherein some charismatic leader uses religion for his or her own personal benefit. Cults are usually centered around one person and isolate people from ordinary functioning in society. They generally end, often in violence, after a short period of time.

A religion like Hinduism that has existed for thousands of years is not centered around any particular personality, and has produced many great people in all walks of life, is not a cult. There are Hindus who are successful in all fields both in the East and the West as scientists, doctors, lawyers, artists and so on. In fact Hindus in America have a much higher standard of education and income than the average American.

Unfortunately according to religious fundamentalists any different or foreign religious group is a cult. Such people are caught in religious prejudice, which they reflect in their condemnation of different religious approaches. They do not recognize any universal Truth or have any tradition of Yoga and meditation, which inner practices they also regard as cults.

From the Hindu point of view any religion which teaches that God is outside of ourselves, and that we must be dependent upon some savior, holy book or church, is a cult because it confuses the internal reality, which is consciousness, with something external. Actually whatever religion asserts a separate identity for itself apart from Universal Truth becomes thereby a cult. Whatever limits Truth, which is Infinite and Eternal, to a particular manifestation is a cult. Yet by this standard most of organized religion is a cult. However, this explains why organized religion has failed to bring us to any real spiritual knowledge or experience.

WHY DO CHRISTIANS AND MUSLIMS SEEK TO CONVERT HINDUS?

Over the centuries Christians and Muslims have sent out not only missionaries but also armies to convert Hindus. Today they are probably spending more money than at any point in history to achieve this aim.

Obviously one does not seek to convert someone whose views one respects. Clearly such Christians and Muslims do not appreciate Hinduism, Sanatana Dharma, its many saints, sages, yogic practices and spiritual philosophies. They do not understand Yoga and Vedanta and may be opposed to such spiritual approaches even in their own traditions. If they appreciated such knowledge they would be coming to the Hindus to learn, as many Westerners have, and not be peddling their own generally inferior doctrines instead. It only shows that they don't know what is of true spiritual value. Hindus who are taken in by them only demonstrate a greater ignorance.

This conversion mentality reflects an outward view of religion, in which religion becomes a social-political institution whose main goal is to increase in numbers. It generally inhibits the internal dimension of religion or the spiritual quest, which it is often opposed to, and which the very groups that it seeks to convert often know much more about. Such missionaries are to be pitied. Though they may have their idealism and their noble sentiments, much like politicians, they have not understood the real purpose of religion which is not to get other people to follow a belief but to awaken the Divine Self in all. They need to be taught the true missionary spirit in religion is not the missionary spirit of conversion but the yogic spirit.

HOW CAN HINDUS FUNCTION AS MINORITIES IN ISLAMIC COUNTRIES?

There are a number of Hindu minorities in Islamic countries. In Pakistan, Bangladesh, Malaysia and Indonesia they are the remnants of the original Hindus of the region. In the Gulf countries they come mainly as workers.

Unfortunately Hindus are not treated well in Islamic countries, particularly as regards their religion. They are often forbidden to practice their religion in public. They are not allowed to teach their religion publicly. They certainly are not allowed to convert Muslims to Hinduism. Nor will any Hindu political parties be tolerated. This is all very different than in India where Muslims are generally allowed to do all these things. In fact Hindus are so oppressed in most Islamic countries that they are often afraid even to speak out. The same is true to a lesser degree in regard to members of other non-Islamic religions in Islamic countries, including Christianity.

Traditionally Arabs employed Hindus as servants and slaves, along with black Africans and other non-Muslims they captured in war. Under Islamic rule in India Hindus were oppressed, forced to pay religious taxes, and otherwise looked down upon, just as the British later discriminated against them. Hence it has not been the tendency of Muslims to appreciate Hindus, and fundamentalist Islam has continued this tradition.

With such a history and under such adverse circumstances Hindus in Islamic countries must hold to the inner truth of their tradition, though it may be difficult to express it outwardly. Above all, they should seek alliance with Hindu groups in other countries, and Hindus in other countries should seek to help them. We live in a global culture today and Hindus must create a common cause with Hindus all over the world. Otherwise Hindus who are suffering oppression will not be helped by anyone.

WHY DID THE POPE CONDEMN YOGIC PRACTICES?

A few years ago the Pope issued a proclamation telling Catholics, particularly monks and priests, to avoid yogic practices and mixing Catholicism with Eastern traditions like the Hindu and Buddhist. In his recent book he was very critical of the Buddhists as well.

Obviously such actions do not show an appreciation of yogic traditions and their practices and does not recognize their importance for the spiritual life. This is not surprising because orthodox Catholicism, such as the Pope supports, has not accepted the doctrines of karma, rebirth and Self-realization that go along with yogic traditions. The church has even sent out priests to convert the great yogis of India, as if such people were in need of salvation!

The Pope needs to be educated more properly as to what the Truth is so that he can promote a true spiritual tradition and not merely a dogmatic religious institution that stifles inner inquiry, which is what his present course appears to be and what Catholicism usually has done. For this Hindus should try to educate Catholics as to the importance of yogic and dharmic teachings, particularly individuals, like the Pope, who have expressed an appreciation of mystical approaches such as have been extensively developed in India.

Unfortunately when religion becomes an institution, maintaining that institution blinds us to the Truth, which transcends all organizations. It causes us to oppose teachings from outside the organization even if they may be more true than those within it. Until this organizational mentality is transcended we will remain trapped in ignorance.

WAS THE PAGAN WORLD MORE SPIRITUAL THAN THE POST-PAGAN WORLD?

According to Hindus generally speaking it was. The pre-Christian Greeks and Romans were generally more spiritual than what they became after adapting Christianity, which as an exclusive religion opposed the great spiritual, philosophical and occult traditions that existed in the Pagan world. The many Pagan temples, deities, festivals and religious observances were obliterated or made to go underground. While we have been given the image of the degenerate Pagans offering Christians to the lions (which has been highly exaggerated), a more accurate image is of fanatical Christians smashing Pagan temples, forcing conversion of Pagans, and sometimes killing Pagan religious leaders. A study of the last Pagans and the early history of the church reveals this (particularly in the fourth and fifth centuries).

The pre-Islamic Arabs also had a great culture and were not simply barbarians. They were known for tolerance and for great spiritual traditions of their own. It is wrong to think that before Islam the Arabs had no spirituality.

We should not divide humanity into the believers and non-believers. The non-believers also have their religions, which have generally been more tolerant, kind and diverse than those of the true believers. We should not close off our human heritage around a belief. All humane culture and religion belongs to us and until we have reclaimed the whole of it we are not truly human or humane. This is the meaning of Sanatana Dharma or a universal tradition.

ISN'T YOUR VIEW CRITICAL OF CHRISTIANITY AND ISLAM?

It is aimed at helping Hindus deal with the ongoing Christian and Islamic efforts to convert them, which are still quite extensive and well-funded. Christian and Islamic groups have projected much criticism of Hinduism, much of it unfair. It is only proper that they hear the Hindu point of view, which is based upon a seeking of universal Truth and is of importance for all human beings. Many Christian and Islamic groups do not recognize Hinduism as a valid religion. While there is some mutual acceptance of Biblical-based religions (Judaism, Christianity and Islam), there is a reluctance to accept religions outside this field. Most Christians and Muslims condemn Hindu-based Yoga and meditation practices. They do not accept God-realization or Self-realization and consider it to be arrogance or delusion. I myself was raised as a Catholic, so I know this first hand.

There is no Hindu counterpart of this form of religious negativity. The main criticism that Hinduism has levelled against other religions is relative to their dogmatism and exclusivism, their insistence that they alone have the Truth, that only their God is the real God and not God called by another name, as well as their failure to discern universal truths of karma, rebirth and liberation.

As the common Christian and Islamic idea of religion as a belief system — which is very different from the Hindu idea of Dharma — is the predominant idea of religion today, it must be questioned in order to show the Hindu idea of religion. The Hindu view, which is religion linked to a spirituality of Self and God-realization, is the essence of religion in its true sense, which means to unite. It is not a matter of Hinduism being opposed to any religious truth but of its placing spiritual realization above any dogma. This naturally places Hinduism in a different position than traditions which make dogma and authority more important than individual spiritual realization.

HOW CAN HINDUS BETTER PROMOTE THEIR RELIGION IN NON-HINDU COUNTRIES?

First it is a matter of communication. Hindus must make it known who they are and what they really believe, so common negative stereotypes about their religion — which breed so much misunderstanding and intolerance — are countered. They must organize themselves, not as a dogma but as a community with the common interest to promote a deeper spiritual knowledge in the world.

They must recognize the value of the Hindu religion for all the world and its great treasures of spiritual and yogic knowledge that are very rare, and sometimes almost unknown in other religions. They must teach Hinduism, particularly Yoga and Vedanta, to non-Hindus, whether such people want to become

Hindus or not. Like the ancient Vedic sages said they should seek to make the entire world spiritual. They must become expansive, open-hearted, fearless, creative and compassionate, not in allegiance to a belief but out of contact with the Divine Self within that is greater than all the world.

SHOULD HINDUS CREATE MISSIONARY MOVEMENTS?

This would probably be better than for them to idly sit by while less spiritual ideologies spread, with little scrutiny, all over the world and in India itself. Yet Hindus need not try to remake Hinduism in the image of militant Islam, the Catholic Church or evangelical Christianity. These groups may have better succeeded socially but they have generally failed in the spiritual quest which is what is of ultimate importance.

Hindus should create educational movements all over the world promoting Yoga, Vedanta, Ayurveda, Jyotish, Sanskrit, Indian music and all aspects of the greater culture of Sanatana Dharma. They should set up teaching centers, schools and universities, retreat centers, and service organizations. While maintaining the diversity of Hinduism, Hindu groups should support one another and also work with any group that accepts dharmic principles and is willing to live according to them.

SHOULD HINDUS BE MORE AGGRESSIVE?

Hindus suffer from passivity and disunity. These are their main enemies. They are not only not aggressive in asserting themselves, they are generally apologetic if they assert themselves at all. A more positive, expansive self-confident spirit in their religion is essential.

This does not require that Hindus become militant or violent, but it does require that they wake up and become active. Perhaps in this process some Hindus may become temporarily over assertive but that is better than being overly passive. The present crisis in the world today, and in India, demands action both inwardly and outwardly. Let us all rise to the occasion and bring the light of Truth and Self-realization into the world.

CAN HINDUS COEXIST WITH OTHER RELIGIONS?

Hindus have throughout the centuries not only coexisted but provided a refuge for many other religious groups including Jews, Christians, Zoroastrians, Muslims, and Bahais. The real question is whether non-Hindus can coexist with Hindus. Hindus have had to endure and still endure great efforts to convert them. While Hindus have generally respected other religions, other religions, particularly Christianity and Islam have not respected them in return, and certainly have never taken any action to help protect Hindus or counter wrong ideas about what Hinduism is. This is particularly sad as Hinduism contains the deeper spiritual teachings that these other traditions often desperately need.

DO YOU THINK HINDUISM IS A SUPERIOR RELIGION?

Hinduism is a religion that includes both the high and the low, which recognizes the spiritual needs of people at all levels. There are no spiritual practices in any religion, whether it is the most simple nature worship or the most exalted meditational approach, without counterparts in Hinduism. Hinduism is thereby probably the most comprehensive religion in the world. This is because it is not trapped in the seeking of superiority but recognizes the same Divine Being and common human aspiration everywhere. Such comprehensiveness in religion is needed today.

However we should seek out the highest Truth, which is to know the Self, and this requires going beyond lesser truths. Recognizing the Self as the real goal of religion, Hinduism partakes of the highest Truth and does not stop short with secondary goals. But that highest Truth exists for all who look deeply into who they really are. No group can claim to own it, though only those who have realized it can really guide us to it.

Yet should some Hindus regard their religion as superior it need not bother anyone. In fact members of all religions tend to think that. Certainly Hindus have many good reasons to do so, with their great spiritual and cultural traditions. Even if we regard our religion as superior we should remain open to the views of others and seek to discover the Truth through developing the higher states of consciousness wherein Truth can be perceived directly within us. It should encourage us to work harder at our own connection with God or Truth, not to sit smugly by and judge others as unholy merely because they don't think the same way we do.

WOULD YOU LIKE TO SEE OTHER PEOPLE BECOME HINDUS?

I think it could be of great benefit for the world, particularly if it is done with a real understanding of the Hindu tradition. The discovery of Sanatana Dharma or the universal teaching is like going home, rediscovering one's Self. The greater the number of people who discover the meaning of Sanatana Dharma and its universal view, the less the warring creeds will be able to divide people and the less materialism will lead people astray.

Becoming a Hindu in the true sense means recognizing that all the spiritual and religious practices of humanity from the most primitive savage to the most exalted yogi have their place in the universal Dharma and should be honored for the genuineness of aspiration behind them, not superficially judged according to their name and form. Such a synthetic view is what we all need today, whether it comes through Hinduism or another source.

Why should it bother us if people join one religion or another? The main thing is that we should join a religion or spiritual group as a means of finding the Truth, the God within, which is our real Self. Otherwise whatever we join is only an illusion. The beauty of becoming a Hindu is that it provides many approaches to Self-knowledge and God-realization.

Part III

APPENDICES

1

The Great Refuge

By Ram Swarup

1. I offer my obeisance to Sanatana Dharma of the Vedas and the Upanishads, the Puranas, the Epics and the many Agamas.

2. I take refuge in this Dharma which has been nourished from generation to generation by great sages and teachers.

3. I take refuge in Sanatana Dharma, whose precepts and practices are pure, which is auspicious in the beginning, auspicious in the middle, and auspicious in the end; whose roots are deep, whose fruits are sweet.

4. I take refuge in Sanatana Dharma whose teaching is pure, whose vision, aspirations and works are pure.

5. I pay my obeisance to Sanatana Dharma which gives us a vision of a higher life, great and immortal life, a life renewed by a higher truth, a life which goes beyond its present limitations.

6. May I be a sharer in its Truth! May I be a worthy sharer in its heritage! May it be given to me to serve this Dharma with all my heart and mind!

7. God grant me that I make its truths my own. Make me a participant in its Truth. May I become worthy of it! Expand and deepen me. Grant me inner vision and enable me to see its horizons and profundities

8. I pay my obeisance to Sanatana Dharma that teaches the oneness of human beings and Gods, the oneness of all life. May I be one with the Gods! May I be one with our ancestors! May I be one with those who have gone before me! May I be one with

those who have yet to come. May I serve those who are immediately around me, and also those who are hidden from my sight. May I serve all beings on all planes of existence!

9. I pay obeisance to Sanatana Dharma which has the power to heal and reconcile, power to awaken and to reform. May this Dharma restore my people and my country! May it bless all humanity and all beings! May all be auspicious toward each other.

10. Sanatana Dharma protects those who protect it. Therefore protect and serve it in order to deserve and claim its protection.

11. Sanatana Dharma is as wide and profound as its subject. Like its Gods, it has a thousand names and facets, but only some of them have been indicated here.

2
The Code of Sanatana Dharma

To strive to do the following with sincerity, commitment and dedication:

TO RECOGNIZE THE SEVEN COSMIC PRINCIPLES

THE SUPREME SELF – Paramatman

To see the Self in all beings and all beings in the Self. To see the entire universe in the Self and the Self in all the universe. To see God as the Self and the Self as God.

REALITY/THE GODHEAD – Para Brahman

To respect the Divine or Truth as the true reality both within and outside all appearances, as Being-Consciousness-Bliss *(Sacchidānanda)*, underlying all the names and forms of the universe.

GOD, DIVINE FATHER/DIVINE MOTHER – Ishvara/Ishvari

To honor the Divine ruler of the universe in both masculine and feminine qualities as creator (*Brahmā-Sarasvatī*), preserver (*Vishṇu-Lakshmī*) and destroyer (*Shiva-Kālī*). To honor His/Her reality on all levels from the deities of nature to the Supreme Lord and Lady of the universe (*Maheshvara/ Maheshvarī*).

NATURE – Prakriti/Shakti

To honor all Nature as the manifestation of the Divine, as the body of the Cosmic Person (*Paramātman*) who is pure consciousness.

To see in Nature the mirror of the Divine Self. This includes honoring the Deities (*Devatās*) functioning through Nature, including the different nature spirits.

COSMIC INTELLIGENCE – Mahat

To observe and respect the workings of cosmic intelligence (*Mahat*) as the main guiding and directing power functioning within the universe. To become citizens of the universe, not partisans of a particular country or cause.

THE LAW OF KARMA/ CAUSE AND EFFECT

To observe and respect the law of karma and rebirth. This includes offering up the fruits of our action and doing our duty for the good of all.

THE SUPPORT OF DHARMA/ NATURAL LAW

To recognize the truth principles (*dharmas*) underlying the universe. To honor and foster the dharma (nature) of others. To follow one's own true nature (*svadharma*), which requires spiritual practices.

TO FOLLOW THE TEN GREAT OBSERVANCES

TRUTHFULNESS – Satya

To always tell the truth, even if it does not make one popular, but to do so in an agreeable and friendly manner.

NON-VIOLENCE – Ahimsa

To respect all life as sacred and to practice non-violence in thought, word and deed, not only relative to people but to animals, plants and all the world of Nature.

CONTROL OF SEXUAL ENERGY – Brahmacharya

To control one's sexual energy and not waste it unnecessarily or in a self-indulgent manner. To direct some portion of it for yogic practices.

NON-STEALING – Asteya

Not to take or to appropriate for oneself something which has not rightfully been given or accrued as the result of one's own efforts.

NON-ATTACHMENT – Aparigraha

Not to cling to any material thing or outward status, or to surround oneself with possessions and property so as to glorify oneself.

CLEANLINESS – Shaucha

To practice purity and cleanliness in body, speech and mind.

CONTENTMENT – Santosha

To remain content whatever circumstances may bring us, good or bad fortune, flattery or insult. To always maintain a happy, cheerful and helpful attitude.

SELF-CONTROL -Tapas

To strive to control one's physical, sensory and mental impulses according to the Divine presence within. To exercise patience and fortitude in all that one does, acting out of peace of mind.

SELF-STUDY – Svadhyaya

To regularly observe and study oneself the spiritual teachings that provide Self-knowledge.

SURRENDER TO GOD – Ishvara-Pranidhana

To surrender the fruits of all actions to God. To recognize the Divine Will as the only real power in the universe.

TO PRACTICE THE FOUR YOGIC PATHS

YOGA OF KNOWLEDGE – Jnana Yoga

To strive to see the Self in all beings and all beings in the Self through self-inquiry (*Ātma-vichāra*) and meditation (*Dhyāna*).

YOGA OF DEVOTION – Bhakti Yoga

To strive to merge into God inwardly through devotional meditation and love. To surrender to the Will of God and be an instrument of grace.

YOGA OF SERVICE – Karma Yoga

To work in the world to fulfill the Divine will through teaching, charity, and social service of a selfless nature.

YOGA OF TECHNIQUE – Raja Yoga

To practice various yogic methods like asana, pranayama, mantra and meditation for purification of body and mind and for realization of Truth.

ADDITIONAL PRACTICES AND OBSERVANCES

RITUAL – Puja

To do regular rituals for harmonizing with cosmic intelligence, purification of the mind, and promoting social welfare.

MANTRA

To do regular prayers and mantras for purification of the mind, communion with Divinity, for the welfare of all creatures, and for world peace.

MEDITATION – Dhyana

To do regular meditation for the purification of the mind and realization of Truth.

PILGRIMAGE – Yatra

To do regular pilgrimages to various sacred sites either as temples or places in Nature.

CHARITY – Dana

To be charitable in our actions and to share our possessions with those less fortunate. To support dharmic activities with our own resources, including temples, schools, and service organizations.

RESPECT FOR PARENTS AND ELDERS

To give honor and appropriate help to our parents. To offer prayers and rituals to our ancestors.

RESPECT FOR THE GURU – Gurupuja

To serve and honor one's teachers and respect all spiritual guides, which means also to put into practice their teachings.

STUDY OF THE TEACHING

To study the Hindu spiritual tradition and its teachings on a regular basis, including scriptural texts like the Vedas, Itihasas, Puranas and Agamas.

TRANSMISSION OF THE TEACHING

To respect Hindu teachings as a valid and universal spiritual path. To strive to pass them on through various forms of instruction. To share whatever we know, particularly with those who are younger than we are.

PROTECTION OF THE EARTH – Bhumi Rakshana

To protect the Earth, its plants and animals, and all its resources. To view the Earth as a manifestation of the Divine

Mother.

VEGETARIANISM or PURITY IN DIET – Shuddha Ahara

To as far as possible be a vegetarian, for purposes of purification of the mind, non-violence, and protection of the Earth. This means also to avoid all intoxicants, drugs and stimulants.

MODERATION/ SIMPLICITY

To be moderate in all of our actions, taking only what is necessary and avoiding excesses. To not make ourselves a burden upon others or upon the Earth.

NON-INTERFERENCE

To not give unsought advice or try to interfere in the lives of others, even if we think that what they are doing is wrong. Not try to impose our views upon others whatever they may think.

UNIVERSALITY – Vishvata

To respect all true spiritual and beneficial views and practices, whatever their name and form, whether they have come from within any particular religion or outside of all of them.

This, however, does not mean that one should respect or compromise with unspiritual and harmful practices done under the veil of religion or anything else.

PEACE – Shanti

To act out of peace and to promote peace in all that one does. To wish only peace for all beings and creatures.

3
Outline of Sanatana Dharma

1. Knowledge (*Veda-Vidyā*)

Higher Knowledge (*Parāvidyā*)
- Knowledge of the Self (*Ātma Vidyā*)
- Knowledge of the Absolute (*Brahma Vidyā*)
- Knowledge of God or the Creator (*Īshvara-Vidyā*)

Lower Knowledge (*Aparāvidyā*)
- Cosmic or World Knowledge (*Prakriti Vidyā*)
- The Gross World – Physical Sciences (*Sthūla Vidyā*)
- The Subtle World – Occult Sciences (*Sūkshma Vidyā*)
- The Causal World – Causal Sciences (*Kāraṇa Vidyā*)

2. Practice (*Yoga*)

Higher Knowledge (*Parāvidya*)

Four Yogas
- Jnana – Knowledge
- Bhakti – Devotion
- Karma – Service
- Kriya – Yoga Techniques

Fourfold Kriya Yoga
- Raja Yoga – Yoga of meditation
- Mantra Yoga – Yoga of mantra
- Laya Yoga – Yoga of the sound current
- Hatha Yoga – Yoga of posture and breath

Lower Knowledge (*Aparāvidyā*), which should be placed in service of the higher

Ritual and Temple Worship (Vedic and Agamic)
History and Mythology (*Itihāsa-Purāṇa*)
Astrology, Astronomy, and Meteorology (*Jyotisha*)
Mathematics and Physical Sciences (*Gaṇita*)
Medicine and Psychology (*Āyurveda*)
Language and Grammar (*Sanskrit*)
Literature, Poetry and Drama (*Kāvya*)
Music and Dance (*Gāndharva Veda*)
Architecture, Sculpture, and Painting (*Sthāpatya Veda*)
Social Sciences (*Varṇāshrama Dharma*)
Law, Politics, Diplomacy (*Nīti Vidyā, Dharma Shāstras*)
Ethics and Morality (*Vinaya*)

4

Glossary of Sanskrit Terms

Diacritical marks have been used very sparingly in the text of this book. They are being provided here in order to indicate the sounds of Sanskrit terms.

Agnihotra – Vedic fire offerings
Ahaṁkāra – ego or self-image
Ahiṁsā – non-violence
Artha – pursuit of wealth or prosperity
Ārya – noble or spiritual
Āsana – yogic postures
Ātman – the inner Self, pure consciousness
Ātmavidyā – Self-knowledge
Atharva Veda – most recent of four Vedas, also mantric text
Āyurveda – Vedic medicine
Bhagavad Gītā – scripture of Sri Krishṇa
Bhakti – devotion
Brahmā – the Divine in its creative or teaching function
Brahmacharya – control of sexual energy
Brahman – God, the Absolute, the Supreme Being, the Uncreate
Brāhmaṇa – member of the Brahmin class, responsible for religious teaching and the performance of rituals
Buddha – the enlightened one, ninth avatar of Vishnu
Buddhi – intelligence, reason
Citta – the field of consciousness, the heart
Deva – God
Devī – Goddess
Dhāraṇā – science of concentration

Dharma – natural law, way of truth

Dhyāna – science of meditation

Guru – teacher, spiritual guide

Homa – Vedic fire offerings

Īshvara – God as the Creator or cosmic lord

Īshvarī – God in the feminine as the Creator and cosmic ruler

Jainism – religion based upon the teachings of Mahāvīra and other Jain *Tīrthaṅkaras*

Jñana – spiritual or Self-knowledge

Jñānī – person of spiritual knowledge

Jyotisha – Vedic astrology

Kāma – desire or enjoyment as a goal of life

Karma – the law of cause and effect

Krishṇa – eighth avatar of Lord Vishṇu

Kshatriya – member of the noble, warrior or ruling class

Kuṇḍalinī – serpent power, energy of the higher mind

Lakshmī – Goddess of beauty, love and prosperity, consort of Vishṇu

Mahābhārata – great epic of the late Vedic age involving the story of Krishṇa and the Pāṇḍavas

Mahesha – name of Shiva

Manas – mind, particularly the outer or sense mind

Mantra – repetition of spiritual words or sounds

Moksha – liberation as the supreme goal of life

Paramātman – the Supreme or Absolute Self

Pārvatī – Goddess of meditation and transformation, consort of Shiva

Patañjali – sage who compiled the Yoga Sūtras

Prakriti – nature, primal matter

Prāṇāyāma – yogic breathing practices

Pūjā – Hindu rituals consisting of various offerings like flowers to the Divine in its various forms

Purāṇas – Hindu scriptures after the Vedic era

Purusha – the conscious being

Rādhā – consort of Lord Krishṇa
Rāma – seventh avatar of Lord Vishṇu
Rāmāyaṇa – story of Rāma and his wife Sītā
Rig Veda – oldest Veda and repository of mantra
Sacchidānanda – Being-Consciousness-Bliss
Sāma Veda – Veda of sound and chanting
Samādhi – spiritual realization
Sanātana Dharma – the universal or eternal tradition of truth
Sāṅkhya – Hindu system of philosophy founded by Kapila
Sarasvatī – Goddess of Wisdom
Satya – Truth or reality
Shaiva – worshipper of the Divine in the form of Shiva
Shākta – worshipper of the Divine in the form of the Goddess
Shankarāchārya – great Advaitic philosopher and sage of the early medieval period
Shānti – peace
Shiva – the Divine in its destructive or transformative function
Shūdra – member of the labor class
Tantra – medieval Hindu texts of Goddess worship and yoga practice
Umā – Divine Mother, form of Pārvatī
Unaryan – a person lacking in spiritual and ethical values
Upanishads – last level of Vedic scriptures relating to Self-realization
Vaishṇava – worshipper of the Divine in the form of Vishṇu
Vaishya – member of the trading or farming classes
Vedas – the Hindu scriptures or source teachings
Vedānta – the science and philosophy of Self-realization
Vishṇu – the Divine in its protective and preserving function
Yajur Veda – Veda of ritual
Yoga – spiritual practices leading to Self-realization
Yoga Sūtras – classical work on yogic spirituality

Index